Assessing
Undergraduate
Learning
in Psychology

Assessing **Undergraduate Learning** in Psychology

Strategies for Measuring and
Improving Student Performance

Edited by Susan A. Nolan,
Christopher M. Hakala,
and R. Eric Landrum

 AMERICAN PSYCHOLOGICAL ASSOCIATION

Published by
American Psychological Association
750 First Street, NE
Washington, DC 20002
https://www.apa.org

Order Department
https://www.apa.org/pubs/books
order@apa.org

In the U.K., Europe, Africa, and the Middle East, copies may be ordered from Eurospan
https://www.eurospanbookstore.com/apa
info@eurospangroup.com

Typeset in Meridien and Ortodoxa by Circle Graphics, Inc., Reisterstown, MD

Printer: Sheridan Books, Chelsea, MI
Cover Designer: Gwen J. Grafft, Minneapolis, MN

Library of Congress Cataloging-in-Publication Data

Names: Nolan, Susan A., editor. | Hakala, Chris, editor. | Landrum, R. Eric, editor.
Title: Assessing undergraduate learning in psychology : strategies for measuring and
  improving student performance / edited by Susan A. Nolan, Christopher M. Hakala,
  and R. Eric Landrum.
Description: Washington, DC : American Psychological Association, [2021] |
  Includes bibliographical references and index.
Identifiers: LCCN 2020012754 (print) | LCCN 2020012755 (ebook) |
  ISBN 9781433832277 (paperback) | ISBN 9781433832284 (ebook)
Subjects: LCSH: Psychology—Study and teaching (Higher) | Curriculum evaluation.
Classification: LCC BF77 .A87 2021 (print) | LCC BF77 (ebook) | DDC 150.76—dc23
LC record available at https://lccn.loc.gov/2020012754
LC ebook record available at https://lccn.loc.gov/2020012755

https://doi.org/10.1037/0000183-000

Printed in the United States of America

10 9 8 7 6 5 4 3 2 1

CONTENTS

CONTRIBUTORS

Kris Acheson, PhD, Purdue University, West Lafayette, IN, United States

Suzanne C. Baker, PhD, Department of Psychology, James Madison University, Harrisonburg, VA, United States

Melissa Beers, PhD, The Ohio State University, Columbus, OH, United States

Victor A. Benassi, PhD, University of New Hampshire, Durham, NH, United States

Roger Benjamin, PhD, Council for Aid to Education, New York, NY, United States

Jacquelyn Cranney, PhD, School of Psychology, The University of New South Wales, Sydney, Australia

Dana S. Dunn, PhD, Moravian College, Bethlehem, PA, United States

Ashley Finley, PhD, Association of American Colleges & Universities, Washington, DC, United States

Regan A. R. Gurung, PhD, Center for Teaching and Learning, Oregon State University, Corvallis, OR, United States

Christopher M. Hakala, PhD, Springfield College, Springfield, MA, United States

Jane S. Halonen, PhD, Department of Psychology, University of West Florida, Pensacola, FL, United States

Bridgette Martin Hard, PhD, Department of Psychology and Neuroscience, Duke University, Durham, NC, United States

Louis Hickman, MS, Purdue University, West Lafayette, IN, United States

Danae L. Hudson, PhD, Department of Psychology, Missouri State University, Springfield, MO, United States

Julie A. Hulme, PhD, School of Psychology, Keele University, Keele, Staffordshire, United Kingdom

Remo Job, Dott. Psic., Department of Psychology and Cognitive Science, University of Trento, Rovereto, Italy

R. Eric Landrum, PhD, Department of Psychological Science, Boise State University, Boise, ID, United States

Jonathan Lehrfeld, MA, Council for Aid to Education, New York, NY, United States

Rob McEntarffer, PhD, Lincoln Public Schools, Lincoln, NE, United States

Susan A. Nolan, PhD, Department of Psychology, Seton Hall University, South Orange, NJ, United States

Catherine E. Overson, PhD, Center for Excellence and Innovation in Teaching & Learning, University of New Hampshire, Durham, NH, United States

Eva Seifried, PhD, Department of Psychology, Heidelberg University, Heidelberg, Germany

Raymond J. Shaw, PhD, Department of Psychology, Merrimack College, North Andover, MA, United States

Craig Shealy, PhD, Department of Graduate Psychology, James Madison University, Harrisonburg, VA, and Executive Director of the International Beliefs and Values Institute, Mary Baldwin University, Staunton, VA, United States

Birgit Spinath, PhD, Department of Psychology, Heidelberg University, Heidelberg, Germany

Claudia J. Stanny, PhD, Department of Psychology, Center for University Teaching, Learning, and Assessment, University of West Florida, Pensacola, FL, United States

Lee Sternberger, PhD, Institute for Global Engagement, Western Washington University, Bellingham, WA, United States

Julia Suleeman, PhD, Faculty of Psychology, Universitas Indonesia, Depok Jawa Barat, Indonesia

Jason S. Todd, PhD, Department of English and Center for the Advancement of Teaching and Faculty Development, Xavier University of Louisiana, New Orleans, LA, United States

Dirk Van Damme, PhD, Organisation for Economic Co-operation and Development, Paris, France

Elizabeth Yost Hammer, PhD, Department of Psychology and Center for the Advancement of Teaching and Faculty Development, Xavier University of Louisiana, New Orleans, LA, United States

Doris Zahner, PhD, Council for Aid to Education, New York, NY, United States

Assessing
Undergraduate
Learning
in Psychology

Introduction

Assessment Assessment Everywhere—
And What Are We to Think?[1]

Susan A. Nolan, Christopher M. Hakala, and R. Eric Landrum

"Not another book on assessment?" you ask with a bit of a sigh. We're guessing that if you're reading this chapter, you don't entirely share this sentiment, but we feel that we'd be remiss not to acknowledge the shrug or the eye roll that so often accompanies earnest attempts at such conversation. In this opening chapter, we hope to convince you that there's much more to say about assessment and that the particular authors who have shared their ideas and research in this volume do indeed have something to add to the conversation. So, stay with us. We strongly believe this book will leave you with new ideas to ponder, research to explore, and concrete suggestions to try out in the safety of your classroom. *Do* try this at home! (And in your course.)

Assessment-driven pressures increasingly shape higher education at all levels. Until not that long ago, it was sufficient for faculty members to assess their students via course grades without consideration of what they were actually learning. Relatedly, instructors were seldom encouraged to engage in any deep consideration of the skills students were expected to learn in their courses; after all, it's far easier to give an exam that measures knowledge of content than one that measures attainment of skills. Sure, there have long been discussions about, say, how best to teach communication or critical thinking,

---

[1]With apologies to Samuel Taylor Coleridge (1798/1863) regarding the famous line from the poem *The Rime of the Ancient Mariner*: "Water, water, every where/Nor any drop to drink."

https://doi.org/10.1037/0000183-001
Assessing Undergraduate Learning in Psychology: Strategies for Measuring and Improving Student Performance, S. A. Nolan, C. M. Hakala, and R. E. Landrum (Editors)

but how often were we really asked to measure students' acquisition of these skills? Moreover, instructors were generally not beholden to assessment-related expectations from their institutions, and, in turn, institutions were not typically asked questions about assessment by the relevant accrediting or governing bodies. Few were asking questions about what, exactly, our students were learning.

Now, however, individual faculty members face pressures from department chairs and administrators to tie their content and pedagogy to clearly outlined learning goals, to develop measures of assessment that map directly onto stated learning goals, and to engage in a process of continual change based on those measures—to "close the loop," in assessment-ese. Departments and other institutional units face pressures from accrediting bodies or governmental agencies, depending on the institution's country, to create and document assessment protocols across all levels of the institution that demonstrate what students are learning and, often, the relevance of their education beyond our campuses—for employers and the broader community. And as our world becomes increasingly interconnected, a variety of pressures are affecting how we think about assessment from an international standpoint, posing some tricky questions for which assessment must be part of the answer. For example, how can we facilitate the mobility of students and instructors across regional and national borders? How can we compare courses and degrees? How can a degree-holder document what a credential from one place actually means when relocating to another place for further study or employment?

These varying demands have already led to dialog among faculty members and administrators in higher education, but the conversation is just beginning. The goal of this book is to further the dialog by exploring the three main types of assessment pressures—individual, institutional, and international—from a range of perspectives. Throughout the chapters, authors offer case examples, best practices, and evidence-informed discussions. Much of it consists of concrete suggestions that others could adopt or adapt. We hope these contributions will spur additional dialog that might forge connections among people and institutions across borders, connections that can lead to excellent, assessment-driven higher education.

The issue is to quite simply begin to imagine assessment in a way that transcends modern attitudes about assessment. That is, we intend to produce a volume that shows how to assess your students in class for better learning, how to use those data to inform course-level performance and program-level performance, and, ultimately, how that information could help us work toward an international Tuning standard to focus on learning and not performance. And indeed, assessment isn't easy, and there are many reasons why it is often not done well: Faculty don't receive training in assessment in many doctoral programs, faculty feel pressure to assess in ways that they don't control, and faculty feel that assessment robs them of academic freedom. In this volume, we hope to disavow faculty of most of these assertions by showing how to do it in your class, how to make use of the data to improve student learning, and, eventually, how to use it to ensure that our students are ready to compete in the global economy.

THE STRUCTURE OF THIS BOOK: FROM MICRO TO MACRO

To further our goal of spurring conversation about assessment and sparking ideas in faculty members and administrators, this book examines assessment across three levels—but we'll start in the middle. At the in-between level, seven chapters explore assessment at the program or institution level, the level at which most assessment work occurs. We then zoom in to the micro level, where four chapters explore assessment from the perspective of individual faculty members. Finally, at the macro level, four chapters offer a big-picture view of how assessment looks when we implement it at a global level.

Institutional Perspectives

As our institutions begin to address assessment questions in meaningful ways, new policies have emerged as well as a new sense of responsibility. In terms of policies, more and more programs are requiring an external accreditation body to evaluate the effectiveness of a program, and colleges and universities are requiring that programs that don't have an external accreditation organization retain the services of an external consultant to evaluate a department. In addition, regional accreditation bodies are also placing larger demands on colleges for accountability.

The goal of this section is to provide the reader with context regarding the way assessment really does happen at the course level, the program level, and the institution level. In addition, the way that assessment takes shape and the results of those assessments help hone our educational practices so that our students have the highest probability of succeeding in their learning.

To kick off this section, Regan A. R. Gurung discusses in Chapter 1 how the scholarship of teaching and learning serves to inform our assessment practices. With the results of the studies, we are able to make informed decisions that not only impact individual courses but also serve to guide the development of programmatic changes to best serve our students.

Melissa Beers follows in Chapter 2 with a call to develop a teaching support and pedagogical team. In her chapter, Beers describes how alignment of learning objectives across similar sections of courses can provide students with similar outcomes as well as ensure that faculty have a deeper understanding not only of what they are teaching but also of what they should expect from students in their courses.

In Chapter 3, Jane S. Halonen and Dana S. Dunn address the role of program review and how such a review can begin to help a college or university align assessment practices in ways that best serve student learning at the institutional level. Halonen and Dunn outline how program review can uncover which assessment practices are effective and which are ineffective. They also provide practical advice to guide the reader through the program review process.

In line with this, Rob McEntarffer, a high school educator, talks in Chapter 4 about how the terminology of assessment, including the use of formative assessment, often clouds the issue. McEntarffer argues that a clearer sense of purpose is obtained by using feedback or responsive teaching, which not only lends credence to the mission of assessment but also provides an opportunity for faculty to engage in it without feeling as though their academic freedom is being impinged upon. High school educators often approach assessment differently than do undergraduate educators, in part because of the expectations of different stakeholders. All of us who engage in assessment efforts can benefit from dialog with our counterparts at other levels.

In Chapter 5, Jason S. Todd and Elizabeth Yost Hammer lend advice on how a teaching center can, through faculty development, begin to develop a culture of assessment on campus by tying the notion of assessment more closely to student learning and moving away from assessment as a requirement. The chapter pairs discussions of effective practices that promote a culture of assessment (e.g., workshops and programming, midcourse reviews) with concrete advice for the faculty developers who might implement these practices.

In Chapter 6, Claudia J. Stanny describes how assessment processes can be used to improve curriculum and teaching in ways that involve considering using faculty development as a mechanism for campus change. Specifically, she outlines how institution-level initiatives can support instructors as they not only develop assessments tied to learning outcomes but also use those assessments to make changes at the course and program levels. In particular, Stanny promotes interdisciplinary approaches that place individual courses within the context of overarching curricula.

In the last chapter of this section (Chapter 7), Catherine E. Overson and Victor A. Benassi provide guidelines for using backward design, with the assistance of a teaching and learning center. Backward design places assessment in the forefront of the course and helps instructors use that evidence to better design learning experiences for students. With backward design, instructors begin by developing learning goals for the course as well as assessments for those goals; they then use that structure to develop instructional activities and assignments that align with the goals and assessments. Overson and Benassi make a strong case for backward design using in-depth examples from their own experiences.

Individual Perspectives

Perhaps you have heard the phrase "think globally, act locally." Meaningful assessment practices start with individual faculty member efforts, and our edited volume offers four different perspectives and approaches for how faculty members approach assessment in their own work. In Chapter 8, the first chapter in this section, Bridgette Martin Hard shares her own personal, developmental changes as a researcher as she became interested in exploring pedagogical science using what she likes to call a "stealthy approach." By leveraging the processes of assessment and harnessing what existing grade data can tell us, Hard presents multiple examples of how she has changed her own teaching practices by closing the loop with her own assessment data. She generously ends her chapter with steps for how to get started on your own journey with pedagogical science.

In Chapter 9, Danae L. Hudson presents a departmental journey of evidence-based course (re)design, using the experiences of her own introductory psychology collaboration at Missouri State University. From design to implementation to refinement, using her own case study experiences, she presents the ups and downs of the process in clear detail, generously sharing with all of us.

Raymond J. Shaw addresses in Chapter 10 the push–pull situation of being caught in the middle regarding assessment; that is, the faculty member is the person who performs assessment work often, collecting data from students (which might make the faculty member unpopular at times), and then the faculty member reports these assessment outcomes to stakeholders such as department chairs and deans, who at times may not find the data very valuable. In this context, he makes a cogent argument that finding a personal, meaningful reason for putting time and effort into assessment can lead to a process and outcome that is first self-satisfying and then secondarily satisfies other necessary audiences.

Eva Seifried and Birgit Spinath provide readers in Chapter 11 with a deeply rich framework for self-assessment in educational psychology courses that they label inquiry-based teaching, which has a number of iterative cycles that has teachers as researchers checking the effectiveness of their teaching practices, much like an action researcher would, and using that cycle of continuous improvement to always be striving to improve one's teaching. Not only do they draw parallels between how students learn and how faculty members improve, but they also present multiple additional strategies for faculty members who are engaging in meaningful self-assessment practices over time.

International Perspectives

Increasingly, universities and other organizations that focus on higher education are taking an international approach to assessment. Indeed, the United States, a world leader in some aspects of higher education, lags behind much of the world in other aspects, including outcomes-based assessment (Adelman, 2008, 2009; Gaston, 2012). In much of the world beyond the borders of the United States, outcomes are increasingly based on input from a broad range of stakeholders that includes not only direct university constituents such as students and alumni but also employers, policymakers, and the general public. The consensus gold standard for such a market-driven, outcomes-based model is the Bologna Process. Briefly, the Bologna Process is a collaboration among 48 European countries that together form the European Higher Education Area. These countries aim to develop comparable programs and outcomes with the dual goals of employability of graduates and mobility for students and faculty members across the region. (For a primer on the Bologna Process, particularly for those in the United States, we recommend Clifford Adelman's 2009 essay *The Bologna Process for U.S. Eyes: Re-Learning Higher Education in the Age of Convergence.*)

With Bologna as the seminal program, these processes are programs of international cooperation that have developed relatively interchangeable programs in terms of preparation for future study and for careers. Through the flexible process called Tuning (see http://www.tuningacademy.org), higher education programs in various global regions are harmonized rather than standardized, so that a student from any participating program may relatively seamlessly continue their education at another member institution, yet each country and institution maintains a degree of academic freedom that true standardization would obstruct. These efforts toward harmonization provide models for how the United States—or other areas that are lagging—might improve.

We, as coeditors of this book, believe that the United States must work to overcome reluctance and resistance to join our international counterparts in harmonization, at least to some degree; however, more urgently, we want to address ways in which we can work toward these goals in the meantime.

To kick off our exploration of international assessment, in Chapter 12 we hear from a multinational team of assessment experts: Jacquelyn Cranney (Australia), Julie A. Hulme (United Kingdom), Julia Suleeman (Indonesia), Remo Job (Italy), and Dana S. Dunn (United States). They identify overlap among assessment initiatives across the five countries that they represent, including pressures from a broader range of stakeholders than in the past and a lack of training and resources related to assessment. They also offer recommendations, including an increased emphasis on assessment of skills (e.g., scientific thinking) and assessment of programmatic outcomes, rather than just individual courses. And they highlight the importance of professional organizations in effecting improvements in assessment.

Next, in Chapter 13, the Australian and U.S. team of Jacquelyn Cranney, Dana S. Dunn, and Suzanne C. Baker asks us to consider ways in which faculty members and programs around the globe might begin to approach assessment in similar ways. They outline an internationally recognized procedure that scaffolds the development of assessments, the Assessment Design Decision Framework, a method that "aims to keep the focus on both the learner's experience as well as the educator's reality." The authors outline the framework's six categories related to assessment decisions, provide international perspectives, and offer a range of practical resources and suggestions for faculty members and institutions.

The final two chapters in this section describe specific assessment initiatives that expand beyond the usual (assessment) suspects in innovative ways: One explores a dynamic assessment of skills, and the other delves into assessments of values and worldviews. In Chapter 14, Doris Zahner, Roger Benjamin, and Jonathan Lehrfeld from the Council for Aid to Education (CAE) and Dirk Van Damme from the Organisation for Economic Co-operation and Development (OECD) introduce global assessment initiatives that are not tied to any particular Tuning region. They introduce readers to the Collegiate Learning Assessment (CLA+) International, a measure of generic skills developed by the CAE and endorsed by the OECD. Measures such as the CLA+ can help students to market their skills, including via digital badges, and can help employers to find talented students. Moreover, CAE and OECD are developing benchmarks that allow for international comparisons.

Finally, in Chapter 15, a team of researchers from U.S. universities and the Association of American Colleges and Universities (AAC&U)—Kris Acheson, Ashley Finley, Louis Hickman, Lee Sternberger, and Craig Shealy—aims to expand our perspectives regarding what we even think to assess in the first place. They particularly emphasize assessment of our students' understanding of and values related to cultural and global issues. The chapter introduces the Beliefs, Events, and Values Inventory (BEVI), the AAC&U's Valid Assessment of Learning in Undergraduate Education rubrics, and the Cultural Controllability Scale, all of which move us beyond the typical constructs targeted by assessments. The BEVI, for example, has scales that assess constructs such as Sociocultural Openness, which measures how open students are to cultures other than their own, and Global Resonance, which assesses global engagement.

The dream goal of truly international mobility may be out of reach at the moment; however, we can all start thinking more internationally in terms of how we highlight commonalities in our approaches, use frameworks that move us toward similarities in how we approach the development of assessments in the first place, nurture a growing international emphasis on assessing skills and not just knowledge, and assess our cultural and international mind-sets themselves.

REFERENCES

Adelman, C. (2008). *The Bologna club: What U.S. higher education can learn from a decade of European reconstruction.* Institute for Higher Education Policy. https://files.eric.ed.gov/fulltext/ED501332.pdf

Adelman, C. (2009). *The Bologna Process for U.S. eyes: Re-learning higher education in the age of convergence.* Institute for Higher Education Policy. http://files.eric.ed.gov/fulltext/ED504904.pdf

Coleridge, S. T. (1863). *The rime of the ancient mariner.* Art-union. (Original work published 1798)

Gaston, P. L. (2012). *The challenge of Bologna: What United States higher education has to learn from Europe, and why it matters that we learn it.* Stylus Publishing.

INSTITUTIONAL
APPROACHES

1

Scholarship of Teaching and Learning and Assessment

Advancing a Collaborative Model

Regan A. R. Gurung

For some academics, *assessment* is a dirty word. This is perhaps because when the assessment movement appeared on college campuses in the United States, the key purpose was to respond to a federal mandate for institutional effectiveness and accountability (Ewell, 2009). Assessment has traditionally been a process seemingly forced on faculty by administrators who, in turn, are pressured by accrediting bodies to provide evidence that students are learning. After years of academic freedom, faculty were called on to, for all practical purposes, publicly justify their effectiveness. Multiple efforts over the past few years have attempted to change the meaning and significance of the word. For example, Halonen and colleagues crafted an assessment guide for psychology teachers clearly defining assessment as "the process of gathering evidence of student success and teaching effectiveness" (American Psychological Association, 2018, p. 4). This definition of assessment and the suggested process for teachers sound very similar to the processes encompassed by scholarship of teaching and learning (SoTL).

Although SoTL has many definitions (McKinney, 2007; Pan, 2009), I see it as encompassing many critical aspects and being "the focus on theoretical underpinnings of how we learn; the intentional, systematic modifications of pedagogy; and assessments of resulting changes in learning" (Gurung & Landrum, 2014, p. 1). Nuances in how the term is used have obscured the fact that researchers using SoTL focus on attaining evidence of learning, which makes it a critical tool for anyone interested in assessment. Likewise, the fact

https://doi.org/10.1037/0000183-002
Assessing Undergraduate Learning in Psychology: Strategies for Measuring and Improving Student Performance, S. A. Nolan, C. M. Hakala, and R. E. Landrum (Editors)

that at the heart of the assessment movement is a focus on student learning is lost on some SoTL practitioners. In this chapter, I illustrate the relationship between SoTL and assessment, demonstrating how each informs and advances the other. First, I provide a brief history of SoTL, followed by highlighting how assessment is a part of SoTL. I conclude with helpful tips for using SoTL for assessment.

SCHOLARSHIP OF TEACHING AND LEARNING IN HIGHER EDUCATION

SoTL is currently practiced across academic disciplines (Hake, 2015; McKinney et al., 2017) at research and teaching institutions (Bernstein, 2013) around the world. Ideally, it is used to drive curricular practice and reform (Hubball et al., 2013) and has a long history. The term *scholarship of teaching* was popularized by Boyer (1990) and expanded to SoTL by the Carnegie Academy for the Scholarship of Teaching and Learning. Boyer's (1990) landmark redefinition of scholarship also provided assessment with scholarly status (Maki, 2011). Definitions and distinctions become important because some variations of SoTL do not involve assessment to the same degree as others and in some cases assessment may be more qualitative than quantitative. Most important is the difference between SoTL and scholarly teaching (Potter & Kustra, 2011). Scholarly teachers create course design portfolios to document systematically collected observations for further reflection and course modification (Richlin, 2006). This use of an organized methodology and literature review is conducted primarily for the teachers' own benefit to make their next class semester better. Conducting formal investigations of teaching and learning (regardless of method), placing the results in the context of relevant published pedagogical literature, and then submitting the results for peer-reviewed publication catapults the scholarly teacher to a contributor to the SoTL literature.

Following Boyer's (1990) model, Halpern and colleagues (1998) attempted to broaden the construct of scholarship in psychology to include activities that investigate pedagogy and student learning within psychology. Halpern and colleagues (1998) provided the field of psychology with a "paradigm for the twenty-first century" (p. 1292)—a five-part definition of scholarship that included (a) original research, (b) integration of knowledge, (c) application of knowledge, (d) the scholarship of pedagogy, and (e) the scholarship of teaching in psychology. Invigorated by Halpern and colleagues (1998), the American Psychological Association (APA)'s Division 2, the Society for the Teaching of Psychology, created multiple task forces charged with advancing SoTL in psychology. In 2008, members of one task force reported on the state of SoTL in psychology in a special issue of the *Teaching of Psychology* (Gurung et al., 2008).

In the first national published study of SoTL in psychology, Gurung and colleagues (2008) surveyed 142 U.S. teachers of psychology, modifying a 2004 survey used by Cox, Huber, and Hutchings (in Huber & Hutchings, 2005).

The researchers assessed the level of support faculty perceived in their departments and institutions as well as the role of SoTL in personnel decisions and obstacles to conducting SoTL. In general, "survey respondents failed to report a prevailing sentiment of support" (p. 257). Gurung and colleagues (2008) found that participants reported low levels of institutional support and claimed more support was needed.

More recently, Gurung and colleagues (2019) reported data from a national survey of faculty (N = 366) that examined SoTL research across seven dimensions of productivity, comparing current perceptions of SoTL with previous findings (Gurung et al., 2008). They found that faculty today perceive SoTL as a ubiquitous part of their daily teaching routines, and they perceived more departmental support for SoTL work than in the past. However, there were also similarities across time, including faculty perceptions of insufficient reassignment time to conduct SoTL work and peer-reviewed publications being the most valued product. Psychology faculty, relative to nonpsychology faculty, also believed that their departmental colleagues were more supportive of SoTL efforts and that their departments supported such work. These researchers suggested SoTL is evolving into an accepted form of scholarship in the United States; however, SoTL may be more accepted and valued in psychology than in other disciplines.

PARALLELS BETWEEN ASSESSMENT AND SCHOLARSHIP OF TEACHING AND LEARNING: ASSESSMENT-INFORMED SCHOLARSHIP OF TEACHING AND LEARNING

SoTL and assessment, by most common definitions of each, are interlocking processes. To a large extent, it is a question of the level at which questions are asked about student learning. When one measures learning at a department, program, college, or university level, the process is labeled *assessment*, a "global term used to refer to the authentic evaluation of teaching and learning outcomes" (Dunn, McCarthy, Baker, Halonen, & Boyer, 2011, p. 145). When faculty ask the same questions in regard to a single course for their personal evaluations of teaching and learning without an administrative or accreditation mandate, the enterprise is more commonly labeled *SoTL*. Both assessment and SoTL may involve intentional changes in pedagogy and measurement of the effectiveness of the change on student learning. Making no changes but just establishing measures of learning and examining grade distributions is basic assessment. SoTL (and in most cases scholarly teaching) involves assessment of learning (what all teachers should be doing) but distinguishes itself with its iterative use of systematic changes. Note, some may decide to call any examination of student learning (whether at the course, department, or institution) SoTL, and they may even refer to class-level examinations as assessment.

SoTL and assessment can and should coexist and sometimes do. Most psychology faculty conducting SoTL have been trained how to do research even though they may not have been trained how to teach. If they try a new pedagogical strategy or change an assignment, the effects of this change, essentially an intervention, can be tested using the scientific method. Correspondingly, it should be easier for psychologists to use the scientific method to evaluate their teaching and student learning, but there is no clear evidence that enough do (Chew et al., 2018). In the context of higher education, the dependent variable, as it were, is learning. Measuring learning effectively and in a valid and reliable way is the result of good assessment training. Although many faculty have not been trained in assessment, all educators know they have to assign a grade and measure learning in a classroom and could benefit from learning the hows and whys of robust assessment. Furthermore, incorporating the best practices of assessment can enhance the quality of SoTL. This assessment-informed SoTL will be more likely to advance higher education than will SoTL that does not utilize the fruits of existing assessment methodology.

To easily see how assessment can inform SoTL, compare the steps advocated for each (APA, 2018; Dickson & Treml, 2013). The assessment cycle involves identifying the purpose of assessment; choosing an appropriate format and strategy; adopting, writing, and revising assessment items or tasks; collecting data; evaluating the effectiveness of assessments; and then closing the loop or using assessment data effectively and ethically (APA, 2018). These assessment steps mirror the path taken in SoTL, which involves asking a question about teaching and learning, examining relevant published research, intentionally and systematically modifying pedagogy, and evaluating the effects of the change to better inform future pedagogy. In light of the parallels, it is not surprising that educators have urged a combination of efforts. Beyond assessment-informed SoTL, Dickson and Treml (2013) encouraged the breaking down of "the artificial boundaries between courses, among faculty, and between teaching and research in order to highlight connections and contributions across these student-centered endeavors" (p. 8).

Objective Versus Subjective Assessments

Contributors to the assessment literature provide numerous helpful discussions that can inform SoTL. One is the use of objective versus subjective dimensions. Although placement of items along this artificial dimension is debatable, this organizational scheme helps us better comprehend the literature (Gurung & Landrum, 2012). Objective assessments are those that possess absolute correct and incorrect answers although there are many variations on a theme (Wright, 1994). There is only one correct answer for an objective test item (e.g., multiple-choice, true/false, matching questions; Suskie, 2018). Objective assessments tend to yield quantitative outcomes, a quality that appeals to many psychologists. The advantages of objective assessment are that (a) they are efficient, with the capability of delivering a large amount of information about student knowledge utilizing little time; (b) large numbers of students can be assessed simultaneously; (c) they are easy and quick to score, although their creation is neither easy nor quick; and (d) a singular score (e.g., performance indicator) can be calculated, making this approach popular for summarizing outcomes to third parties (Suskie, 2018).

Subjective assessments produce data where a machine-scorable answer is not feasible, and skilled judgments are needed to determine learning outcomes. In other words, subjective assessments result in numerous possible answers with variable quality, and assessment requires the judgment of a professional to provide a score (Suskie, 2018)—often yielding a qualitative outcome. Rubrics aid the assessment of student work that falls to the subjective side of the continuum. Multiple resources exist to aid psychology educators who wish to utilize rubrics to facilitate subjective assessments (e.g., Stevens & Levi, 2011).

The advantages of subjective assessments are numerous. Subjective assessments (a) provide the ability to measure many important skills that objective tests cannot measure, including organization, synthesis, problem solving, creativity, and originality; (b) allow for the assessment of skills, such as having a psychology major write a literature review on a research topic (rather than answer multiple-choice questions about how to write a literature review); (c) promote deep learning and help to establish skills that outlast the rote memorization of textbook information; and (d) allow for nuanced scoring, such as giving partial credit (Suskie, 2018).

Direct Versus Indirect Assessments

Another important dimension used in assessment is the direct–indirect dimension. Direct measures of student learning are what most would call grading—that is, the individual evaluation of student work (e.g., exams, writing assignments). Indirect measures of student learning may be perceptual in nature—that is, asking students about their opinions or attitudes about how much they learned, alumni surveys, and surveys of employers (Walvoord, 2004).

SCHOLARSHIP OF TEACHING AND LEARNING AND ASSESSMENT: USING STUDENT LEARNING OUTCOMES

To know whether students are learning, one has to first clarify what it is students should be learning. Student learning outcomes (SLOs) are the "knowledge, skills, attitudes, and habits of mind that students take with them from a learning experience" (Suskie, 2018, p. 117). Setting SLOs is critical for SoTL and assessment as faculty conceptualize their courses from the standpoint of the goals that should be reached. Clear-cut SLOs allow faculty to align their courses with both the department and the institution. Pragmatically, SLOs are how SoTL researchers operationally define their dependent variables to measure learning.

The systematic measurement of SLOs provides evidence that learning occurred. Being knowledgeable about how to write SLOs is a key skill of a model teacher (Richmond et al., 2016), and many excellent guides for SLO development exist (Gurung & Landrum, 2012; Suskie, 2018). Instructional designers typically recommend that the course design process start with SLOs and design the course "backward" (Wiggins & McTighe, 1998). Instructors develop SLOs, then design assessments to evaluate the extent to which SLOs have been achieved, then determine ways to ensure students can accomplish the SLOs (design delivery of content and design the course). Adequately measuring SLOs is challenging, but, again, detailed instructions on how to conduct assessments exist (e.g., Dunn, McCarthy, Baker, & Halonen, 2011; Maki, 2011).

One excellent example of coordinating SoTL and assessment—blending course-level, department-level, and institution-level activities—is focusing on a research question that applies beyond a class. In a recent review of published work on the introductory psychology class, Gurung and Hackathorn (2018) highlighted 11 key SoTL questions in need of urgent attention. Many of the questions relate to the quality of education in a single class (e.g., Does class size influence learning?), but most questions can also be used across courses within a department and even across departments on campus (e.g., What are the best ways to study for the class?).

ADVANCING SCHOLARSHIP OF TEACHING AND LEARNING: BE ROBUST AND OBJECTIVE

The presence of strong measurement is one indicator of SoTL and is tied to a larger issue relating to how SoTL is valued. In other words, are faculty who publish in SoTL publishing "real" research? Many assessment experts may see SoTL as not sufficiently rigorous. The momentum of the SoTL movement is also thwarted by an internal turf battle over which discipline's methodology should take center stage (Chick, 2014). Some of the discussion in SoTL seems to imply that quantitative methodologies and the scientific method are the keys to producing quality SoTL work (Maurer, 2011). Addressing pressures felt by some SoTL researchers to use the scientific method, Grauerholz and Main (2013) discussed how the scientific method is not appropriate in every classroom context. Poole (2013) took this discussion a step further to unpack what is (and should be) meant by SoTL research.

The good news is that a recent national study of faculty across disciplines suggests the value of SoTL is improving (Gurung et al., 2019), but the battle for credibility is not over. To conduct efficient SoTL and correspondingly better assessment, a number of criteria have been established. Glassick, Huber, and Maeroff (1997) included the following six standards to assess the quality of any type of research: clear goals, adequate preparation, appropriate methods, significant results, effective communication, and reflective critique.

More recently, Wilson-Doenges and Gurung (2013) established gold standard benchmarks for SoTL in psychology. Gold standards include a grounding in theory, a longitudinal design, large sample sizes, diverse samples, advanced statistical techniques, mixed-methods approaches, and high standards of ethics. The good news is many studies in psychology already fit the benchmarks (Wilson-Doenges et al., 2016).

Whether SoTL or assessment, the best measures of student learning include objective approaches (Bartsch, 2013). For example, major journal outlets for SoTL in psychology—*Teaching of Psychology*, *Psychology Learning and Teaching*, and *Scholarship of Teaching and Learning in Psychology*—strongly urge contributors to include objective assessments of learning. A meta-analysis of SoTL bears this out. In one meta-analysis of 197 studies published in *Teaching of Psychology* from 1974 to 2006, Tomcho and Foels (2008) found that, on average, studies evidenced a medium effect size ($z_{Fisher} = .378$) across types of learning outcomes.

BLENDING ASSESSMENT AND SCHOLARSHIP OF TEACHING AND LEARNING

Assessment in the context of SoTL is fraught with many of the same challenges as assessment at the university or department level, including faculty resistance and insufficient know-how. Faculty in general are resistant to mandates to conduct specific assessments. I have had many colleagues balk when asked to embed assessments to ascertain how students attain general education or even department outcomes. A major barrier to the continued growth, acceptance, and valuation of SoTL efforts may lie with the lack of faculty assessment expertise and with the corollary belief that assessment is "not their job." Paradoxically, every faculty member who evaluates student work and assigns grades at the end of the semester is performing an essential component of assessment already. All that needs to be done in such cases is provide better training and support for faculty to help them make the link between assessment and SoTL. In some cases, this will involve enhancing knowledge about the development of SLOs and assessing the extent to which students are accomplishing specific outcomes, something not captured by the omnibus end-of-semester course grade. Some faculty may see SoTL under the purview of formal outcomes assessment and thus a responsibility of their institutional research office. In some cases, faculty members may fear that the assessments will be used as evaluations of their own performance (Dunn, McCarthy, Baker, & Halonen, 2011), a fear not without basis (Halpern, 2004).

Three major types of SoTL work can also double up to serve assessment purposes (McKinney, 2007; Nelson, 2003): (a) reports on particular classes or courses to gather qualitative or quantitative data from students before and after some change in teaching practice; (b) quantitative and/or qualitative comparisons of multiple courses or sections with a shared or similar measurement instrument; and (c) syntheses of extant SoTL via quantitative meta-analyses (e.g., Hattie, 2009).

Within these major categories of work are also myriad ways of measuring classroom learning and teaching (Angelo & Cross, 1993). In general, instructors can use course portfolios or blogs, interviews, focus groups, observational research, questionnaires, content analysis of student papers or assignments, secondary analysis of institutional data (e.g., university scores on the National Survey of Student Engagement), and experimental and quasiexperimental designs to gather quantitative and rich qualitative data. Aggregated rationally, these forms of classroom evidence of learning can also be leveraged for department-level assessment. For example, a faculty member might collect minute papers each week and track the effectiveness of the teaching as the students make progress toward the course learning goals.

CLOSING THOUGHTS

The rigor of measurement available in the assessment movement has yet to be fully tapped by faculty doing SoTL. Moreover, innovative measures of learning conducted by SoTL practitioners can enhance assessment work. One does not have to become well versed in educational theory or even statistical analysis to use assessment know-how in SoTL, but one needs to be open to what assessment can provide. If faculty see robust SoTL as a way to get ahead of accreditation requests, perhaps more assessment-informed SoTL can take place. If faculty have not talked to colleagues who oversee assessment and accreditation, I suggest a coffee meeting is in order. The more that faculty and administrators coordinate efforts to measure student learning, the easier and more satisfying all our jobs become.

Higher education is under attack (Berlinerblau, 2017), with growing fears that students are not learning (Arum & Roksa, 2010). SoTL can join the assessment movement to show what is really going on in our classrooms. SoTL advocates need to continue to spread the word about the beneficial effects of an SoTL approach to teaching (Hutchings et al., 2011). Educators who are passionate about student learning want to know that the course, major, and institutional experiences are leading to the cultivation of educated citizens. Assessment and scholarly teaching are individually important, but when they are combined systematically, SoTL emerges with the potential to impact students and student learning worldwide.

REFERENCES

American Psychological Association. (2018). *Assessment guide for psychology teachers.* https://www.apa.org/ed/precollege/topss/assessment-guide.pdf

Angelo, T. A., & Cross, K. P. (1993). *Classroom assessment techniques: A handbook for college teachers* (2nd ed.). Jossey-Bass.

Arum, R., & Roksa, J. (2010). *Academically adrift: Limited learning on college campuses.* University of Chicago Press. https://doi.org/10.7208/chicago/9780226028576.001.0001

Bartsch, R. A. (2013). Designing SoTL studies-Part I: Validity. In R. A. R. Gurung & J. H. Wilson (Eds.), *Doing the scholarship of teaching and learning: Measuring systematic changes to teaching and improvements in learning* (pp. 17–34). Jossey-Bass.

Berlinerblau, J. (2017). *Campus confidential: How college works, or doesn't, for professors, parents, and students.* Melville House.

Bernstein, D. (2013). How SoTL-active faculty members can be cosmopolitan assets to an institution. *Teaching & Learning Inquiry, 1*(1), 35–40. https://doi.org/10.20343/teachlearninqu.1.1.35

Boyer, E. L. (1990). *Scholarship reconsidered: Priorities of the professoriate.* Jossey-Bass.

Chew, S. L., Halonen, J. S., McCarthy, M. A., Gurung, R. A. R., Beers, M. J., McEntarffer, R., & Landrum, R. E. (2018). Practice what we teach: Improving teaching and learning in psychology. *Teaching of Psychology, 45*(3), 239–245. https://doi.org/10.1177/0098628318779264

Chick, N. L. (2014). Methodologically sound 'under the big tent': An ongoing conversation. *International Journal for the Scholarship of Teaching and Learning, 8*(2), Article 1. https://doi.org/10.20429/ijsotl.2014.080201

Dickson, K. L., & Treml, M. M. (2013). Using assessment and SoTL to enhance student learning. In R. A. R. Gurung & J. H. Wilson (Eds.), *Doing the scholarship of teaching and learning: Measuring systematic changes to teaching and improvements in learning* (pp. 7–16). Jossey-Bass.

Dunn, D. S., McCarthy, M. A., Baker, S. C., & Halonen, J. S. (Eds.). (2011). *Using quality benchmarks for assessing and developing undergraduate programs.* Jossey-Bass.

Dunn, D. S., McCarthy, M. A., Baker, S. C., Halonen, J. S., & Boyer, S. (2011). Understanding faculty reluctance to assess teaching and learning. In D. Mashek & E. Y. Hammer (Eds.), *Empirical research in teaching and learning: Contributions from social psychology* (pp. 143–159). Wiley-Blackwell. https://doi.org/10.1002/9781444395341.ch9

Ewell, P. T. (2009). *Assessment, accountability, and improvement: Revisiting the tension.* National Institute for Learning Outcomes Assessment, University of Illinois.

Glassick, C. E., Huber, M. T., & Maeroff, G. I. (1997). *Scholarship assessed: Evaluation of the professoriate.* Jossey-Bass.

Grauerholz, L., & Main, E. (2013). Fallacies of SoTL: Rethinking how we conduct our research. In K. McKinney (Ed.), *The scholarship of teaching and learning in and across the disciplines* (pp. 152–168). Indiana University Press.

Gurung, R. A. R., Ansburg, P. I., Alexander, P. A., Lawrence, N. K., & Johnson, D. E. (2008). The state of scholarship of teaching and learning in psychology. *Teaching of Psychology, 35*(4), 249–261. https://doi.org/10.1080/00986280802374203

Gurung, R. A. R., & Hackathorn, J. (2018). Ramp it up: A call for more research in introductory psychology. *Teaching of Psychology, 45*(4), 302–311. https://doi.org/10.1177/0098628318796413

Gurung, R. A. R., & Landrum, R. E. (2012). Assessment and the scholarship of teaching and learning. In D. Dunn, S. C. Baker, C. M. Mehrotra, R. E. Landrum, & M. A. McCarthy (Eds.), *Assessing teaching and learning in psychology: Current and future perspectives* (pp. 159–171). Wadsworth.

Gurung, R. A. R., & Landrum, R. E. (2014). Editorial. *Scholarship of Teaching and Learning, 1*(Suppl. 1), 1–2.

Gurung, R. A. R., Richmond, A., Drouin, M., Landrum, R. E., & Christopher, A. N. (2019). The past, present, and future of scholarship of teaching and learning in psychology. *Scholarship of Teaching and Learning in Psychology, 5*(2), 97–120. https://doi.org/10.1037/stl0000143

Hake, R. R. (2015). What might psychologists learn from scholarship of teaching and learning in physics? *Scholarship of Teaching and Learning in Psychology, 1*(1), 100–106. https://doi.org/10.1037/stl0000022

Halpern, D. F. (2004). Outcomes assessment 101. In D. S. Dunn, C. M. Mehrotra, & J. S. Halonen (Eds.), *Measuring up: Educational assessment challenges and practices for psychology* (pp. 11–26). American Psychological Association. https://doi.org/10.1037/10807-001

Halpern, D. F., Smothergill, D. W., Allen, M., Baker, S., Baum, C., Best, D., Ferrari, J., Geisinger, K. F., Gilden, E. R., Hester, M., Keith-Spiegel, P., Kierniesky, N. C., McGovern, T. V., McKeachie, W. J., Prokasy, W. F., Szuchman, L. T., Vasta, R., & Weaver, K. (1998). Scholarship in psychology: A paradigm for the twenty-first century. *American Psychologist, 53*(12), 1292–1297. https://doi.org/10.1037/0003-066X.53.12.1292

Hattie, J. (2009). *Visible learning: A synthesis of over 800 meta-analyses relating to achievement.* Routledge.

Hubball, H., Pearson, M. L., & Clarke, A. (2013). SoTL inquiry in broader curricular and institutional contexts: Theoretical underpinnings and emerging trends. *Teaching & Learning Inquiry, 1*(1), 41–57. https://doi.org/10.2979/teachlearninqu.1.1.41

Huber, M. T., & Hutchings, P. (2005). *The advancement of learning: Building the teaching commons.* Jossey-Bass.

Hutchings, P., Huber, M. T., & Ciccone, A. (2011). *The scholarship of teaching and learning reconsidered: Institutional integration and impact.* Jossey-Bass.

Maki, P. L. (2011). *Assessing for learning: Building a sustainable commitment across the institution.* Stylus.

Maurer, T. (2011). On publishing SoTL articles. *International Journal for the Scholarship of Teaching and Learning, 5*(1), Article 32. https://doi.org/10.20429/ijsotl.2011.050132

McKinney, K. (2007). *Enhancing learning through the scholarship of teaching and learning.* Anker.

McKinney, K., Atkinson, M., & Flockhart, T. (2017). A sampling of what psychologists engaged in SoTL might learn from sociology. *Scholarship of Teaching and Learning in Psychology, 3*(2), 178–190. https://doi.org/10.1037/stl0000080

Nelson, C. (2003). Doing it: Examples of several of the different genres of the scholarship of teaching and learning. *Journal on Excellence in College Teaching, 14*(2), 85–94.

Pan, D. (2009). What scholarship of teaching? Why bother? *International Journal for the Scholarship of Teaching and Learning, 3*(1), Article 2. https://doi.org/10.20429/ijsotl.2009.030102

Poole, G. (2013). Square one: What is research? In K. McKinney (Ed.), *The scholarship of teaching and learning in and across the disciplines* (pp. 135–151). Indiana University Press.

Potter, M. K., & Kustra, E. (2011). The relationship between scholarly teaching and SoTL: Models, distinctions, and clarifications. *International Journal for the Scholarship of Teaching and Learning, 5*(1), Article 23. https://doi.org/10.20429/ijsotl.2011.050123

Richlin, L. (2006). *Blueprint for learning: Constructing college courses to facilitate, assess, and document learning.* Stylus.

Richmond, A., Boysen, G., & Gurung, R. A. R. (2016). *An evidence-based guide to college and university teaching: Model teaching competencies.* Routledge. https://doi.org/10.4324/9781315642529

Stevens, D. D., & Levi, A. (2011). *Introduction to rubrics: An assessment tool to save grading time, convey effective feedback, and promote student learning.* Stylus.

Suskie, L. (2018). *Assessing student learning: A common sense guide* (3rd ed.). Jossey-Bass/Wiley.

Tomcho, T. J., & Foels, R. (2008). Assessing effective teaching of psychology: A meta-analytic integration of learning outcomes. *Teaching of Psychology, 35*(4), 286–296. https://doi.org/10.1080/00986280802374575

Walvoord, B. E. (2004). *Assessment clear and simple: A practical guide for institutions, departments, and general education.* Jossey-Bass.

Wiggins, G., & McTighe, J. (1998). *Understanding by design*. Merrill/Prentice Hall.

Wilson-Doenges, G., & Gurung, R. A. R. (2013). Benchmarks for scholarly investigations of teaching and learning. *Australian Journal of Psychology*, *65*(1), 63–70. https://doi.org/10.1111/ajpy.12011

Wilson-Doenges, G., Troisi, J. D., & Bartsch, R. A. (2016). Exemplars of the gold standard in SoTL for psychology. *Scholarship of Teaching and Learning in Psychology*, *2*(1), 1–12. https://doi.org/10.1037/stl0000050

Wright, D. L. (1994). Grading student achievement. In K. W. Pritchard & R. M. Sawyer (Eds.), *Handbook of college teaching: Theory and applications* (pp. 439–449). Greenwood Press.

2

A Framework for Setting Educational Priorities

Melissa Beers

Imagine you are traveling through a city divided by a river. You have to cross this river to reach your destination. Fortunately, there are many bridges, and all will get you to the other side—but, less fortunately, you don't get to choose which bridge you take. At the outset, all your options look about the same, but it's not until you are well over the water that you find out exactly what it will really take to cross this bridge. Will you find yourself stalled in traffic? How many tolls and traffic signals await you? Making matters worse, across the water you see that traffic is flowing quite differently on other bridges. They aren't quite the same after all.

If this situation isn't frustrating enough, imagine that it isn't until after you overcome these obstacles that you find out whether you have actually arrived where you want to be. As it turns out, travelers over this river don't know exactly where they will end up until they get to the other side. You might wind up much further north or south than your intended destination and have to travel quite a bit further before you get where you really want to be.

As improbable as this scenario may seem, there is a disconcerting parallel in higher education. Consider, for example, an institution that offers many sections of an introductory course. Like the bridges, these courses all seem the same at the outset. It might seem safe to assume that any one of these classes will get students to the same destination, but this is not always the case. The reality is that two sections of the same course may actually be quite different. They may use different textbooks or require different online resources. The

https://doi.org/10.1037/0000183-003

Assessing Undergraduate Learning in Psychology: Strategies for Measuring and Improving Student Performance, S. A. Nolan, C. M. Hakala, and R. E. Landrum (Editors)

instructors teaching these courses may not even know one another. Most likely, the instructors construct their syllabi independently and never see how others are approaching assignments or are making instructional design decisions within other sections of the same course. Faculty might even take pride in teaching the same course quite differently than their colleagues do, invoking the privilege of academic freedom. If learning objectives do appear on these syllabi, there is no guarantee they will be the same across courses. In fact, even if well-intentioned authorities[1] mandate objectives to appear on syllabi, listing objectives is no guarantee that a course will be aligned with them or with any other section of the course. Much like the aforementioned bridges, these courses may appear equivalent at the outset but only well into the journey does it become evident they don't necessarily lead students to the same place.

All courses at an institution are designed to meet certain expectations and fill specific goals; multiple sections of the same course are typically offered in a term or across an academic year to meet demand. When multiple instructors teach the same course, it is reasonable to consider them part of an instructional team. By any definition, a *team* is a number of individuals who work together toward a common goal—in this case, to meet a course's learning objectives. However, in many institutions, especially large and research-intensive institutions, it's not uncommon for multiple sections to be taught more or less independently, with little if any coordination between instructors in terms of textbooks, assignments, or even content. Although the full impact of this independence on student learning outcomes remains unknown in higher education, a lack of coordination between U.S. public K–12 and postsecondary (higher education) systems has long been recognized as negatively impacting students' success in transitioning from high school to college (Kirst & Venezia, 2001). In light of the scale of student enrollment in introductory psychology courses in the United States each year (conservatively estimated to be 1.2 million–1.6 million students; Steuer & Ham, 2008), a lack of curricular coordination and collaboration in assessment— within or across institutions—is not simply a missed opportunity but may negatively impact students as they transition through their program of study.

Assessment in such a context can play a critical role, both for the benefit of students and for creating community and enhancing collaboration within the team. The process of assessment is one that is naturally aligned with the core values of psychological science. In its simplest form, assessment involves

---

[1]In the United States, requirements to include specific learning objectives on course syllabi may be issued from several possible sources. For example, a department may require specific objectives as part of the major program assessment. Courses approved to meet certain college- or university-level requirements may be required to include those objectives on syllabi as well. Even government agencies may require learning objectives. For example, the Ohio Department of Higher Education requires certain foundational courses to meet specific learning objectives so students can easily transfer credit when taking courses at multiple institutions in the state (see https://www.ohiohighered.org/transfer/tag).

setting learning goals, collecting evidence to determine whether (or not) students are achieving these goals, and using that evidence to inform instructional decisions in the course. Assessment requires the instructor's active engagement in identifying instructional priorities, aligning instruction with goals, and intentionally using assessment data to inform teaching practice. But assessment also can play a critical role in faculty development, especially in multisection and general education courses. Working as part of a cohesive team affords all instructors the opportunity to learn from one another and teach in a way that emphasizes clear instructional priorities. Assessment can be the catalyst that brings it all together.

A FRAMEWORK FOR TRANSFORMING LOOSE GROUPS INTO COHESIVE TEAMS

Establishing an identity as an instructional team is a critical first step in developing and sustaining successful course assessment practices. Too often, instructional faculty are organized in what has been described as a loose group—they may have a common goal (student learning) but don't function as a cohesive team. Without intentional development and organization, members of such groups will continue to function independently, and the team will not evolve or achieve its goals. Sheard and Kakabadse (2002) identified nine key factors that differentiate loose groups from effective teams and how each factor manifests itself (see Table 2.1).

In the application of this framework to the context of curricula and instruction, a critical first step is to introduce the idea of working as an instructional team and focus on the task of setting goals and priorities for student learning. This means that new faculty members, even one-term instructors, understand the big picture of program goals and where the course(s) they teach fall in the larger curriculum. Faculty conceptualize the role of curricula differently and may have different underlying assumptions about the goals and objectives of a course (Fraser & Bosanquet, 2006). In practical implementation, curricula in a course or program can be conceptualized as "intended," "enacted" (e.g., taught), and "assessed" (Porter & Smithson, 2001); intentional and explicit alignment is needed as gaps can emerge between any of these levels.

A potential barrier to success at this phase can often be a disconnect between curricular teams developing instructional goals and the individuals teaching the courses. Without a sustained and concerted effort, the intentions of curricular committees may not be clearly communicated to faculty on the front lines. Because of many factors, including faculty retirement and attrition, turnover among graduate teaching associates, increases in adjunct and part-time faculty, and curriculum revision or renewal, curricula can drift over time; the original or intended goals for a course may evolve or may simply not be well understood. Even if a course is taught faithfully to its intended objectives, external changes to courses in a department or program may impinge upon the course's ability to fulfill its curricular role.

TABLE 2.1. Key Factors That Differentiate Loose Groups From Effective Teams

Element of need	Key factor	Loose group	Effective team
Task	1. Clearly defined goals the team is required to deliver	Individuals opt out of assessment of goals when they are not understood.	Learning goals are understood and acknowledged by all.
	2. Priorities are established by the organization.	It is unclear what activities are most valued, leading individuals to focus on their own priorities.	Team is cohesively aligned with instructional priorities.
Individual	3. Roles and responsibilities	Individuals' responsibilities are unclear with gaps and overlap, lack of accountability.	Roles and responsibilities are agreed upon and understood by all team members.
	4. Self-awareness; individuals understand the impact and consequences of their actions.	Individuals are guarded, are uncertain, lack trust, avoid engaging in assessment.	Individuals act in a way that constructively supports the team needs.
Group	5. Leadership	Directive—focused on concrete tasks; leadership sets goals	Catalytic—collaborative, supportive, and empowers team to set goals
	6. Group dynamics	Individuals are guarded and act in their own best interests.	The team is established and accepted as a social system.
	7. Communications	Formal, guarded	Open dialogue
Environment	8. Context	Task-focused, independent of other organizational goals	Decisions are influenced, not controlled, by the organization.
	9. Infrastructure—resources and support available to the team	Task-focused, disconnected from other organizational priorities	Stable support from organizational structure; strategy is translated into action in a way teams can tackle.

Note. From "From Loose Groups to Effective Teams: The Nine Key Factors of the Team Landscape," by A. G. Sheard and A. P. Kakabadse, 2002, *Journal of Management Development, 21*(2), p. 138. Copyright 2002 by Emerald Publishing. Adapted with permission.

The term *curriculum drift* has been used to describe a gap that develops over time between an intended curriculum and an enacted curriculum; it is a particular risk when individuals work in "unmonitored silos" (van de Mortel & Bird, 2010; Woods, 2015). Such a scenario is not uncommon in institutions where independence in the classroom is normative and seen as a component of academic freedom—even though most definitions of academic freedom reinforce faculty members' responsibility for teaching within a defined curriculum (albeit with latitude and discretion in how to do this).

Without some measure of coordination across courses, the results over time are problematic, as Donald (1997) described: "What might initially have been a well-designed and well-integrated course, with careful scaffolding across the course and the purposeful embedding of graduate attributes, can become a set of separate units."

Drift is also likely when instructional teams experience a high degree of turnover, which occurs when courses are primarily staffed by contingent faculty. In such cases, intentionality is needed to communicate course goals and learning objectives and to open lines of communication about intended objectives and how they will be assessed. The number of contingent or non–tenure-track faculty is rapidly growing in U.S. institutions (Benjamin, 2015). According to the American Association of University Professors (n.d.), non–tenure-track positions constitute the majority of U.S. positions. Non–tenure-track faculty teach an ever-growing share of undergraduate courses but typically work outside established communication structures; they may not be included in faculty meetings or formal communication networks. Consequently, instructors may be assigned to teach courses without being fully informed of course goals, why the goals were established, or where the course fits within the department or institution. Similarly, without explicit communication and guidance, graduate instructors may be assigned to teach or assist where curricular goals may not be communicated clearly—a particular issue in general education courses. And, as many institutions offer an increasing number of online courses, instructors may manage courses remotely and not have a regular physical presence on campus. Without understanding the goals from the start, how can instructors teach in a way that supports them?

At the individual level, even if curricular goals and priorities are communicated to members of an instructional team, it may not be clear what instructors' specific roles and responsibilities are with respect to curricula and assessment. In the worst case, instructors may not be aware of their assessment responsibilities until well after the course has been designed. Much like an unexpected toll levied halfway across a bridge, surprising instructors with new requirements midway through a semester (or worse, after the course has ended) undermines the integrity of the assessment process, the quality of the data, and potentially the instructors' trust.

At the group level, instructional teams can be defined at the level of an individual course, across multiple courses, or in a department as a whole. However the goals are defined, open dialogue, collaboration, and shared decision making around instructional goals and assessment both improve outcomes and move the team away from a loose structure toward teamwork. If instructors, especially graduate instructors or non–tenure-stream faculty, consider the assessment process as something "done unto" them as opposed to a process in which they play an active role, they cannot develop the kind of self-awareness and efficacy needed to improve team functioning. Establishing leaders who empower all members of the team to take an active role in assessment can both build community and reduce diffusion of responsibility.

Finally, the role of the surrounding environment with respect to the tone and tenor of conversations around assessment cannot be underestimated. Is there interest in and meaningful support for assessment at the course, department, and institutional levels? Does the institution invest in necessary infrastructure at the local (e.g., departmental, course) and institutional levels? Are there dedicated personnel committed to assessment who work to build community, or do administrators dictate assessment practices to be implemented by instructors independently? Are time and resources consistently devoted to assessment or are resources only marshaled in a scramble when accreditation reports are due? All these factors will either contribute to or detract from the effectiveness of instruction, assessment, and, consequently, student learning.

STRATEGIES TO ENHANCE TEACHING AND ASSESSMENT IN INSTRUCTIONAL TEAMS

Over the past 15 years, I have served as director for two sizeable instructional programs at a large, research-intensive university in the midwestern United States. One course, Introduction to Psychology, has had enrollments of up to 5,000 students per year in as many as 30 different sections per term. Introduction to Psychology serves as a prerequisite to every course in the major as well as a general education requirement. A second course, Introduction to Social Psychology, serves as a major program requirement and a general education requirement for second-level writing. Both courses are taught primarily by graduate student instructors (graduate teaching associates, or GTAs) and non–tenure-track lecturers. Instructors typically teach each course for 1 to 2 years, with nearly 100% turnover approximately every 4 years.

In this context, instructors at my institution are responsible for conducting assessment of relevant general education learning outcomes every term. In such large and rapidly changing course contexts, one might expect to encounter many of the characteristics of a loose group and anticipate that a sustained emphasis on assessment would be unlikely. However, we have established a set of sustained, integrated assessment practices that support student learning and simultaneously support instructor development. After many years of experience, we have identified six key strategies that enhance teaching and assessment in an instructional team:

- Understand the meaning and relevance of key learning objectives.
- Relate specific content to key learning objectives.
- Listen to students.
- Pool resources and collaborate.
- Create room for individual variation or degrees of freedom in instructional approaches.
- Assess, discuss, and reflect.

Each strategy can be adapted to varying course structures, sizes, and contexts with a goal of strengthening and sustaining assessment practices and cultivating a strong instructional team.

Understand the Meaning and Relevance of Learning Objectives in Your Course

It is not uncommon for instructors to teach classes that are on the edges of their professional expertise. Introduction to Psychology, for example, is a particularly challenging course for instructors because of the breadth of topics included in the course. The vast majority of psychologists today are trained as specialists rather than generalists, so at least some portion of the content takes an instructor out of their comfort zone. Further, it's not uncommon for last-minute reassignment to a class that is slightly outside of an instructor's primary area of expertise. Yet, content mastery does not in itself equip an instructor to assess higher order objectives, such as "Develop meaningful professional direction for life after graduation" (American Psychological Association [APA], 2013), or general education expected learning outcomes. Consider, for example, the following three general education expected learning outcomes for our social science courses:

- Students understand the theories and methods of social scientific inquiry as they apply to the study of individuals and groups.

- Students understand the behavior of individuals, differences and similarities in social and cultural contexts of human existence, and group processes.

- Students comprehend and assess individual and group values and their importance in social problem solving and policymaking.

These objectives are intentionally abstract so they can apply broadly to multiple courses in any social science discipline: economics, anthropology, sociology, political science, and, of course, psychology. However, this abstraction presents a significant challenge for instructors tasked with aligning instruction to and ultimately assessing these objectives. Before we can even begin to address the question of equivalency across courses and disciplines, what do these objectives mean in the context of an instructor's course? It is not uncommon for instructors, especially new ones, to struggle with the interpretation of learning objectives—and how can we teach what we don't understand? Assuming all objectives are equally clear and understandable to all instructors leaves the team vulnerable to pluralistic ignorance—a state in which no one is really confident about their own interpretation of the learning objectives or how to assess them.

Clear communication about required objectives is critical and can't be taken for granted, even for courses that have been on the books for a long time. The history of a course may be lost due to administrative or personnel changes, or the original intention for a course to meet a particular curricular requirement may be undocumented and forgotten. In such situations, the onus for understanding the history and evolution of a course can fall to the individual instructor to investigate: Who originally proposed the course and why? How has it been assessed in the past? If it is a general education course, who requested general education status, and is that paperwork available to review?

Taking these steps can help instructors align their instruction to the goals of the course at the outset. However, if the instructor doesn't have access to this kind of information, or if institutional or organizational norms don't support assessment, it is unlikely that instructors will have the motivation or ability to take these steps on their own.

In a cohesive instructional team, instructors should be oriented to understand objectives from the outset. In our program, for example, new graduate instructors complete a training course prior to teaching for the first time. Key learning objectives are addressed in the curriculum of the training course as well as in instructor handbooks and teaching manuals. As new instructors develop their course materials, they receive feedback from course administrators and experienced peers on how well their plans align with the learning objectives.

We regularly hold professional development events for both new and experienced instructors teaching general education courses. Taking time to discuss learning objectives in your instructional team improves shared understanding of the objectives as they relate to specific courses and helps instructors appreciate the value and importance of the objectives. For example, most introductory psychology instructors likely can generate strategies to assess how well students understand or apply specific concepts, such as correlation or operant conditioning, but it is much harder to identify strategies relevant to individual and group values and their importance in social problem solving and policy making. Once they understand the meaning, instructors can take the step to make the objective more concrete and have a greater appreciation of its value in their course. In instructor surveys at the end of the academic year, we found a relationship between instructors' self-reported understanding of general education learning objectives and their perception of how important the objectives are in their courses ($r(16) = .61$, $p = .007$), as well as between instructors' self-reported understanding of the general education learning objectives associated with their courses and their understanding of why the university wants instructors to address those learning objectives in their courses ($r(16) = .66$, $p = .004$).

Finally, it is important to invest the time to create community among instructors. Instructors in our program have organized both formal and informal mechanisms to share teaching strategies and resources. Organized professional events, department conferences, or other formal channels convey institutional support, and informal lunch meetings, social hours, or mixers also help to develop community and collaboration.

Relate Specific Content and Activities to the Learning Objectives

Even if instructors understand the meaning and significance of a learning objective in their course, this doesn't guarantee that they will understand how to align instruction to those objectives. Ideally, all courses would be developed in a backward-design approach (e.g., Wiggins & McTighe, 1998).

In a backward-design approach, learning objectives are identified first, and then relevant content and assignments are developed and prioritized to support those goals. Although pedagogically sound, this is not, unfortunately, how many (if not most) instructors first learned how to design their courses. Guidance and training on principles of backward design in planning a course and developing assignments will benefit individual instructors and the entire instructional team as well.

Yet, sometimes instructors may be assigned to teach a course on short notice, or they may have previously taught a version of the course that focused on different learning objectives. For example, a social psychology course may have a professional skills component, although one version of the course may have a focus on career development and planning and another on communication and writing. An instructor who has experience teaching social psychology may not have previously taught the course with either such objective. In such cases, it is critical to establish resources that support instructors' understanding of how to leverage content and develop assignments and activities that will support key learning objectives.

A key strength of an instructional team is that members can quickly and efficiently work together to crowdsource resources. In our program, this process begins with a curriculum map. This map includes all the major topics covered in the course and cross-references key learning objectives (see Figure 2.1). When new instructors join the team, the curriculum map helps them to connect topics to key objectives and thus understand how to operationalize objectives in their own instruction and assessment, including detail on why this material is relevant and specific suggestions for teaching the connection between the objective and the content. As a process, curriculum mapping helps an instructional team develop shared understanding of priorities and

FIGURE 2.1. Sample Curriculum Map Relating Course Topics to General Education Expected Learning Outcomes

Page	Description	ELO1a: Theories	ELO1b: Methods	ELO2: Culture and Groups	ELO3: Policy Making
109-112	Minimal information: inferring personality from physical appearance	✓	✓	✓	✓
112-113	Misleading firsthand information: pluralistic ignorance	✓		✓	✓
114-116	Misleading secondhand information	✓	✓	✓	✓
116-117	Order effects		✓		✓
117-120	Framing effects		✓		✓
120-121	Temporal framing		✓		✓
121-123	Confirmation bias	✓	✓		✓
123	Motivated confirmation bias	✓		✓	✓
125-129	The influence of schemas	✓	✓	✓	
129-134	Which schemas are activated and applied	✓	✓	✓	✓
136-141	The availability heuristic	✓			✓
141-147	The representativeness heuristic	✓		✓	✓
147-149	The joint operation of availability and representativeness	✓	✓		✓

Note. ELO = expected learning outcome.

goals and can improve team cohesiveness (Stark & Lattuca, 1997; Uchiyama & Radin, 2009; Wijngaards-de Meij & Merx, 2018), making the process of curriculum mapping a form of professional development in itself (Lam & Tsui, 2016).

Mapping the curriculum has the added benefit of helping the team identify gaps in available resources to support instruction and assessment. For example, if a review of the curriculum shows a lack of resources around a particular learning objective, the team may reconsider whether to retain that objective. Alternatively, as is the case in general education courses, if there is a lack of alignment with a required objective, the team can work together to develop content and resources to better meet that objective. In our program, review of general education outcomes resulted in the development of a set of quick reference guides for new instructors to align instruction with general education learning objectives. These tools have helped communicate to new instructors how and why individual topics are relevant, along with ideas to enhance teaching the topics (e.g., videos, activities) as well as assignments and activities to support assessment. On a national scale, APA's Project Assessment (http://pass.apa.org/login) provides assessment activities and resources aligned with the learning outcomes for the psychology major (see Figure 2.2). Seeing examples of assignments aligned to the learning objectives helps instructors better operationalize and implement such assessments in their own courses.

Listen to Students

Just as it is important to build instructors' skills and resources to align the work of an instructional team, it is equally important to listen to students' interpretation of course learning objectives as well as what concepts they see as relevant. Direct assessment methods capture an observable aspect of performance—for example, scores on a rubric or exam. Indirect methods assess an opinion, belief, or attitude—for example, students' perceptions that an assignment, activity, or course meets an expected learning outcome (cf. APA, 2018).

Students actually have a distinct advantage in contributing feedback on course goals and objectives. Consider that students take classes with multiple instructors each term and are thus exposed to a wide range of various teaching approaches. Incorporating opportunities for indirect assessment helps to align the work of the instructional team with the perspective of students. Often students have the opportunity to see a course (and discipline) in a broader context than does the instructor, who many have only limited (if any) opportunities to observe other classrooms.

Strategies to engage students may be as simple as asking at the start of the term which learning objective was most important to them in selecting a class and what they hope to gain by taking the course. Throughout the term, instructors can build in opportunities for students to reflect on how well the class is meeting the expected learning outcomes. Do students

FIGURE 2.2. Sample Resource From Project Assessment

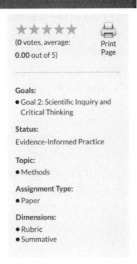

Evaluating a Claim About Human Behavior and the Evidence Presented to Support It

Jon Mueller, PhD
North Central College

Outcomes
2.1: Use scientific reasoning to interpret psychological phenomena

★★★★★
(0 votes, average:
0.00 out of 5)

Print Page

Indicators
2.1b Use psychology concepts to explain personal experiences and recognize the potential flaws in behavioral explanations based on simplistic personal theories 2.1B Develop plausible behavioral explanations that rely on scientific reasoning and evidence rather than anecdotes or pseudoscience 2.1D Generate alternative explanations based on perceived flaws in behavioral claims 2.1E Use strategies to minimize committing common fallacies in thinking that impair accurate conclusions and predictions

Goals:
● Goal 2: Scientific Inquiry and Critical Thinking

Status:
Evidence-Informed Practice

Topic:
● Methods

Assignment Type:
● Paper

Dimensions:
● Rubric
● Summative

Overview
Students witness scientific claims in the media and elsewhere every day. Are students capable of evaluating those claims from a scientific perspective? For this assignment, students locate a claim in the media and evaluate how well the evidence provided supports the claim. A claim is a statement of fact about the world. For example, someone might claim that smoking causes cancer. But one can ask, "Is there sufficient evidence to support the claim?" (Examples of scientific claims can be found at http://jfmueller.faculty.noctrl.edu/100/ correlation_or_causation.htm. Additional assignments or activities for students using the claims can also be found on this page.)

Note. From APA's Project Assessment (https://pass.apa.org). Copyright 2021 by the American Psychological Association.

feel they are developing a strong foundational understanding of the content? Are they building writing and communication skills? Are they developing professional skills and preparing for a future career? Remember, not all assessment must be formal or graded. Compare student perceptions with the results of direct assessments to identify critical gaps—for example, if students are meeting goals on direct assessments but do not perceive the course to be meeting their expectations for an associated objective, why might that be the case?

Instructors can draw students' attention to the relevance of learning objectives throughout the curriculum, being explicit as to why a topic or assignment is relevant. On the syllabus and on assignments, objectives can be cross-referenced to show that they are integrated across the course. Assessment should not simply be something "done to" students; they can take an active role themselves and, as a result, develop a better understanding of their own learning.

Pool Resources and Collaborate

A distinct advantage of working as an instructional team is the opportunity to collaborate and share resources. Team members can work together to refine their understanding of learning objectives, generate teaching strategies, develop common materials, and collaborate on assignments, in-class resources, and assessment tools. Rather than impose instructional decisions on individual instructors, cohesive instructional teams empower instructors to share with one another and contribute their own original content. In our program, instructors participate in exam committees to collaboratively author common exams. Each instructor contributes questions to only one of three exams; everyone contributes, but the workload is shared.

Programs can incentivize resource development and sharing, as we have often done in the form of a friendly competition. Framed as an idea exchange or a friendly "steal my idea" competition, we ask instructors to share their best ideas for assignments, activities, or writing prompts or teaching resources aligned to a learning objective. As an incentive, we have offered the chance to win recognition or small prizes based on the popular vote of the instructional team. For example, when we wanted to increase the number and quality of resources for instructors in teaching writing and communication skills, we put out a call for them to submit their best writing activities. The first-place submission was a class activity designed to help students practice developing transitions. In the activity, students randomly received information describing an event or topic; as a class they then told a story that linked each element together in a meaningful way. All instructors received directions for how to implement this activity, along with copies of all the submissions for use in their own classes. We maintained the resources in a central repository.

When infrastructure is leveraged in one's program, department, or organization, mechanisms to share and maintain resource repositories are essential. This may be a common site in the institution's learning management system; an online file repository such as Box, Dropbox, or Google Drive; or even a course YouTube channel to collect and organize teaching videos. The goal should be to support an environment in which instructors feel empowered and encouraged to identify new resources and contribute to the success of the rest of the team. We continue to work on ways to make resources more accessible to our teaching alumni even after they leave our program for their own academic positions.

Create Room for Individual Variation or Degrees of Freedom in Instructional Approaches

A frequent misconception about teaching in an instructional team involves the perception that it will constrain academic freedom. On the contrary, in a cohesive team, instructors themselves agree upon curricular decisions. Being part of a team does not mean that instructional decisions are imposed upon individual instructors and that courses have to be taught in a cookie-cutter manner but rather that instructors work collaboratively in the decision-making process.

In any team, individual instructors will vary in terms of their experience, focus, strengths, and preferences. Just as we observe individual variation in students, there will be individual variation in members of the instructional team. This is not a limitation but rather a strength on which teams can capitalize. More diverse teams have been observed to be more rigorous in evaluating evidence, more likely to carefully consider alternative points of view, and more likely to introduce new ideas and innovations (Rock & Grant, 2016). Particularly in foundational courses such as Introduction to Psychology, team members who possess expertise in diverse subject areas better support the whole team and can leverage their unique skills and knowledge to support one another. One instructor may be specialized in neuroscience but less experienced in disorders and treatments. Another instructor may be specialized in clinical psychology but less familiar with social psychology. Yet another instructor may be an adjunct working in industry who brings significant expertise on professional skill development but is less familiar with current research. Together they offset one another's individual limitations and add value to one another, to the team, and to students. Forcing all instructors into a course format that limits their ability to leverage their own expertise and teach in an authentic way is detrimental to students and teachers, and it defeats the intended purpose of enhancing student learning outcomes.

It is important to remember that learning objectives provide an emphasis or a direction for members of an instructional team. Shared instructional priorities require not that instructors walk in lockstep, but rather that they orient themselves toward the same target. Strategies to build flexibility and create degrees of freedom in assessment practices may include the following:

- As a team, collaboratively develop multiple assessment strategies, including both direct and indirect measures, and rotate them over the course of a semester or academic year.

- Ask instructors to develop objective-oriented assignments that can take a variety of forms as long as they target one or more specific learning objectives.

- Develop multiple prompts or assignments aligned with the same learning objectives for instructors to choose depending on their instructional preferences and styles.

- Collaboratively develop a set of assessment items to embed in tests or quizzes and ask instructors to use at least a portion of them on exams (e.g., use 10 out of 12 items) and share the results with the team at the end of the semester.

Whatever choice you make in your program of assessment, developing strategies that work for your team in your context with your students should be the priority. Without instructor buy-in and support, you'll find your assessment program hopelessly stalled.

Assess, Discuss, and Reflect

How, then, does an instructional team sustain instructor engagement and support? Instructor investment begins with the institution making assessment a priority and supporting the belief that assessment is important to understand what students and instructors are doing well and where they can improve. At the organizational level, an investment is required to collaboratively discuss assessment results so instructors understand the goals and progress toward meeting them. Taking time to reflect on results underscores that assessment cannot be done independently of what happens in the classroom. Effective teaching requires assessment to ensure the team is obtaining its desired results, and without time to discuss and integrate results into teaching practice, there can be no progress toward goals. Change doesn't necessarily happen quickly, and it doesn't necessarily imply a course overhaul. Leaders of instructional teams must understand how to be patient change agents and support instructors in developing their own solutions in an iterative, incremental fashion.

The relationship between engaging in teaching development, improvement in the quality of teaching, and improved student learning outcomes is well established (Gibbs & Coffey, 2004). To support instructor reflection on their teaching strategies and outcomes, instructional teams should focus on mobilizing the team and providing resources to support them in making the kind of incremental changes necessary to focus on their instructional priorities. For example,

- Review overall assessment results in team meetings at the beginning of each term. Highlight successes and areas of focus for the coming term and let the team discuss ideas to improve outcomes. Meet at the end of the term to debrief and share successes.

- Engage instructors as part of the assessment process. Create working groups to tackle big projects and involve instructors in writing reports and disseminating results.

- Share assessment results with other instructional teams or at teaching conferences to compare results and strategies.

Leaders of instructional teams should not underestimate the power of non-evaluative observation. A growing number of institutions in the United States, including Rice, Vanderbilt, and Loyola, have reportedly established "open classroom" weeks to create an opportunity for observation to serve as teaching development for observers. Formative classroom observation is a novel practice in the United States, where historically classroom observation has been evaluative and part of the tenure and review process. As part of the formative process, instructors observing their colleagues have the opportunity to learn new classroom skills, including high- and low-tech assessment techniques. At one campus, instructors who engaged in such nonevaluative observation for teaching development were motivated by a desire to learn new techniques and, following their observation, intended to use the strategies they observed

(Mueller & Schroeder, 2018). It can be eye-opening to look outside one's own classroom and see the broader environment in our departments and institutions. Doing so can only enrich your students' experiences and your own. Although it is neither a desirable nor attainable goal to expect instructors to teach in a way that is identical to one another, establishing objectives as instructional priorities creates an emphasis or direction for individuals as well as the team as a whole.

CONCLUSION

Much like bridges over a river, instructors transport precious cargo in the context of their courses. In a cohesive instructional team, instructors can support one another to ensure students get where they need to be. Assessment is not the end product but rather a process that has the potential to enhance faculty and graduate student development, improve student learning, and enhance community and collaboration among members of an instructional team.

REFERENCES

American Association of University Professors. (n.d.). *Background facts on contingent faculty positions.* http://www.aaup.org/issues/contingency/background-facts

American Psychological Association. (2013). *APA guidelines for the undergraduate psychology major: Version 2.0.* https://www.apa.org/ed/precollege/about/psymajor-guidelines.pdf

American Psychological Association. (2018). *Assessment guide for psychology teachers.* https://www.apa.org/ed/precollege/topss/assessment-guide.pdf

Benjamin, E. (2015). Overreliance on part-time faculty: An American trend. *International Higher Education, 21,* 7–9. https://doi.org/10.6017/ihe.2000.21.6902

Donald, J. (1997). *Improving the environment for learning: Academic leaders talk about what works.* Jossey-Bass.

Fraser, S. P., & Bosanquet, A. M. (2006). The curriculum? That's just a unit outline, isn't it? *Studies in Higher Education, 31*(3), 269–284. https://doi.org/10.1080/03075070600680521

Gibbs, G., & Coffey, M. (2004). The impact of training of university teachers on their teaching skills, their approach to teaching and the approach to learning of their students. *Active Learning in Higher Education, 5*(1), 87–100. https://doi.org/10.1177/1469787404040463

Kirst, M., & Venezia, A. (2001). Bridging the great divide between secondary schools and postsecondary education. *Phi Delta Kappan, 83*(1), 92–97. https://doi.org/10.1177/003172170108300118

Lam, B. H., & Tsui, K. T. (2016). Curriculum mapping as deliberation—Examining the alignment of subject learning outcomes and course curricula. *Studies in Higher Education, 41*(8), 1371–1388. https://doi.org/10.1080/03075079.2014.968539

Mueller, R., & Schroeder, M. (2018). From seeing to doing: Examining the impact of non-evaluative classroom observation on teaching development. *Innovative Higher Education, 43,* 397–410. https://doi.org/10.1007/s10755-018-9436-0

Porter, A. C., & Smithson, J. L. (2001). *Defining, developing, and using curriculum indicators* (CPRE Research Report Series RR-048). Consortium for Policy Research in Education, University of Pennsylvania Graduate School of Education. http://repository.upenn.edu/cpre_researchreports/69

Rock, D., & Grant, H. (2016, November). Why diverse teams are smarter. *Harvard Business Review*. https://hbr.org/2016/11/why-diverse-teams-are-smarter

Sheard, A. G., & Kakabadse, A. P. (2002). From loose groups to effective teams: The nine key factors of the team landscape. *Journal of Management Development, 21*(2), 133–151. https://doi.org/10.1108/02621710210417439

Stark, J., & Lattuca, L. (1997). *Shaping the college curriculum*. Allyn & Bacon.

Steuer, F. B., & Ham, K. W., II. (2008). Psychology textbooks: Examining their accuracy. *Teaching of Psychology, 35*(3), 160–168. https://doi.org/10.1080/00986280802189197

Uchiyama, K. P., & Radin, J. L. (2009). Curriculum mapping in higher education: A vehicle for collaboration. *Innovative Higher Education, 33*, 271–280. https://doi.org/10.1007/s10755-008-9078-8

van de Mortel, T. F., & Bird, J. L. (2010). Continuous curriculum review in a Bachelor of Nursing program: Preventing curriculum drift and improving quality. *The Journal of Nursing Education, 49*(10), 592–595. https://doi.org/10.3928/01484834-20100730-05

Wiggins, G., & McTighe, J. (1998). *Understanding by design*. Association for Supervision and Curriculum Development.

Wijngaards-de Meij, L., & Merx, S. (2018). Improving curriculum alignment and achieving learning goals by making the curriculum visible. *The International Journal for Academic Development, 23*(3), 219–231. https://doi.org/10.1080/1360144X.2018.1462187

Woods, A. (2015). Exploring unplanned curriculum drift. *The Journal of Nursing Education, 54*(11), 641–644. https://doi.org/10.3928/01484834-20151016-05

3

The Sound and Fury of Academic Program Reviews

What They Reveal About Assessment and Accountability

Jane S. Halonen and Dana S. Dunn

It is a tale told by an idiot,
Full of sound and fury,
Signifying nothing.

—WILLIAM SHAKESPEARE, *MACBETH*, ACT V, SCENE 5

It may seem a stretch to begin an analysis of the status of assessment practices with a quotation from William Shakespeare. However, we have become increasingly concerned that despite the promise of assessment for helping to generate true reform in teaching and learning, such activities may be generating more noise and heat than help for academic departments aspiring to make legitimate changes (Chew et al., 2018). Nearly all departments are now obligated to report annually on their accomplishments and improvement efforts, and most must submit to periodic visits by external reviewers to validate their work. However, these exercises often strike departments as unnecessary busywork with not much substance to show for their efforts.

At the turn of the 21st century, academic program reviews (APRs) were not part of the academic landscape (Bresciani, 2008). More recently, APRs have become a standard operating procedure in higher education accountability in the United States (Allen, 2004; Dill et al., 2010). Whether dictated by local institutional norms or legislative mandate, APRs provide an opportunity for departments to engage in systematic self-reflection regarding what they do and do not do well, followed by careful scrutiny from experts in the

https://doi.org/10.1037/0000183-004
Assessing Undergraduate Learning in Psychology: Strategies for Measuring and Improving Student Performance, S. A. Nolan, C. M. Hakala, and R. E. Landrum (Editors)

41

field—external program reviewers. The experts offer judgment about the relative success a program has achieved in meeting its goals while also identifying areas for development. APRs expose not just specific problems in getting the educational job done but also underlying difficulties that compromise educational objectives and quality of life for both faculty and students alike. The endgame here is continuous program improvement.

We, the authors, have served as external academic program reviewers—either solely or as part of an APR team—at more than 75 institutions. As a consequence, we have seen all manner of approaches for conducting an APR. Some processes are remarkably successful; departments function smoothly to meet their goals and function at optimal levels (Banta et al., 2009). The curriculum is coherent and comprehensive, and it is delivered collegially. These departments' assessment plans are well-designed and efficiently executed and optimize justifiable changes in curricular matters. Such visits are a joy, offering a brief showcase to celebrate academic achievement.

Unfortunately, in our experience, the majority of APR visits do not yield such happy outcomes, and many do not uncover evidence of sound assessment practice. From our vantage point, the insights we have gained suggest that collectively we have not achieved the "culture of evidence" vaunted as a goal by assessment experts (cf. Kuh et al., 2015). Rather than promoting meaningful improvement strategies, we conclude that we are at a disappointing juncture where assessment practices simply do not fulfill the promise of promoting effective change.

The purpose of this chapter is to highlight what we have learned about effective and ineffective assessment practices revealed by the APR process. Well-conceived and well-executed APRs encourage faculty members to reflect critically on what they are doing (or not doing) to advance quality teaching and learning. In contrast, ineffective processes may ultimately signify nothing. We advocate for the need for the metaculture to embrace the potential of assessment to make real and meaningful changes for the benefit of all stakeholders. We summarize what elements may be useful to producing the best outcomes from the process, including the important advantages of involving students in the APR process.

THE TYPICAL APR PROCESS

An official from academic affairs typically oversees the APR process, which usually transpires in a specified cycle for all academic departments (Dunn, McCarthy, Baker, & Halonen, 2011). The department normally has 12 to 18 months to prepare for the formal visit, during which time they will be gathering data, reviewing results, and preparing a self-study.

Departments must typically review a broad range of data, including specific achievements of identified student learning outcomes and performance metrics, such as graduation and retention statistics, enrollment trends, cost per student, and faculty profiles and performance. One of the primary components of the materials the organizers usually provide for the reviewer is the department annual report along with assessment data of student learning outcomes. If one is available, sharing a copy of the more recent APR is also a good idea, one that allows the external reviewer(s) an opportunity to assess whether the previous review led to any lasting changes in the department's curriculum or procedures. The administration may ask the department members to reflect on their strengths and weaknesses, identify resources they need to improve performance, and set goals for improvement. Exhibit 3.1 lists many of the items usually found in a departmental self-study document (see also Dunn, McCarthy, Baker, & Halonen, 2011).

Many resources have emerged to help faculty in their quest to tell a compelling assessment story. For example, professional organizations and advocacy groups have begun to produce guidance for faculty faced with the challenge of developing an assessment plan. The National Institute for Learning Outcomes Assessment (https://www.learningoutcomesassessment.org/) provides workshops and occasional papers that promote current best practices. Similarly, the American Psychological Association (2013) established guidelines for what undergraduate students in psychology should know and be able to do at graduation.

The department and administration normally collaborate on the choice of individuals who will serve as invited external assessors. Sometimes the institution will hire a sole contractor to come in for a 1- to 2-day visit. Many departments hire an experienced faculty member who may be acquainted with a department member, but more routinely departments may go in search of experts who can provide assistance in areas of need. Institutions often strive to get reviewers who themselves work in a similar context (e.g., 4-year colleges look for reviewers who also work in 4-year colleges). To expand the expertise in the review process, the institution may hire a second reviewer or ask members from other departments on campus to assist with fostering

---

EXHIBIT 3.1

Materials Usually Found in a Departmental Self-Study Document

Departmental mission statement

Data on number of psychology majors and minors; percentage of psychology majors in total undergraduate enrollment

Curriculum structure and course sequence; flowchart for majors showing required and elective courses

Chart showing course rotation for 4 years

Course syllabi for recent academic year

Recently assessed student learning outcomes

List of program changes achieved since last academic program review

Departmental budget

Recent annual department report, including issues of concern and planned future directions

Current curriculum vitae for all faculty in the department, including adjunct colleagues

Most recent self-study document

Most recent academic program review

EXHIBIT 3.2

General Outline for an Academic Program Review Report

Charge to external reviewer(s): What is expected through the review process
Description of reviewer's experience(s) in relation to program's needs
Observations drawn from self-study document and campus visit
Reviewer responses to specific needs expressed by the host program in the self-study
    and/or during the campus visit
List of recommendations (with supporting details) for the host program to consider
Conclusions
Appendix: Schedule for reviewer during campus visit

a better understanding of local norms and expectations. In some instances, a student alumnus or alumna may also be invited to serve on a team.

After the visit, the contractor or team drafts a report of the findings. The report may be in response to a formal template that the institution provides, or it may be more open-ended, driven by the priorities and problems uncovered in the report and during the campus visit. Exhibit 3.2 provides a general outline for the content of an APR document. Dunn, McCarthy, Baker, and Halonen (2011) provided a framework for the dimensions that constitute a thorough program review.

The contractor normally submits the report to the department to ensure detail accuracy before sending the official report to the commissioning official (i.e., provost or dean). Once it is reviewed, the administration releases the report to the department, from which it often requires a formal response. At some institutions, other officials may also chime in. For example, the dean may be expected to read and comment on the written materials generated by the process. In turn, the department will offer a plan for how to address the recommendations presented in the review as well as a timetable for achieving them.

CONTEMPORARY ACCOUNTABILITY CHALLENGES

From the vantage point of an academic program reviewer, a variety of problems prevent departments from using assessment strategies effectively to embrace a culture of continuous improvement and fully develop a given department's potential. Some of the challenges have been present since the assessment movement began to take root in the mid-1980s (Hutchings & Marchese, 2010). Other problems have surfaced as programs began to struggle with evolving accountability demands.

Faculty Engagement

In most contexts, administrators expect faculty to engage in assessment practices with little to no training, compensation, or clarity of purpose. Faculty members tend to respond to assessment mandates as time-consuming add-ons that do little to help them deliver a high-quality educational experience (Hutchings, 1990). When top-down assessment demands are exacting, faculty are likely merely to comply with assessment expectations rather than embrace them and have them drive a genuine assessment culture. In effect, faculty may mindlessly execute the specifications required without the process ever touching the core of who they are as teachers.

Allen (2004) argued that a well-developed curriculum should not undermine the freedom faculty exercise to facilitate the best experiences for their students. Establishing common goals does not preclude faculty from placing their unique imprint on course plans. However, faculty may need specific training in learning how to combine their unique talents with the department's standard expectations.

Resistance Is Not Futile

In most contexts there is little consequence for faculty disengagement from assessment (Dunn, McCarthy, Baker, Halonen, & Boyer, 2011). Formal expectations about participation in assessment may merely be window dressing, making it easy to minimize or sidestep any involvement in collaborative department assessment activity. In the absence of evidence that there is a significant and meaningful consequence for the activities, why wouldn't faculty avoid assessment?

As a result, it is not unusual for the academic program reviewer to see half-hearted assessment strategies or lackluster data submitted to affirm quality. The only time a department is likely to receive feedback on the assessment plan is when it is not submitted on time or if a specific problem triggers concern by an accreditor or a reviewer. When faculty adopt the stance of "What is the least we can do to get by?" they are likely trying to preserve their autonomy and discretionary time for more important activities that will have some palpable payoff.

The Unsung Assessment Hero

We occasionally discover an assessment hero in the APR process. The hero steps up when others step back, whether to satisfy intellectual curiosity about the true impact of the program or out of a sense of obligation to the department. That individual typically designs the assessment process, persuades department members to support the proposal, and oversees data collection and reporting. The hero usually undertakes the burden without compensation or release time. In the APR, the hero can hold forth an impressive discussion of design, implementation, and even future goals; however, the rest of the department may voluntarily remain in the dark about actual outcomes and how they might be used to improve delivery of the academic program and may be quite happy about their uninvolved status. The assessment hero can be so enamored of the job—or the perceived power that comes with the job—that they implement the responsibility in a heavy-handed way, further compromising a collegial response to share assessment practices.

The Business of Obfuscation

Ewell (2009) claimed that some tactical blunders transpired in the promotion of accountability practices. In the interest of trying to generate the most objective results of program review, many assessment programs concentrated on developing strategies that were to be set apart from day-to-day classroom operations, including prohibiting the use of classroom grading as part of the data-gathering process. Many faculty objected to being informed that somehow grading didn't count. In addition, the spirit of continuous improvement tends to reflect a management worldview. For example, terms such as *continuous quality improvement, value-added,* and *benchmarking* are all a comfortable fit for business and management faculty, but others may find such terminology to be additional incentives for remaining uninvolved in assessment discussions or activities.

During APR visits, faculty tend to recoil when continuous improvement terminology surfaces. They dislike the notion of students as "customers," especially as customers who may always be presumed to be right in their opinions, demands, and complaints. Instructors' disciplines may not foster comfort with quantitative evidence, nor do they think comfortably in terms of crisp behavioral statements that can serve as the basis for well-defined student learning outcomes.

The Paradox of Expectation

Although all institutions have incorporated assessment mandates as standard operating procedure, institutions differ in terms of the clarity with which they specify what is acceptable practice. On the one hand, the institution may provide no guidance in the hopes that an assessment plan will grow organically out of the departments' values and missions. However, it does not always occur to departments that have limited guidance to consider the degree to which the program should be a direct reflection of the institutional mission.

On the other hand, an institution that is preoccupied with creating tidy reports that make overall data collection easier to accomplish tends to fashion complex charts and templates that must be completed, which can result in fairly bizarre-looking results in the reporting forms. For example, faculty may attempt to cram the qualitative story they really want to tell in a column designed for a summary of quantitative data. The institutional goal of being able to sweep across reports to create a grand perspective on institutional functioning then inadvertently contributes to processes that preclude faculty from pursuing the ideas that matter most in planning and reporting improvements in their programs.

The impact on the APR process in such cases is that annual report documents become dense and hard to decipher. Mismatched data collection processes simply make the department's story harder to communicate and understand. The priority of serving the overall profile then actually interferes with the original intent of the process (i.e., helping the department develop insights into their operations that will lead to improvement).

One other aspect of expectation is worth noting. Faculty often expect that accreditors or APR reviewers have a best practice template in mind that may be recommended at best or foisted upon a department at worst. Good reviewers do not decide a priori what recommendations might be relevant for any given department. Instead of offering prescriptions, they suggest possible options and alternatives, emphasizing that the members of the department must decide together how best to proceed with changes that adhere to departmental folkways. The reviewers recognize that meaningful change will need to grow out of the organic concerns as well as the talents and energies of the faculty. And, in any case, what works in one department on one campus may not turn out to be effective in a different program at a different institution— local traditions will always trump best practices until appropriate adjustments are made.

Failure to Close the Loop

In optimal circumstances, assessment activities should drive ongoing curricular change (Hutchings & Marchese, 2010). However, as APR reviewers we see two problems that compromise this principle. The first is that faculty may become very enthusiastic about the collection of data but do not see it connected to program reform in any meaningful way. They have mountains of information but do not recognize that the point of data gathering is to serve as an impetus for eventual and meaningful changes to the existing program.

Second, faculty may not respect that curricular decisions should be informed by data. Faculty members have traditionally navigated curricula through normal processes of faculty debate, hunch, tradition, and even whim. If such tactics have worked in the past, why bother with gathering data? During APR reviews, the process by which faculty decide how to move the curriculum reveals a great deal about limited reliance on the data they collect.

Content Loyalty Overshadows Skill Development

Barr and Tagg (1995) argued that faculty members needed to transform how they teach to emphasize skill development rather than content transmission. Their learning-centered arguments resonated with many educators. However, the majority of faculty members still maintain loyalty to the traditions of content coverage as their primary mode of operating. In other words, it's the material taught that matters, not the skills students can and should learn in that context.

Examining syllabi in the APR gives disappointing insight into how few faculty have embraced Barr and Tagg's (1995) proposal about the needed transformation in higher education from content-centered to learning-focused pedagogy. Some syllabi fail to address learning outcomes at all, but the majority of goals concentrate on the lowest levels of Bloom's taxonomy (Anderson & Krathwohl, 2001), such as remembering facts rather than achieving loftier aspirations that engage higher levels of critical thinking.

The Threat of a Cookie-Cutter Curriculum

Many faculty view assessment as a threat to what makes the department unique. Faculty members sometimes harbor expectations that a site reviewer will dictate solutions that represent standardization and threaten program creativity. Accreditors and APR reviewers are more likely to recommend particular best practices rather than impose or require predetermined solutions to the problems they encounter in their campus visits.

With the promulgation of national standards in any discipline, many faculty members expect the next natural development would be a nationally endorsed examination to test student learning and prove department value. Not only does this stance favor content retention as the most important objective achieved in the undergraduate curriculum, but it also runs the risk of faculty narrowing the scope of their work to improve their standings. If they care about department status, they will "teach to the test" to help students maximize the success profile of the department. Something magical about a department's unique vision will then truly be lost.

The Continually Moving Target

An emerging expectation in some institutions is that assessment questions need to be freshly chosen each year. As a consequence, departments may be asked to develop a 5- to 7-year plan that guarantees coverage of all outcomes specified in the department's assessment plan. The rationale for this paradigm is that a department should target a weakness based on data, fashion an intervention to make an improvement, document those improvements, and then move on to the next weakness while maintaining whatever new effort might have been required by the last intervention.

We suggest that it may be unrealistic to set this type of expectation for this pace of continuous improvement. It is legitimate to report sustained achievement, not just targets for improvement, particularly if the program is operating at high levels of function. We argue that departments should be given some latitude to tell their achievement stories in a way that does justice to their discipline and its values as well as to determine the selection of goals that will be in the best interest of their students. Moving from goal to goal each year may not be an effective way to accomplish genuine continuous improvement.

The Weaponized APR

In our experience, sometimes APRs become the nail in the coffin for departments or chairs who are in trouble with higher level administration. Campus officials may recognize that a department is not functioning well and legitimately want to get assistance in figuring out how to get that group of faculty back on track. However, we occasionally see administrators whose focal questions represent a "gotcha" perspective and whose hopes rest on whether the reviewer can dredge up sufficient evidence from "an objective viewpoint" that justifies the officials taking actions that they want (i.e., remove an ineffective chairperson) but may not have sufficient justification in the absence of external validation.

When an antagonistic relationship develops between a department and its overseers, then assessment activities magnify the intensity of the trouble. Administrators may pay differential attention to assessment planning and are more likely to challenge the accuracy of the data or commitment to the plan. It is understandable that faculty would not be eager to surrender data that might impugn what they are currently doing or value as important. Like most humans, faculty members are not crazy about getting feedback that potentially highlights their imperfections. Throw in the sense of self-importance tied to many faculty members' self-views as well, and there is the real risk of triggering narcissistic rage upon the delivery of the inevitable bad news.

If a department has fallen into disfavor, then no amount of assessment data or praise from an objective review will suffice to change minds. If an APR generates evidence favorable to the department, it can easily be ignored by administrators whose confirmation bias promotes disregarding viewpoints that conflict with their closely held perspectives. In such cases, assessment becomes an exercise in hypocrisy if administrators ignore findings that don't jibe with their personal truths about the department.

Quantitative Evidence Outweighs Qualitative Concerns

Measuring high-quality learning is obviously challenging. However, in the absence of widely endorsed strategies for affirming learning, institutions find that demands have ramped up for performance metrics that at best imply educational quality rather than measure it directly. As U.S. state legislatures have signed onto holding higher education more accountable for how tax dollars are invested, their focus tends to be economically driven. They attend to how many freshmen are retained or 6-year graduation rates rather than the quality of the education that transpires during that period. Although some metrics do provide comparative evidence about the efficient operations of an institution, they do not have any meaningful relationship to the quality of the learning experience the institution provides. This criticism is especially relevant when legislators choose entry-level salaries after graduation as proof that high-quality education has transpired.

Sadly, we are seeing archival reports drive high-stakes decisions in performance-based funding. Although that level of attention is warranted to address efficiency, it fails to inspire confidence that quality education is even a concern for those allocating higher education budgets. A well-designed assessment story should be able to make a persuasive argument about the quality of student learning, but, at present, there would be no willing audience to listen.

Assessment Creep

What may have started out as a legitimate demand for accountability appears to be proliferating into an assessment nightmare for ambitious programs. Largely because of the growth of online programming, accrediting bodies and academic reviewers have begun to request evidence that programs are treating all learners equitably regardless of the mode of delivery. Thus, faculty may need to harvest data specifically for every permutation of the degree, certificate, and delivery mode at every level of education from general education through graduate training. What used to be a very simple question—"How are the students doing?"—now becomes a complex matrix of how the online students are doing in the general psychology course compared with the face-to-face variation or whether adjunct faculty can deliver the same high-quality education as full-time faculty, and so on.

Although we recognize that asking questions about equivalence in programs is relevant and interesting, we also know that asking for comparisons at this nuanced level quickly moves assessment from providing basic information about program quality to something that may require almost full-time attention to gathering and analyzing data regarding course activities. If departments cannot manage basic assessment questions, then the quality of nuanced comparisons is likely to be poorly executed.

The Scarce-Resource Trump Card

Under ideal circumstances, positive APR results should help galvanize arguments for resources to meet unmet needs. If a department is high functioning and can document evidence that additional resources would make them even more effective, then an APR should provide the advocacy necessary to capture those resources. Under those circumstances, faculty may engage in assessment activity with enthusiasm and confidence that their efforts will not be wasted.

However, even when data clearly emphasize badly needed resources to achieve goals, these rewards may not be forthcoming. Regardless of the caliber of the evidence, a university may be unable to free up resources as a suitable reward. It is also quite possible that the department's mission may simply be at odds with current institutional priorities. For example, local nursing shortages may divert resources to meeting the health care needs of the community rather than cranking out more liberal arts majors irrespective of the quality of performance by competing departments. Where there is no obvious connection between APR results and distribution of scarce resources, the APR feels at best like a futile exercise and at worst like a sham. At the very least, administrators need to be clear about what potential rewards, if any, may accrue to a strong APR performance. If the results of the exercise will not influence budget decisions, then the illusion should not stand.

HOW TO OPTIMIZE THE APR EXPERIENCE

With all of its attendant complicated problems (see Maki, 2010), how should departments respond to the demands associated with APR? We still believe the APR can be a legitimate vehicle to assist faculty in improving learning outcomes as well as the quality of life for both faculty and students alike, if undertaken in the proper spirit. We offer a few principles to facilitate the best outcomes, whether the activity has impact beyond department operations or not.

Set the Context for Moving From "Having" to "Wanting" to Do Assessment

Do not assume that all faculty members understand the assessment mandate or will agree with it once it is understood. Convene a conversation in which faculty can fully air their concerns about the APR specifically and assessment in general. It may be useful to have a dean's representative meet with the faculty rather than simply having the chair translate what the administration expects. Dedicate time in faculty meetings to providing conversation related to assessment and avoid making comments or jokes that undermine the continuous improvement intent of the mandate. Avoid top-loading assessment concerns into one—sometimes deadly—session per year to respond to minimum requirements in an institution's assessment plan.

Choose Assessment Targets Wisely

Informal gatherings of faculty often result in the airing of concerns about how poorly students may be functioning. Forging an assessment plan that addresses their most pressing concerns should produce a greater commitment from faculty at this juncture to shared goals about ways to improve the program. Part of continuous improvement involves maintenance of gains achieved in the curriculum. As such, departments can be encouraged to provide evidence to support the activities that they are doing well and not just focus on weaknesses.

Embed Assessment

Gathering objective evidence of quality is a challenge; however, separating assessment from frontline activities in the department virtually guarantees distancing and resistance. Walvoord (2004) made a compelling case that faculty members' grading practices should be at the core of a department's assessment plan. Rather than investing in high-profile exit exams that concentrate on content mastery, figuring out critical junctures in the program where the department can compile assessment data on skill development will reinforce individual faculty contributions to assessment.

Similarly, having faculty develop shared assessment strategies may promote a stronger sense of ownership. Departments should strive to embed assessment in existing coursework wherever possible to simplify the process (Halonen, 2018). One simple step is to encourage a department rubric or style sheet to be used with project reports and presentations. Collaboration in design of the rubrics clarifies what good communication performance should look like. Students with repeated exposures to a commonly deployed rubric are likely to absorb effective communication principles and use the rubric in their own personal improvement plans beyond their experiences in the classroom.

For those faculty members who remain committed to the importance of content over skills, collaborating on an exit exam can be useful. Testing the content students acquire in their required courses can give faculty insights into how their individual courses contribute to a coherent and cohesive curriculum. However, avoid using a standard exit exam in situations in which students are not required to take all of the courses covered by the exam.

Facilitate Smart Data Collection via Technology

Digital learning systems (e.g., CANVAS, Blackboard) have begun to adopt data-harvesting options to help faculty with their assessment demands. Although these strategies may be challenging to learn, building a technology-friendly assessment program can liberate faculty from the drudgery of collecting data. With the push of a button, outcome-based programming can efficiently provide patterns of student performance that can populate an annual report or an APR. In addition, achievement patterns from prior semesters can be shared with new students to give them an advantage in achieving at a higher level.

Distribute the APR Workload

Although it may be useful to have an overall coordinator to get a report across the finish line, assessment experts agree that the assessment burden should not fall on just one person (cf. Hutchings, 2010). That strategy leads to a shallow departmental commitment that will surface when the assessment hero tells the story. Asking each faculty member to contribute at a level that corresponds to their experience and expertise offers a greater chance that department members see the value of an improvement-oriented climate. It also emphasizes that to be fair to all department colleagues, whether junior or senior, assessment efforts must be shared and undertaken by all.

Enact Sufficient Lead Time

Program self-studies that are haphazardly assembled are clear indications of how little faculty members care about the goal of program improvement. If the program review is a singular opportunity to have attention focused on the program—even if it is just once every 7 or so years—then a department needs to gear its work toward making the most impressive case. That intention requires substantial time to develop appropriate questions and design the proper process for answering them.

Give Assessment Engagement Incentives and Consequences

We recommend that incentives are going to be most effective to promote full engagement of faculty. Where resource distribution can be aligned with proven performance, faculty members are more likely to engage willingly. However, as long as disengaged faculty also have no negative consequences that follow their lack of collaboration, it is unlikely that a culture of assessment (cf. Kuh et al., 2015) can thrive. At minimum, faculty should be able to make the case that involvement in the scholarship of teaching and learning, including publishing the results of assessment, should render credit for personnel decisions, such as tenure and promotion.

Where Possible, Reward Good Performance Linked to Evidence of Quality

If the institution values evidence of effectiveness, then several steps can be taken to underscore that commitment. These can include providing some release time to facilitate completion of data collection and report writing. As well, departments might develop a wish list that is embedded and annually updated regarding the resources they need to make strides in program improvement. Funding retreats, big-screen televisions to announce activities, and additional graduate assistantships committed to assessment planning, among other possible options, affirms that good performance will be not just expected but also rewarded.

Be Rational About Securing New Faculty Lines

Faculty lines—that is, new faculty positions allocated to the department—tend to be the most important currency administrators have at their disposal to manage their departments and acknowledge appreciation for program achievement. During a typical APR exit interview, virtually every dean hears that a program needs more lines to do a better job. As a consequence, virtually every dean has developed a rather thick skin about that APR recommendation. In fact, many may adopt a defensive posture from the outset, suggesting that the APR team needs to help the department figure out how to do more with less rather than expecting the report to culminate in faculty lines being granted. Realistically, most administrators have very little leeway to use faculty lines as a means to validate that the program is functioning well, but they should strive to find other vehicles to endorse high-quality functioning. For example, an administrator might agree to increase some graduate assistantships or sponsor a retreat so the faculty can tackle their next objective more efficiently.

Involve Students Meaningfully in the APR

Reviewers know that departments tend to recruit their best and brightest to show off how accomplished their students are. Astute reviewers recognize that all programs have high-caliber students who are unlikely to provide an unbiased view of the program's accomplishments. Although it is reasonable to conduct an interview session with leaders in Psi Chi, for example, reviewers should insist on talking to a class or a group of students in which abilities are likely to be more normally distributed.

When we do a campus visit for an APR, we routinely have one or more meetings with undergraduate and often graduate students. Rarely has the department chair or self-study team informed them about the rationale behind our visit. They are usually given some vague notion that we are "looking over the department" or "doing a routine evaluation of our program." That's fine as far as it goes, but by neglecting to explain the larger purpose behind an APR, department colleagues have missed an opportunity to expand students' understanding of what makes for a good education in psychology. When students are involved in the review process, they get a sense of the larger picture behind their education and why the psychology curriculum and course assignments are crafted as they are.

Require a Formal Response From Overseers

To ensure that program reports have some kind of impact on what is done in a program, those who require the report to be written should be required to read and respond to it within a fixed period. Although it does not have to be an extensive response, a formal response that reflects the highest achievements, the most pressing needs, and the most significant challenges at least provides some validation that the activities done by the program faculty members matter.

CONCLUSION

As Simon Sinek (2017) tweeted, "Accountability is hard. Blame is easy. One builds trust[;] the other destroys it." Astute assessment planners acknowledge that the process is a fragile one, fraught with threats from above and below.

However, we believe that an APR process becomes a powerful tool to help departments truly achieve increasing quality. The process should not be idiotic, abrasive, or driven by fury, but it should be a thoughtful process that improves quality for all stakeholders.

How should departments avoid the doldrums and frustrations of bad assessment design? First, adopt appropriate humility about the likely achievements of your program and let your curiosity about what aspects of the program are truly effective shine through. Second, strive to foster a legitimate assessment culture in which conversations about program quality transpire regularly rather than as an annual hollow or drab exercise. Third, when you have the opportunity to work with external academic program reviewers, choose them wisely. Make contracts with individuals whose expertise matches the improvement directions that have emerged from your own solid planning. Finally, embark on APRs as an important investment that department members will make to maximize their impact on the department's future direction. Regardless of the insights gained from your external visitors, the true value of the APR lies in honest conversation that will unfold in departments that have embraced the value of practicing in a culture of assessment.

REFERENCES

Allen, M. (2004). *Assessing academic programs in higher education*. Anker.

American Psychological Association. (2013). *APA guidelines for the undergraduate psychology major: Version 2.0*. https://www.apa.org/ed/precollege/about/psymajor-guidelines.pdf

Anderson, L. W., & Krathwohl, D. R. (Eds.). (2001). *A taxonomy for learning, teaching, and assessing: A revision of Bloom's taxonomy of educational objectives*. Allyn & Bacon.

Banta, T. W., Jones, E. A., & Black, K. E. (2009). *Designing effective assessment: Principles and profiles of good practice*. Jossey-Bass.

Barr, R. B., & Tagg, J. (1995). From teaching to learning: A new paradigm for undergraduate education. *Change, 27*(6), 12–26. https://doi.org/10.1080/00091383.1995.10544672

Bresciani, M. J. (2008). *Outcomes based academic and co-curriculum program review: A compilation of institutional good practices*. Stylus.

Chew, S., Halonen, J. S., Beers, M. J., McCarthy, M. A., Gurung, R. A. R., McEntarffer, R., & Landrum, R. E. (2018). We should practice what we teach: Improving teaching and learning in psychology. *Teaching of Psychology, 45*(3), 239–245. https://doi.org/10.1177/0098628318779264

Dill, D. D., Massy, W. F., Williams, P. R., & Cook, C. M. (2010). Accreditation and academic quality assurance: Can we get there from here? *Change, 28*(5), 17–24. https://doi.org/10.1080/00091383.1996.9937136

Dunn, D. S., McCarthy, M. A., Baker, S. C., & Halonen, J. S. (2011). *Using quality benchmarks for assessing and developing undergraduate programs*. Jossey-Bass.

Dunn, D. S., McCarthy, M. A., Baker, S. C., Halonen, J. S., & Boyer, S. (2011). Understanding faculty reluctance as reactance and opportunity for persuasion: A social psychology of assessment. In D. Mashek & E. Y. Hammer (Eds.), *Empirical research in teaching and learning: Contributions from social psychology* (pp. 143–159). Wiley. https://doi.org/10.1002/9781444395341.ch9

Ewell, P. T. (2009, November). *Assessment, accountability, and improvement: Revisiting the tension* (NILOA Occasional Paper No. 1). University of Illinois and Indiana University, National Institute for Learning Outcomes Assessment. https://www.learningoutcomesassessment.org/wp-content/uploads/2019/02/OccasionalPaper1.pdf

Halonen, J. S. (2018, June 23). *KISS assessment for general education and the major: A workshop* [Conference session]. Eastern Teaching of Psychology Conference, Staunton, VA, United States.

Hutchings, P. (1990, June 30). *Assessment and the way we work* [Closing plenary]. 5th American Association of Higher Education Conference on Assessment, Washington, DC, United States.

Hutchings, P. (2010, April). *Opening doors to faculty involvement in assessment* (NILOA Occasional Paper No. 4). University of Illinois and Indiana University, National Institute for Learning Outcomes Assessment. http://www.learningoutcomeassessment.org/documents/PatHutchings_000.pdf

Hutchings, P., & Marchese, T. (2010). Watching assessment: Questions, stories, prospects. *Change, 22*(5), 12–38. https://doi.org/10.1080/00091383.1990.9937653

Kuh, G. D., Ikenberry, S. O., Jankowski, N. A., Cain, T. R., Ewell, P. T., Hutchings, P., & Kinzie, J. (2015). *Using evidence of student learning to improve higher education.* Jossey-Bass.

Maki, P. L. (2010). *Assessing for learning: Building a sustainable commitment across the institution* (2nd ed.). Stylus.

Sinek, S. (2017, July 20). *Accountability is hard. Blame is easy. One builds trust, the other destroys it* [Tweet]. https://twitter.com/simonsinek/status/888111803669946368?lang=en

Walvoord, B. E. (2004). *Assessment clear and simple: A practical guide for institutions, departments, and general education.* Jossey-Bass.

4

Replacing the Term *Formative Assessment*

A Modest Proposal

Rob McEntarffer

The term *formative assessment* originated in the context of program evaluation (Scriven, 1967) and is now in widespread use in the context of classroom assessment. Although commonly used, the term is frequently misunderstood and used by students, teachers, and textbook publishers in several different ways. These conflicting definitions impede research and discussion about classroom assessment processes (Andrade & Cizek, 2010). Formative assessment refers to important uses of assessment data by teachers and students, but the term is problematic because it seemingly refers to a type or kind of assessment instead of the process of using assessment data. The term *formative assessment* can be usefully replaced by two other more descriptive terms: *responsive teaching* and *student practice*. Replacing the term *formative assessment* with these two more descriptive terms emphasizes specific uses of information from classroom assessments and could help teachers and students communicate more effectively about these important classroom assessment processes.

The 21,537 students in the school district where I work hear and use the term *formative assessment* almost daily during their conversations with teachers. Formative assessment is a category in the online gradebook system for all 1,729 middle and high school teachers. Teachers use this assessment category in their gradebooks for dozens of activities and assignments in each class. But if you ask these students what formative assessment means, you get very different answers. Because of its ubiquity in gradebooks, many students hear "formative assessment" and immediately think "homework" or "an assignment

https://doi.org/10.1037/0000183-005
Assessing Undergraduate Learning in Psychology: Strategies for Measuring and Improving Student Performance, S. A. Nolan, C. M. Hakala, and R. E. Landrum (Editors)

not worth many points." Teachers hear about the importance of formative assessment during professional development sessions, but many would struggle to verbalize a specific definition of the term or what makes one kind of activity or assignment a formative assessment. This confusion isn't their fault: Debates about the definition of this term have been raging for years (Popham, 2008), and educators and researchers disagree about how this term should be used. Maybe it's time to stop banging our heads against the wall and replace the term with more specific terms that better communicate when we mean as teachers. In this chapter, I briefly review the history of the term *formative assessment*, discuss limitations of this term in classroom contexts, and propose new terminology to address these limitations.

BACKGROUND: WHAT IS FORMATIVE ASSESSMENT?

The term *formative assessment* was first used in the context of program evaluation, not classroom assessment (Scriven, 1967). Some evaluators used the term *summative evaluation* to refer to evidence about the quality of an intervention that was completed and the term *formative evaluation* to refer to ongoing evidence and improvement advice about an intervention while it was taking place. A few decades later, Black and Wiliam (1998) used the term *formative assessment* to refer to

> activities undertaken by teachers—and by their students in assessing themselves—
> that provide information to be used as feedback to modify teaching and learning
> activities. Such assessment becomes formative assessment when the evidence is
> actually used to adapt the teaching to meet student needs. (p. 140)

This early definition of formative assessment emphasizes different data uses rather than defining formative assessment as a type of assessment. Assessment becomes formative when it is used by teachers to make instructional decisions: "These terms are therefore not descriptions of kinds of assessment but rather of *the use to which information arising from the assessments is put*" (Wiliam, 2000, p. 2, italics in original). Under this definition, an assessment instrument is neither formative nor summative until data from that instrument are used, and data from the same instrument could be used in either summative (used for course grades) or formative processes. This basic distinction between formative and summative assessments is important to remember when examining different definitions of how the term *formative assessment* has been used.

   In the United States, several education organizations attempted to clarify the definition of formative assessment, with varying degrees of success. The Council of Chief State School Officers (CCSSO) is one of the most recognized expert groups by school administrators. In 2006, this group formed a consortium of members to deal specifically with the task of defining formative assessment. This consortium, known as the FAST SCASS (Formative Assessment for Students and Teachers State Collaborative on Assessment and Student Standards), examined different definitions of formative assessment and eventually agreed on this one: "Formative assessment is a process used by teachers and students during instruction that provides feedback to adjust ongoing teaching and learning to improve students' achievement of educational outcomes" (McManus, 2008, p. 3). This definition also indicates that data use defines whether an assessment is either formative or summative, but includes the idea that either students or teachers may use the same assessment data in formative or summative ways. Popham (2008) tried to clarify the CCSSO definition further: "Formative Assessment is a planned process in which teachers or students use assessment-based evidence to adjust what they're currently doing" (p. 6). This clarification implies that any time a teacher or a student uses assessment data to reflect on and make a change in the teaching/learning process, that action was a formative assessment process. Note that very different examples of data use are included in this umbrella definition of formative assessment: Teachers using feedback from a classroom assessment to change a lesson plan, students using a comment on a paper to revise their work, teachers using data from a quiz to clarify misconceptions, and students looking at exam results and deciding to study a specific section of a textbook are all formative assessment events under this definition.

Other attempts to clarify the term *formative assessment* rely on distinguishing between the purposes of different kinds of assessment. Stiggins and Chappuis (2006) proposed two new terms: *assessment for learning* and *assessment of learning*. They proposed that chronology is important when thinking about formative and summative assessments. Some assessments occurred after learning was finished and the purpose was to summarize or evaluate learning after it was complete (assessment *of* learning). Some assessments occurred during the learning process, and the purpose was to diagnose ongoing learning and make adjustments (assessment *for* learning). These terms may help emphasize the importance of data use, but they ignore the reality that different users (teachers, students, and others) may use assessment data at any time during the learning process for either formative or summative purposes. The same assessment results might be used by students to evaluate learning after they consider it done (summative, assessment *of* learning) but at the same time by the teacher to identify ongoing student misconceptions and adjust instruction accordingly (formative, assessment *for* learning).

Although there is widespread agreement about the potential for formative assessment to help students learn (Black & Wiliam, 1998; Hattie, 2008), confusion and disagreement about the definition of the term get in the way of effective research and implementation of formative assessment in classrooms (Andrade & Cizek, 2010). The term *formative assessment* has been used in schools for at least 2 decades, but confusion still abounds. Test and textbook publishers muddy the waters further as they try to use the term for educational products and services (Shepard, 2000). The existing efforts to precisely define the terms already described apparently are not enough to clarify these terms in practice for many stakeholders.

Why is it so difficult to define formative assessment? Ayala et al.'s (2008) work with teachers may provide insights about other obstacles to the understanding of formative assessment in the context of classroom assessment. Ayala led a research team whose goal was to help teachers integrate formative assessment practices into their classrooms. The team struggled at the beginning of the project as they worked with teachers to design interventions. Teachers kept thinking of and designing assessments for the grading purposes instead of formative practices (feedback for teachers or students and changing the teaching/learning process). Ayala concluded that the teachers in the project were operating under "summative assessment scripts;" when they thought about assessment, their cognitive script led them to immediately think of evaluation and grades instead of the role of assessment and feedback in learning. They concluded that this summative assessment script is so dominant that it leads teachers to immediately associate the term *assessment* with the use of scores to summarize or make conclusions about student achievement and ignore potential uses of assessment data as feedback about learning as it is occurring.

Every teacher and student can relate to the spirit of formative assessment: using assessment information and feedback to improve learning (Andrade & Cizek, 2010). Widespread agreement on precise definitions may elude us, but every teacher and student I've ever encountered agrees that using feedback helps humans learn. If this spirit of formative assessment is the important core idea, perhaps the problem is the term itself.

WHY THE TERM *FORMATIVE ASSESSMENT* SHOULD BE RETIRED

If the purpose of the term *formative assessment* is to label an important part of teaching and learning, does it really matter what term we use for that idea? The label has important implications in education systems because it leads to implementations that distort the purposes of formative assessment.

For example, in the school district where I work, the term became integrated into the curriculum purchased for teachers and students. The reading and math curriculum materials purchased in my district include frequent uses of "formative assessment." But what does this term mean in this context? Curriculum materials used by school districts typically include these components:

- traditional (print) textbooks,
- teacher's editions of textbooks,
- online portals to digital versions of the student and teacher's editions of the text,
- slide collections (sets of slides teachers can use and modify based on textbook content),
- digital test banks (or other collections of assessment items), and
- online and print assessment tools (typically incorporating items from the digital test bank or other assessment items and tasks aligned with the text).

The term *formative assessment* is used often and with abandon in this final category: assessment tools. Any smaller assignment, such as a quiz, worksheet, or single assessment task, includes the label *formative assessment*. Sales representatives for the publisher make sure teachers and administrators know that the textbook and supplements include a variety of different kinds of assessments, and they justify this claim by listing the number of formative and summative assessments included in the textbook package. Some textbooks incorporate formative assessments directly in the text (typically a small number of assessment items or tasks at the end of each section of the text).

In what ways do these assessments that are labeled by publishers as formative assessments match the definitions and purposes of formative assessment described earlier? The different definitions all agree that formative assessments are defined by how data are used: either teachers using assessment data to make instructional decisions or students using assessment data to revise their work or make other changes in their learning. Materials provided by publishers, even if they are labeled "formative assessments," aren't likely to match either of these purposes. It would be difficult or impossible for textbook publishers to provide support for formative assessment processes because formative assessment processes consist of teacher and student behaviors within specific learning contexts. Teachers might use an assessment to gather information that they then use to make a teaching decision (such as reteaching, addressing common misconceptions, or using student thinking to create an extension activity). Students might use assessment data during a revision process or to identify effective and ineffective studying methods before another assessment event. These processes aren't easily packaged in published curriculum materials. Curriculum materials cannot be specifically tailored to specific pedagogical techniques because curriculum needs to be useful across a wide variety of instructional contexts. Because formative assessments are processes embedded in instructional contexts, the best that curriculum publishers can do is apply the label *formative assessment* to assignments, activities, and assessments that teachers and students may or may not use in formative processes.

This same misleading use of the term occurs in another context in school districts: online gradebooks. The online gradebook that teachers use in my district provides teachers with ways to assign, record, and combine grades on assignments and activities in their classrooms. Teachers create assignments or activities in the gradebook and decide on details about that assignment (e.g., how many points they are worth, due dates). These digital gradebooks facilitate communication with students and parents and across classrooms because the gradebook can be seen at any time online (access is controlled so that students and their parents see only their own grades, but groups of teachers and administrators can share gradebooks to make decisions about student interventions).

The online gradebook also includes the ability to categorize assignments as formative or summative. The company that publishes the gradebook included this feature as a selling point: Formative and summative assignments are weighted differently in the online gradebook to impact the overall grade differently. The rationale provided in my district is that summative assignments should determine the majority of the student's overall grade, whereas formative grades should only slightly influence a student's overall average.

This decision, although well intentioned, distorts the meaning and intent of the term *formative assessment*. Because of this feature of the online gradebook, teachers and students use the terms *formative grade* and *formative assignment* more often than they use *formative assessment*. The purpose and nature of the formative assessment (feedback teachers or students use to make changes in teaching/learning) is lost. Because of this representation in the gradebook, students are likely to think of formative assessments as "assignments worth fewer points" rather than learning experiences that provide feedback that they use. Teachers are strongly encouraged to assign points to activities they categorize as formative assessments, and this focus on grading formative assessments clouds what should be the purpose of these assignments. The time teachers spend grading and recording grades for formative assessments should be spent using data from those assessments to make teaching decisions. The formative/summative categories in the gradebook become nothing more than a replacement for categories that teachers saw in the past: tests/quizzes, assignments/homework, and so on. Formative assessments are again misrepresented as a kind of assessment rather than processes involving teachers and students using assessment data to change learning.

As the term *formative assessment* became more integrated into my school district, it became less recognizable. Well-intentioned administrators and teachers excitedly implemented the term, and that process ironically changed formative assessment into practices that are not at all connected to or supported by the formative assessment research that caused teachers and administrators to advocate for the term. We learned (again) that "culture eats strategy for breakfast" (Drucker, as cited in Coffman & Sorensen, 2013, p. 5). The culture of points and traditional letter grades dominates secondary education, and that culture transformed the good idea of formative assessment into something else. Teachers and administrators looked at the term *formative assessment*, and because it included the word "assessment," they figured out ways to incorporate it into existing gradebooks. This seemingly obvious and innocent choice changed what was meant to be a process into something secondary teachers and schools were used to dealing with: a kind of assessment that can be assigned points and absorbed into the existing grading system.

LET'S CHANGE THE TERM

In my conversations with K–12 teachers and administrators, I encounter one common error that may be one of the root causes of misunderstandings about the term *formative assessment*. The error stems from a grammar issue: the term *formative assessment* looks like a noun. Teachers know what an assessment is:

a tool used to get information about student learning. The term *formative assessment* seems like an adjective ("formative") describing a noun ("assessment"). This is where the misunderstandings may start. Conceiving of formative assessment as a kind of assessment (a tool used to gather information about student learning) points teachers in the wrong direction. Because the term looks like a noun, many teachers and students think about formative assessments as kinds of assessments, which leads them to group assessments into formative and summative categories by irrelevant criteria. For example, homework is often considered to be a formative assessment by many teachers in my district. According to the definitions of formative assessment cited earlier, homework is not necessarily formative or summative: It depends on what is done with the information from the homework assignment. The appearance of the term *formative assessment* is deceptive to many students and teachers in my district. The term sounds like it describes a specific kind of assessment rather than a use of assessment data.

If the term *formative assessment* is getting in the way of an important idea, perhaps it's time to change the term. Recently, Dylan Wiliam said that the term he and Paul Black helped popularize in 1998 may have been a poor choice of words. Wiliam wondered if he should have used the term *responsive teaching* instead to refer to the process of teachers using assessment data to make teaching decisions (Ashman, 2018; Wiliam, 2018). The term *responsive teaching* includes one of the most important functions of formative assessment in the term itself: teaching that responds to information about student understanding. The term *responsive teaching* would clarify this process with teachers. In an undergraduate or high school introductory psychology class, this might involve using a quick, low-stakes assessment of student understanding and adapting your teaching based on the result. After a discussion of the concept of operational definitions, an instructor could ask the class to share an example of an operational definition of *altruism*. The instructor could review student operational definitions to determine if most of the class understands the concept well enough to develop reasonable methods of measuring altruism and address misconceptions about operational definitions in the next class. Every teacher I know wants to change their teaching to respond to information about what students know and are currently able to do. Using the term *responsive teaching* emphasizes an important part of the spirit of formative assessment: teachers responding to evidence about student learning by making teaching choices.

But the original definition of formative assessment included another important component that is separate from the idea of responsive teaching. The definitions of formative assessment mentioned earlier include the process of students (not teachers) using assessment data to improve learning. The term *responsive teaching* does not refer to this element of formative assessment, so another term is needed. I suggest the term *student practice*. When I discuss the student practice process with groups of teachers, I use a series of questions: I ask the group if any of them were ever involved in athletics or performing arts.

After many teachers raise their hands, I ask if they practiced ("yes"). I ask why they practiced ("to get better"). I ask if they got feedback when they practiced ("yes"). I ask if they used that feedback ("yes"). And finally, I ask if using that feedback improved their performance ("yes"). This series of seemingly silly questions captures the essence of what I propose we call *student practice*. The process is a cycle or loop: Students get feedback, students use that feedback, students see that their performance improves. The term *student practice* will be more immediately understandable to teachers and students. The term identifies who is doing the process (students), and most teachers and students are very familiar with the idea and value of practice. In an undergraduate or high school introductory psychology class, a student practice process could involve students turning in a draft of a hypothesis, including clearly identified independent and dependent variables and realistic operational definitions. The instructor could review these draft submissions and provide feedback about the operational definitions, and students could revise their operational definitions using this feedback.

Replacing one term with two terms may seem counterintuitive, but this change will help remedy a basic issue with the term *formative assessment*. All the definitions provided earlier referred to two distinct processes: teachers using assessment data to change their teaching and students using assessment data to improve their performance. These processes are different enough to justify two separate terms.

The term *formative assessment* leads many teachers and students to conclude that formative assessment is a kind of assessment, rather than the process of using assessment data to improve learning. Replacing the term *formative assessment* with the terms *responsive teaching* and *student practice* could help the 21,537 middle and high school students and 1,729 middle and high school teachers in the school district where I work understand what is important about the processes that the term *formative assessment* was intended to refer to. Every teacher wants students to use feedback to learn (student practice). Teachers want to get feedback about what students know and can do in order to plan changes in their teaching (responsive teaching). Replacing the term *formative assessment* with the terms *responsive teaching* and *student practice* can help teachers and students say what they mean and get on with the important work of using assessment data to make changes in their teaching and learning.

REFERENCES

Andrade, H., & Cizek, G. (Eds.). (2010). *Handbook of formative assessment*. Routledge.
Ashman, G. (2018, August 11). An interview with Dylan Wiliam [Blog post]. https://gregashman.wordpress.com/2018/08/11/an-interview-with-dylan-wiliam
Ayala, C. C., Shavelson, R. J., Araceli Ruiz-Primo, M., Brandon, P. R., Yin, Y., Furtak, E. M., Young, D. B., & Tomita, M. K. (2008). From formal embedded assessments to reflective lessons. *Applied Measurement in Education, 21*(4), 315–334. https://doi.org/10.1080/08957340802347787
Black, P., & Wiliam, D. (1998). Inside the black box. *Phi Delta Kappan, 80*(2), 139–147.

Coffman, C., & Sorensen, K. (2013). *Culture eats strategy for lunch: The secret of extraordinary results, igniting the passion within.* BookBaby.

Hattie, J. (2008). *Visible learning.* Routledge. https://doi.org/10.4324/9780203887332

McManus, S. (2008). *Attributes of effective formative assessment.* The Council of Chief State School Officers. https://ccsso.org/resource-library/attributes-effective-formative-assessment

Popham, J. (2008). *Transformative assessment.* Association for Supervision and Curriculum Development.

Scriven, M. (1967). The methodology of evaluation. In R. W. Tyler, R. M. Gange, & M. Scriven (Eds.), *Perspectives of curriculum evaluation* (Vol. I, pp. 39–83). Rand McNally.

Shepard, L. (2000). The role of assessment in a learning culture. *Educational Researcher, 29*(7), 4–14. https://doi.org/10.3102/0013189X029007004

Stiggins, R., & Chappuis, J. (2006). What a difference a word makes: Assessment "for" learning rather than assessment "of" learning helps students succeed. *Journal of Staff Development, 27*(1), 10–14.

Wiliam, D. (2000, August). *Integrating formative and summative functions of assessment.* Paper presented to Working Group 10 of the International Congress on Mathematics Education, Makuhari, Tokyo.

Wiliam, D. (2018, March 25). The point I was making—years ago now—is that it would have been much easier if we had called [Tweet]. https://twitter.com/dylanwiliam/status/977820000558858240

5

How to Create a Culture of Assessment

Jason S. Todd and Elizabeth Yost Hammer

We call it the "a-word," turning it into a curse, perhaps because that's how we faculty see it: a malignancy imposed upon us, an imposition that darkens our days and distracts us from our calling. It is something ugly, something other. Some of us see it as a punishment; others, a practical joke; others still, the end of academic freedom. For all of us, it is yet another deadline that must be met, another demand that must be satisfied, another rule that doesn't make sense. This reaction is rather extreme and is a generalization, of course, but many American faculty have negative (often highly negative) opinions about assessment. Whether we see it as an attack on our academic freedom or an invasion into our sacred classroom space or as a nonacademic demand imposed by some bureaucracy to simply do something at which we are not adept, many faculty respond to the very idea of academic assessment with fear (Kramer, 2008). These are all valid concerns. Assessment is often something faculty are simply told to do, and let's face it, faculty, as a rule, don't like to be told what to do. For many of us, it's still new, some trendy buzzword that administrators like to toss around. Furthermore, and perhaps most critically, in the United States, academic assessment is something very few of us were trained to do in graduate school.[1] Faculty developers (and faculty development

---

[1]Fortunately, some American graduate programs are beginning to recognize the need to provide their students, who will be the faculty of tomorrow, with effective training in the assessment of student learning. In 2017, following a 3-year pilot project with a number of large American universities, the Council of Graduate Schools released *Strategies to Prepare Future Faculty to Assess Student Learning* (Denecke et al., 2017) to provide institutions with better practices for incorporating the pedagogy of assessment into their programs.

https://doi.org/10.1037/0000183-006
Assessing Undergraduate Learning in Psychology: Strategies for Measuring and Improving Student Performance, S. A. Nolan, C. M. Hakala, and R. E. Landrum (Editors)

centers), by definition, exist to help faculty learn what they didn't learn about teaching in graduate school. For some, that means learning new pedagogical methods, such as just-in-time teaching and game-based learning. For others, it means learning how to teach beyond the basics of the lecture–test–review model. For still others, it means learning to think about teaching beyond the classroom, for example, with service learning or community partnerships.

In recognizing that faculty are trained as disciplinary experts, not classroom instructors, many institutions have created faculty development centers or have hired faculty developers, and indeed these efforts have paid off. Condon and colleagues (2016) conducted a multiyear, multisite study and found that "when faculty improve their teaching, students learn more and their performance on course work improves" (p. 125). As the field of faculty development has matured, many centers have come to see their work as helping faculty with more than just their teaching. To provide context, we (the authors) are the director and associate director for the Center for the Advancement of Teaching and Faculty Development at Xavier University of Louisiana, a historically Black and Catholic liberal arts institution. A few years ago, when our Center celebrated its 20th anniversary, we revisited our mission—and our purpose— and after much reflection, we recognized that we needed to help Xavier's faculty "across all career stages and areas of professional responsibility" (see http://cat.xula.edu for our complete mission) because, as we all know, being a faculty member requires a lot more than just teaching, and many of those requirements were not taught to us in graduate school. In response to this expansion, we also changed the name from the Center for the Advancement of Teaching to the Center for the Advancement of Teaching and Faculty Development (CAT+FD). Many other centers now offer a more holistic approach to faculty development to meet the changing demands of faculty (Lockhart & Stoop, 2018), and this includes the a-word.

Except for those of us who have degrees in the field of education, assessment is yet another area we probably didn't learn about as teaching assistants in graduate school. Sure, we learned something about grading assignments and exams, and we got to make horrible mistakes as we, as students, graded our own students' work. But how many of us learned about academic assessment— that task that isn't grading, even though it often sounds a lot like grading— that task that can't be grading and yet is often done alongside grading? One of the problems with assessment, we think, is that it is a reconceptualization of what we already do. We assess by grading our students, don't we? But how often have our deans and assessment directors and accreditation liaisons told us that grades can't be used as a means of formal assessment? This, sadly, is stated all too often at many institutions, in our experience.

AN ARGUMENT FOR ASSESSMENT

My (Jason's) first experience with what I then thought of as the a-word was when I was working as the Writing Center director at our institution. One day the woman who worked down the hall from the Writing Center, someone

I'd seen dozens of times but whose name I didn't know, asked to meet with me. She wanted to talk about the kind of data I kept about the tutoring sessions that took place in the Writing Center. I told her I had a database I'd inherited from the previous director in which we recorded information about every session: the student's name, the student's major, the assignment the student wanted help with, the class that assignment came from, the professor of that class, the topics discussed in the tutoring session, and the start and end times of the session. She wanted to know if we did anything to test whether the student had actually learned anything as a result of the session. I said we had an exit survey that asked the student to self-report helpfulness and if they thought they might come back to the center. "You don't *test* them, though?" she asked. I told her our sessions were only 50 minutes long (assuming the student was willing to stay for the full 50 minutes) and that there was no way we could do any sort of formal testing, particularly not the pretesting and posttesting she seemed to be suggesting, in that little bit of time. We often don't know what the student needs help with until we start to work with the student, I explained, and generally, the student doesn't know either. It was frustrating having this administrator with no experience with the kind of intensive, intimate, and immediate work that goes on in a writing center second-guessing me. It was frustrating to be told that although what we were doing made sense when we explained it, it wasn't going to look good enough on paper in the report that I eventually understood was being assembled for the school's decennial accreditation visit. I later learned that this kind of meeting was going on all over campus and that the message received by the faculty was that something—anything—had to go into this assessment report. Because the resulting reports were so mixed and the data so poorly coordinated, it became clear that there was a strong need for improved efforts at assessment.

My (Elizabeth's) first experience was in my first academic position at Belmont University. Accreditation was upcoming and the psychology department, along with all other departments, was told we had to "assess" our program. To my knowledge, that was the extent of the training and support (hit the panic button, especially as a newer faculty member). However, being the social scientists that we are, we sat down as a department and talked about what we wanted our graduates to know or be able to do and what data we could gather to determine if we had hit our mark. We decided on a portfolio approach, divided the workload, and then actually used the data we collected to make changes to improve both our program and our assessment tools. This open-minded and beneficial approach to assessment has stayed with me as a faculty developer.

In some ways, assessment is simply the documentation of what we already do in our heads. If half the students in a research methods class are turning in papers that don't have a clear and appropriate hypothesis, then, we hope, the instructor knows to work with the students on that concept more. Our teaching gut knows the students aren't getting it. Why then does that instructor need to document that in a spreadsheet, or in a report, or in the software an institutional research office spent a lot of money on? When asked this question by our faculty, we ask them this in return: "Do you allow students to simply say they know by their gut that something is true, or do you insist, as a way to build their critical thinking skills, that they provide evidence?" Most of us respond, "Show me the data." What's the difference, then, between students presenting their own opinion as fact and us saying we know implicitly when our teaching (or program) is good or not? We should hold ourselves to the same standard for our own professional practices as we hold our students for course content.

FACULTY DEVELOPERS AND ASSESSMENT

If you buy this argument that we all need to do assessment, then it follows that we all need to learn how to do assessment. How faculty are taught to approach assessment is critical to the success of a culture of assessment at any campus.

A lot changed at our institution as a result of the accreditation visit in 2010 we mentioned above. SACSCOC, the Southern Association of Colleges and Schools Commission on Colleges, is one of six U.S. regional accreditors. In the early 2000s, SACSCOC was blazing a new path for accountability in higher education, in part by insisting that assessment be a critical component of the university's ecosystem (Watson, 2015). In addition to numerous other requirements, we had to develop a quality enhancement plan (QEP), a 5-year program to address a specific academic problem point for the university. Xavier's QEP, developed by a group of faculty, students, and staff, was named *Read Today, Lead Tomorrow* and was designed to improve the culture of reading on campus, focusing, in particular, on what we called active and engaged reading. Looking back upon it, we can see that the QEP requirement that SACSCOC initiated in the early 2000s is simply a large-scale demonstration of the assessment cycle: That is, the university uses data to identify a problem point in student learning, the university develops a set of actions to improve student learning, the university develops a plan to assess that set of actions, and the university uses the results of that ongoing assessment to adapt the plan and to continue to improve learning.

Xavier's QEP was extensive, but its primary focus was in the classroom, where faculty members were given a variety of opportunities to implement their own plans to improve active reading in their classes. All faculty who participated—some were required to do so through a department-level mandate, whereas others chose to do so through incentivization such as minigrants—were required to incorporate assessment at the classroom level that could also be used at the institutional level. This created a challenging but meaningful learning curve, as we were able to initiate the discussion of assessment with the question "What do you want your students to learn?" instead of "What data can you give us?" By laying the foundation for the assessment process in this way, we received significantly less pushback from the faculty. Assessment for the QEP was not seen as a silly administrative demand (well, by most people); rather, it was a purposeful component of effective pedagogy. Indeed, many of the faculty who participated in the QEP in this way have gone on to be the standard-bearers for assessment in their departments and divisions, even after the end of the QEP.

Encouragingly, as a university-wide program, Xavier's QEP ultimately proved to have a small but significant change for student reading engagement. However, one of the greatest impacts the QEP had at Xavier was to demonstrate to many faculty how assessment, even though it might be required by the administration, could be used to improve their own teaching (and their students' learning) while also providing a meaningful evaluation of an academic program or even an entire curriculum.

Throughout all of this, our Center was instrumental in working with faculty on these pedagogical implementations. CAT+FD has a long-standing reputation at Xavier as a safe space for faculty to take risks and try new things. Teaching our faculty how to effectively use assessment in that safe space was a critical component of our success with the QEP (and beyond), especially in ensuring it had a rigorous and meaningful assessment component, as required by SACSCOC. Faculty could reflect upon and discuss how assessment might be used within their specific projects (and departmental programs) in a meaningful way; as a result, faculty were empowered to develop assessment plans that were useful both to them as instructors and to the institution.

From this experience, we learned that faculty developers can play an important role in the creation of a culture of assessment at their institution by helping faculty see the tangible, pedagogical benefit of this level of analysis. Certainly, assessment can be used to improve entire curricula, specific programs, or commonly taught courses, but it can also be used to make one individual class better and even to make the teaching of a specific concept better. In addition to illuminating the tangible benefits of assessment, faculty developers also can help to create a culture of assessment at their campus by reminding faculty (and administrators) that everything we do needs to be done to help our students learn. Assessment can be used to improve student learning— at the curricular, program, course, or lesson level. By helping faculty to see how an ongoing cycle of assessment can improve their teaching—not for the sake of some report or for the bemusement of some administrator, but for themselves—faculty developers can help to firmly establish a culture of assessment at their institutions.

SUCCESSFUL FACULTY DEVELOPMENT PROGRAMS FOR ASSESSMENT

Despite a seemingly endless array of assessment tools, there are just two overarching categories of assessment: formative and summative. This topic is covered elsewhere in this volume (see Chapter 4), so we remain brief here and keep our focus on faculty developers. Carnegie Mellon University's Eberly Center for Teaching Excellence & Educational Innovation defines formative assessment as having the goal of "monitor[ing] student learning to provide ongoing feedback that can be used by instructors to improve their teaching and by students to improve their learning" (Carnegie Mellon University, Eberly Center, n.d.). These are low-stakes, often in-class activities that allow students to see where they fall short in their knowledge so they can address it. In contrast, summative assessments are given to "evaluate student learning at the end of an instructional unit by comparing it against some standard" (Carnegie Mellon University, Eberly Center, n.d.). In any course, the best teachers use formative assessments before summative assessment so that students can test their own knowledge and so that the instructors themselves can know where to target a lesson. At a minimum, faculty developers should assist faculty in understanding this sequence and introduce them to tools and better practices for each. However, there are many other ways that faculty developers can be successful in creating a more open and useful culture of assessment, and we want to introduce you to some of the things we have done.

Workshops and Programming

The most basic way to introduce faculty to the benefits of using assessment is to provide programming around the topic. Obviously, one can do this without titling the program "The Benefits of Assessment." For example, we regularly offer workshops on topics such as active learning, the flipped classroom, or enhancing metacognition. Many of the activities we describe in these workshops are drawn directly from Angelo and Cross's *Classroom Assessment Techniques* (1993) and Bean's *Engaging Ideas* (2011). We introduce the idea of using these activities as a way to teach specific concepts or skills as well as a way to assess where students are, then respond through instruction by either moving on or remediating. It sounds like the familiar assessment cycle, doesn't it? By getting faculty buy-in at the student activity level and by demonstrating the effectiveness of the process, we are able to make inroads at the curricular and programmatic levels.

Beyond the one-shot workshop, we also incorporate sessions on writing student learning outcomes and assessing student learning outcomes in any intensive programming we do. For example, we offer a weeklong, intensive seminar each summer to support faculty in planning and implementing innovative curricular projects over the course of an academic year. Each year we have a different focus such as internationalizing the curriculum, teaching for social responsibility, and utilizing educational technology. In addition to the specific assessment-related sessions during the week, we also require participants to submit an assessment report of their student learning outcomes upon completion of their projects. Moreover, we ourselves begin the seminar with clear outcomes that we assess and use in our future planning. Taken together, our programming has allowed our Center to become a place where faculty engage with assessment.

Recommendation for faculty developers: The best way to get your faculty involved in something, whether a pedagogical innovation or an assessment tool, is to introduce it to them and model it for them. Make sure your workshops have outcomes, utilize evidence-based practices, and follow the assessment cycle.

Midcourse Reviews

One way to demonstrate the importance of formative assessment for students is to get instructors to see the importance of it for themselves, for their own teaching. Since 2007, our Center has offered to conduct midcourse reviews (MCRs) for interested faculty. MCRs are a form of small-group instructional diagnosis, described by Clark and Bekey (1979) as a means of collecting anonymous feedback from students to enable faculty members to improve their teaching while the class is still ongoing. About a month into the semester, faculty can request to have a reviewer visit their class. During a 20-minute session with the faculty member out of the room, the reviewer works with the students to develop three lists:

- What is helping you learn in the class?
- What is getting in the way of your learning?
- What improvements would you suggest for this class?

Anonymity is key. The reviewer ensures that there is no indication of who has said what. Instead, it is the class that is agreeing upon and determining the feedback that will be provided. This is also a critical distinction between MCRs and end-of-semester reviews. The small-group structure allows the students and the evaluator (and ultimately the instructor) to see patterns and what strengths and weaknesses are impacting most, if not all, of the students (Medina, 2011). Following the session, the reviewer types up a summary report and meets with the faculty member to discuss the results. Following that meeting, which often turns into a discussion of better classroom techniques, the faculty member reflects upon the results and reports back to the class to discuss how they will be implementing some of the feedback they've received.

Most of our faculty would not describe this as typical assessment, perhaps because it focuses not on what students are learning but rather on how well students are learning. Yet the process followed for our MCRs is clearly a demonstration of the assessment cycle: Outcomes are determined, actions are taken to achieve those outcomes, data are gathered, results are reflected upon, and changes are made in direct response to the data gathered. Perhaps another reason why faculty might not see this as assessment is because there is no external reporting. Faculty are free to do with the report what they wish. Although some may include it in their teaching portfolios or in their materials compiled for tenure or promotion, others simply use it to improve their teaching. Regardless of how the information is used outside of the classroom, we stress the importance of following the entire process, of closing the loop, as assessment experts like to say, in the classroom, for evaluation is useful only if it is actually used.

Recommendation for faculty developers: MCRs are a relatively easy, low-cost initiative to implement, and they provide a great bang for your buck. If you are looking to begin or increase the culture of faculty development on your campus, start here, and make the explicit connection to assessment for faculty.

Assessment Toolbox

One challenge faculty developers can face when discussing assessment with faculty members is getting those faculty members to see that there are more ways to assess student learning than just having students take tests and write essays. Although most faculty developers may have Angelo and Cross's (1993) and Bean's (2011) books on their bookshelves, the average faculty member likely does not. As a result, some faculty development centers have created assessment toolboxes on their websites. These toolboxes provide faculty with a wide variety of easy-to-implement assessment techniques (e.g., word journals, directed paraphrasing, minute papers), often categorized by assessment type, that can be used, as we said above, to both teach and assess. As Mueller (2005)—who established one of the earliest assessment toolboxes—explained, many faculty simply are not familiar with the extensive options they have to assess student learning, whereas others are simply unaware that the things they are doing in the classroom are actually effective assessment techniques.

At CAT+FD, we like to make sure that anything posted to the assessment toolbox gives viewers not only a description of the assessment technique but also references to demonstrate that the technique is based on good research as well as examples to better clarify the ideas described. Such offerings let faculty see a wide variety of easy-to-implement, easy-to-adapt, and evidence-based techniques they can use in their classes to assess student learning.

Recommendation for faculty developers: Be familiar with various assessment tools and make them available to faculty in an easy-to-access, easy-to-digest way. There's no need to recreate the wheel; you can link to toolkits that already exist.

Learning Management System Assessment Tools

Another way we support the assessment efforts of instructors is by showcasing how it can be done effectively through our school's learning management system (LMS). When our institution moved from Blackboard to Brightspace in 2018, our Center was tasked with providing the faculty with training in the new system. We used this as an opportunity to stress how the LMS can facilitate assessment while still allowing the faculty the freedom to run their classes as they see best.

For example, many LMSs now offer robust ePortfolio systems available to the entire campus. Increasingly, ePortfolios are being seen as a possible means of streamlining program-level and college-level assessments. To help our faculty see the potential benefits of using ePortfolios, in addition to offering focused workshops on their use, we have begun incorporating ePortfolios into some of our other initiatives, like our Teaching Portfolio Working Group. Since its founding in 1994, our Center has offered faculty the opportunity to spend an academic year developing a portfolio to reflect upon their teaching. During the 2018–2019 academic year, the group members created ePortfolios via Brightspace instead of the traditional paper-and-binder portfolios. In doing so, they were not only learning how to construct an ePortfolio (so that they can then teach it to their students) but also seeing the various benefits of ePortfolios for the students who create them and the teachers who assign them. In the process, they are becoming more comfortable with one of the technological options we have for assessment.

Recommendation for faculty developers: Be familiar with the various assessment tools available to faculty through your LMS, and find ways to model those tools in your programming.

CONCLUSION

In this chapter, we offer concrete suggestions to faculty developers interested in supporting the work of assessment on their campuses. These are based on our experiences and what has worked well with our faculty. Of course, this is not an exhaustive list of recommendations. Hutchings (2010) provided a thorough summary of ways to involve faculty in assessment that includes building an understanding of assessment into graduate preparation and involving undergraduate students in assessment efforts, and Angelo (2002) suggested that we faculty developers reframe the work of assessment as academic scholarship. However, at the heart of all these suggestions is the belief that we must encourage faculty to see the importance of assessment and then train them how to do it well.

Finally, we'd like to leave you with this thought: We can't teach our faculty better practices in assessment or support them in their assessment efforts if we don't know these ourselves. As such, faculty developers must keep up to date on assessment practices and principles in teaching and learning. If you are reading this chapter, you are likely interested in faculty development. Nunn-Ellison et al. (2015) challenged us, as faculty developers, to "practice what we preach." We must model the very assessment cycle that we encourage our faculty to follow. We must gather appropriate data that show the impact of our offerings (and that are ideally aligned with the strategic goals of institutions), going beyond attendance and satisfaction data. Then we must use these data in our planning and adapt accordingly (Diaz et al., 2009). To maximize our impact, we must model authentic assessment for faculty, who in turn model requiring evidence for students, thus bringing the focus back to them.

REFERENCES

Angelo, T. (2002). Engaging and supporting faculty in the scholarship of assessment. In T. Banta (Ed.), *Building a scholarship of assessment* (pp. 185–200). Jossey-Bass.

Angelo, T. A., & Cross, K. P. (1993). *Classroom assessment techniques: A handbook for college teachers.* Jossey-Bass.

Bean, J. C. (2011). *Engaging ideas: The professor's guide to integrating writing, critical thinking, and active learning in the classroom.* Jossey-Bass.

Carnegie Mellon University, Eberly Center. (n.d.). *What is the difference between formative and summative assessment?* https://www.cmu.edu/teaching/assessment/basics/formative-summative.html

Clark, D. J., & Bekey, J. (1979). Use of small groups in instructional evaluation. *POD Quarterly: The Journal of the Professional and Organizational Development Network in Higher Education, 1*(2). http://digitalcommons.unl.edu/podqtrly/10

Condon, W., Iverson, E. R., Mandica, C. A., Rutz, C., & Willett, G. (2016). *Faculty development and student learning: Assessing the connections.* Indiana University Press.

Denecke, D., Michaels, J., & Stone, K. (2017). *Strategies to prepare future faculty to assess student learning.* Council of Graduate Schools. http://www.teaglefoundation.org/Teagle/media/GlobalMediaLibrary/documents/resources/CGS_PFFASL_Pub_web_final.pdf?ext=.pdf

Diaz, V., Garrett, P. B., Kinley, E. R., Moore, J. F., Schwartz, C. M., & Kohrman, P. (2009, May/June). Faculty development for the 21st century. *EDUCAUSE Review, 44,* 46–55. https://er.educause.edu/~/media/files/article-downloads/erm0933.pdfy

Hutchings, P. (2010, April). *Opening doors to faculty involvement in assessment* (NILOA Occasional Paper No. 4). University of Illinois and Indiana University, National Institute for Learning Outcomes Assessment.

Kramer, P. I. (2008). The art of making assessment anti-venom: Injecting assessment in small doses to create a faculty culture of assessment. *Assessment Update, 21*(6), 8–10.

Lockhart, M. S., & Stoop, C. (2018). Assessing a faculty development program in a changing environment. *Journal of Faculty Development, 32*(2), 13–21.

Medina, B. (2011, October 30). As emphasis on student evaluations grows, professors increasingly seek midcourse feedback. *The Chronicle of Higher Education.* https://www.chronicle.com/article/As-Emphasis-on-Student/129566

Mueller, J. (2005). The authentic assessment toolbox: Enhancing student learning through online faculty development. *Journal of Online Learning and Teaching, 1*(1), 1–7.

Nunn-Ellison, K., Kapka, L., Myers, J., McGrew, H., Bernheisel, J., & Cutler, J. (2015, January). *Practice what you preach!* University of Illinois and Indiana University, National Institute for Learning Outcomes Assessment.

Watson, J. E. (2015, March 19). Belle Wheelan's drive pays off for higher education. *Diverse Issues in Education.* https://diverseeducation.com/article/70934

6

Overcoming Obstacles That Stop Student Learning

The Bottleneck Model of Structural Reform

Claudia J. Stanny

Leading a campus-wide discussion about assessment of student learning can be complicated by conflicting messages. Mandates from external accreditation agencies, professional organizations associated with disciplines (e.g., education, business), and government agencies, often with high-stakes consequences, create an urgency that focuses attention on compliance. Pressures to meet accreditation standards or government mandates require conducting and documenting assessment activities, which sends the message that the primary purpose is to create reports. On the other hand, assessment directors and staff of centers for teaching and learning advocate gathering and using assessment data to inform decisions about how to improve curriculum, teaching, and learning (Kuh et al., 2015; Stanny, 2018; Suskie, 2015). Faculty who resist assessment initiatives note the pressure to comply with external demands and characterize assessment as a resource-sapping activity that feeds an insatiable data monster (Gilbert, 2018; Worthen, 2018).

Assessment advocates argue that assessment provides the empirical evidence that faculty need to inform their decisions about curriculum, teaching, and learning (Fulcher et al., 2014; McConnell, 2018). For example, evidence-based decisions have been responsible for significant advances in medicine (e.g., Gawande, 2004).

When faculty reflect on evidence about student learning and use evidence to inform decisions about curriculum and teaching strategies, they can craft programs that facilitate student learning. Published examples of institutions

https://doi.org/10.1037/0000183-007
Assessing Undergraduate Learning in Psychology: Strategies for Measuring and Improving Student Performance, S. A. Nolan, C. M. Hakala, and R. E. Landrum (Editors)

that experience these benefits illustrate the power of assessment to motivate and inform large-scale improvements in academic programs and student learning (e.g., Isabella & McGovern, 2018; Kuh et al., 2015; Latuca et al., 2006; Magruder et al., 1997; O'Neill et al., 2018; Suskie, 2018). For example, two composition programs used assessments of student writing to guide revisions to their curriculum and addressed faculty development needs associated with teaching disciplinary writing (Isabella & McGovern, 2018; O'Neill et al., 2018). In both cases, assessment evidence identified aspects of student writing that could be improved, which informed faculty reflection on their goals for student writing and the pedagogies used in writing classes. Faculty revised learning outcomes, adopted new teaching strategies, and restructured the writing curriculum (Isabella & McGovern, 2018). Over several years, faculty trans- formed a basic skills program into a writing curriculum that addressed complex writing skills such as writing for different audiences, evaluating sources, and improving writing through revision. Similarly, when faculty disaggregated assessments of writing by course, they found that writing-intensive courses in disciplines were "facilitating student learning about writing in ways that the first-year ENGL 101 course was not" (O'Neill et al., 2018, p. 100). As a result, the institution increased the role of writing-intensive courses in the curriculum and offered professional development to disciplinary faculty about writing.

When institutions focus on using assessment evidence to inform faculty efforts to improve teaching and learning, compliance issues tend to resolve (National Institute for Learning Outcomes Assessment [NILOA], 2016; Suskie, 2018). Assessment leaders should create structures and institutional cultures that promote assessment as a reflective process focused on improvement (NILOA, 2016; Stanny, Stone, & Cook, 2018; Suskie, 2018). In this chapter, I describe institution-level structures and strategies that encourage faculty not only to gather assessment data to answer questions about student learning but also to reflect on findings and identify actions they can take to improve student learning in classes and academic programs—in short, to stop the bottle- neck and share assessment strategies to better inform teaching and learning.

PROFESSIONAL DEVELOPMENT ISSUES AND STRATEGIES

Faculty learn to conduct research in their graduate programs but seldom receive explicit training in teaching or in assessment. The increased expectation to engage in meaningful assessment of student learning, including use of assess- ment findings to inform improvement efforts, creates a need to develop faculty skills with both assessment methods and the pedagogy of teaching and learning in higher education (Condon et al., 2016; Kuh et al., 2015; Maki, 2010b; Stanny & Halonen, 2011).

Faculty expertise with assessment varies widely across disciplines. Several disciplines have a long history of specialized accreditation in the United States with strong assessment expectations. Examples include the Accreditation Board for Engineering and Technology, Inc.; The Association to Advance Collegiate Schools of Business, Council on Social Work Education, Council for the Accreditation of Educator Preparation, and a variety of health sciences disciplines (National Accrediting Agency for Clinical Laboratory Sciences, Commission on Collegiate Nursing Education, and Council on Education for Public Health). Many academic departments in the United States had only begun to attend to assessment processes when assessment moved to the forefront of national conversations about higher education and the assessment of student learning received more attention, driven by pressure from the Spellings Commission (U.S. Department of Education, 2006) and regional accreditation bodies (Kuh et al., 2015; Maki, 2010a).

The bottleneck framework can be fruitfully applied to understanding the obstacles institutions face while attempting to establish a meaningful culture of assessment (Venkatraman, 2007). Bottlenecks are points in a course or the curriculum where large numbers of students get derailed in their learning. Students stuck in a bottleneck may encounter significant delays in their learning or even change majors. The obstacles that prevent or inhibit progress in learning include various cognitive, affective, procedural, and technical problems (Middendorf & Pace, 2004; Pace, 2017). Concepts that are merely difficult to learn may create a bottleneck, but a subset of bottlenecks—threshold concepts—represents obstacles that carry an emotional burden (Meyer & Land, 2005). Myths, misconceptions, and false assumptions may contribute to both bottlenecks and threshold concepts. Threshold concepts represent a special case, in which emotional ties to prior (and fundamental) assumptions produce resistance to revising these beliefs or accepting new assumptions or concepts. Although mastery of a bottleneck concept will enable a learner to progress, mastery of a threshold concept may be transformative. In contrast, bottleneck concepts may simply be associated with difficult concepts or procedural problems such as a failure to identify or execute key steps in a process or difficulty applying abstract understanding to a concrete problem.

Whether problems understanding and implementing meaningful assessment are a cognitive bottleneck or a threshold concept might depend on the underlying culture of a given institution. In either case, misunderstandings about the goals and procedures for assessing student learning can subvert efforts to develop a culture of assessment and impede efforts to gather and use assessment evidence to improve academic programs. Each of the following conceptual obstacles represents both a need for professional development and an opportunity to create institutional structures and incentives that promote meaningful and productive assessment processes.

Confusion About the Purpose of Assessment

Faculty are often confused about the purpose of assessment. Crisis responses to satisfy external mandates to conduct and document systematic assessment processes may mistakenly target compliance as the primary purpose of assessment. Institutions that outsource assessment tasks to external providers or internal professional staff, who are not actively engaged in teaching, may inadvertently promote a culture of compliance, in which submitting a report becomes the practical endpoint of the assessment process. Outsourced assessment processes often focus on data that are easy to measure but may be irrelevant to questions and concerns faculty have about teaching and learning (NILOA, 2016). Institutional leaders must defuse this misperception by articulating the purpose of assessment as the process by which faculty reflect on and attempt to improve student learning in courses and academic programs. Faculty engagement with the interpretation and use of assessment findings reinforces the notion that the purpose of assessment is to improve student learning (NILOA, 2016; Stanny, 2018).

Interdependence of Courses in the Curriculum

Faculty are engaged with student learning in their courses but may not have a clear sense of the way the curriculum as a whole develops disciplinary skills, attitudes, and expertise. When faculty focus only on the courses they teach and student learning in those courses, they fail to address how a sequence of courses creates a progression of learning activities that scaffold and develop skills such as critical thinking, analysis of evidence, and writing. Department chairs should facilitate collective discussions about how courses create paths for the development of expertise and facilitate discussions about how courses prepare students for learning experiences in subsequent courses.

A curriculum map provides a snapshot of the courses that comprise the curriculum. When constructing a curriculum map, faculty should reflect on the relations between required courses. In addition, faculty should engage in regular discussions about how the learning experiences in one course prepare students for learning experiences they will encounter in subsequent courses. Do students experience repeated opportunities to practice and develop complex cognitive skills such as writing for a professional audience in the discipline or integrating content and skills encountered in multiple courses? How do faculty work together to discourage students from "siloing" knowledge and skills they learn in one course? How can faculty encourage students to retain and apply skills they learned in a previous course when they complete assignments and projects in our courses?

Misunderstanding the Relation Between Grading and the Collection of Assessment Evidence

Misunderstandings about the relation between how faculty assign grades and how faculty gather and report assessment evidence create impediments to fruitful assessment work. Assessment professionals and accrediting bodies admonish faculty that grades do not satisfy expectations for assessment of student learning. However, when faculty hear that "grades are not assessment," they may feel that calls for direct measures of student learning question the validity of the grades that faculty determine for students in their courses.

Faculty underestimate the degree to which grades blur and obscure the diagnostic information about student performance that faculty need to properly assess student learning outcomes and identify opportunities for improvement. Grades aggregate student performance across multiple learning outcomes. Grades may also include performance factors unrelated to learning such as penalties for late work, points earned for attending class regularly, or extra credit awarded for participating in service projects, departmental research, or other activities that do not align with learning goals. The grading process can yield legitimate and useful assessment data, however, provided instructors record and report the components they use to determine the grade. For example, rubric elements align well with specific learning outcomes and provide useful information about strengths and weaknesses in student learning that is blurred in the overall grade. Similarly, faculty might identify specific exam questions that align with a single learning outcome and report this score as assessment data (instead of reporting the overall exam grade).

Figure 6.1 illustrates how different patterns of strengths and weaknesses in student learning can produce the same grade. Data presented in Figure 6.1

FIGURE 6.1. Percentage of Points Earned for Rubric Elements (Four Student Artifacts)

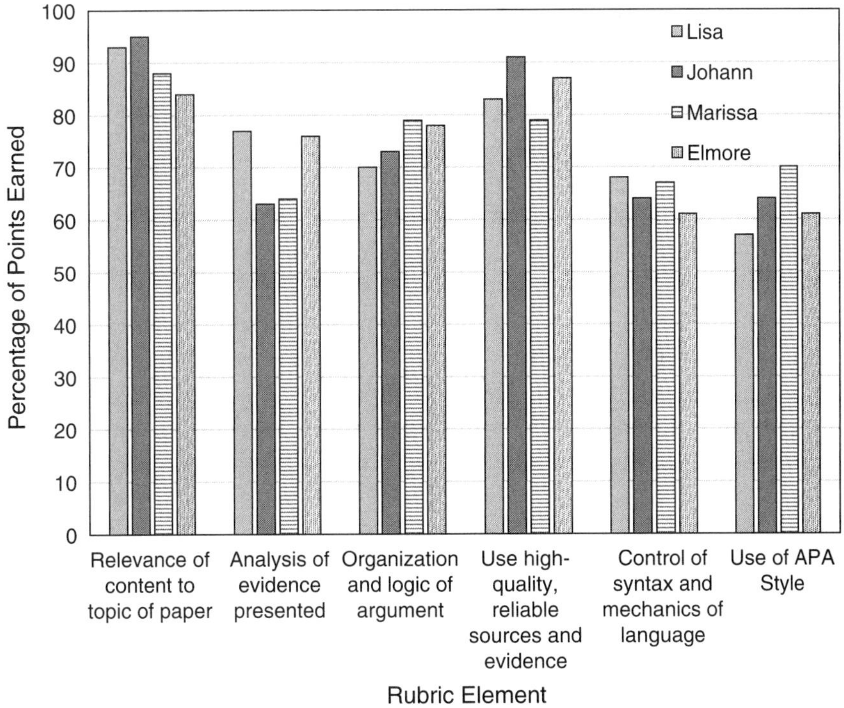

Note. APA = American Psychological Association.

represent the percentage of points earned by each of four students, whose work was evaluated on six rubric elements. The students earned identical grades on the assignment. The scores on individual rubric elements support the primary goal of assessment (to identify opportunities to improve student learning) because they provide useful, diagnostic, actionable information that is obscured in the overall rubric score (or assignment grade). Rubric element scores identify strengths and weaknesses in specific skills. Instructors can propose new activities or teaching strategies that might improve future student performance. In this example, students are performing well in identifying high-quality, reliable sources. Their essays are generally focused on the topic of the assignment. However, students need more guidance on how to analyze the evidence they present and how to organize it as a logical argument. They also need more feedback and practice with writing and use of American Psychological Association style. In contrast, the overall assignment grade (75%) does not suggest how an instructor might alter the course to improve future student performance.

Procedures that track and record granular information about student work require additional effort, but they require less effort than does creating and completing a second, independent scoring process to generate assessment data. Faculty create unnecessary work for themselves when they evaluate an assignment twice: once to determine the grade and a second time to generate assessment evidence. Naturally, this extra work creates resentment and resistance to assessment.

Misunderstanding the Meaning of Academic Freedom

Academic freedom is frequently misunderstood as freedom of speech in the classroom. Faculty sometimes invoke academic freedom to justify a variety of behaviors, including a refusal to engage in assessment activities. However, academic freedom simply entitles faculty to "freedom in the classroom in discussing their subject" and the right to conduct research on topics that might generate controversy within their discipline (American Association of University Professors [AAUP], 1940, p. 1). A discussion among leaders of three major U.S. faculty unions specifically addressed the relation between academic freedom, curriculum design, and the assessment of student learning (Gold et al., 2011). The AAUP, the American Federation of Teachers (AFT), and the National Education Association (NEA) underscored the role of faculty in determining the design, structure, and pedagogy of their courses and curriculum. These activities include the collective tasks of identifying student learning outcomes, conducting assessments of student learning, and revising the curriculum as needed, based in part on assessment findings. Thus, these organizations regard the assessment of student learning and efforts to revise and improve academic programs as "core academic activities" for faculty work (Gold et al., 2011, p. 7).

Fearing the Relation Between Assessment Findings and the Evaluation of Faculty As Teachers

Faculty legitimately fear that the ultimate goal of assessment is to generate evidence about student learning that colleagues will use to evaluate individual faculty. They worry that administrators will use disappointing assessment findings to target individual faculty as defective teachers. Assessment works best when faculty trust that less-than-flattering findings will only motivate efforts to improve programs, not punish individuals (Suskie, 2015). Institutional leaders must institute policies and create credible buffers between assessment findings and the identities of individual faculty members to establish trust and ensure that assessment evidence is used only for program improvement.

Program-level assessment is not necessarily about learning in individual courses but rather about how the curriculum functions as a whole to promote learning goals. A curriculum that relies on a single course, taught by a single faculty member, to ensure student learning on a specific program-level learning outcome is inherently flawed because the outcome receives little formal support. Expertise develops over time, requiring multiple years of deliberate practice (Ericsson et al., 1993). How can we expect students to gain competence in complex cognitive skills such as critical analysis of evidence or disciplinary writing during a 14-week course? Thus, faculty should not be surprised to discover that student performance on an outcome that is supported by only one course is disappointing. Although the AAUP, AFT, and NEA endorse the notion that faculty are responsible for assessing student learning and using assessment evidence to improve academic programs, they clearly oppose using these activities "for the purpose of evaluating faculty, academic programs or institutions" (Gold et al., 2011, p. 9).

The Perfect Is the Enemy of the Good

Faculty sometimes assume that assessment methods must meet standards for psychometric rigor associated with published tests. Institutions need to ensure that demands for perfect data do not subvert the collection and interpretation of assessment data that are "good enough" (Fulcher et al., 2014; Suskie, 2018). For example, when I need to know whether to wear a coat or not, a quick-and-dirty assessment like stepping outdoors is adequate. Moreover, the biggest impacts on student learning are likely to be achieved by correcting the most glaring or extensive problems with student learning. We do not need precise measures designed to detect marbles when we need to find basketballs. Simple assessment measures have the advantage of being cheap and easy to implement. Although simple measures may be more prone to error than an expensive but psychometrically rigorous method would be, the cost of making an error is relatively low. We might err when we decide to make a change to teaching or curriculum that is unnecessary. We might even make a change that is not helpful. But the worst that will happen is that students do no better (or do a bit worse) the next time we assess the outcome. If a new initiative does not work as planned, we can modify it, replace it, or revert to the old strategy the next time the course is taught. If we assess regularly, the mistake will be detected (and corrected) quickly. Even the most psychometrically rigorous assessments do not guarantee that an improvement initiative we decide to implement will produce the intended benefits. Moreover, if we decide to make no changes because we discounted evidence as insufficiently rigorous, we can incur a high cost if we ignore a problem until we have compelling evidence from a more reliable assessment.

STRATEGIES FOR IDENTIFYING AND IMPLEMENTING ACTIONS FOR IMPROVEMENT

The greatest assessment challenge academic programs face is the need to reflect on assessment findings and identify specific, concrete actions or initiatives that might improve future student learning (known as "closing the loop" in assessment jargon). If programs never implement change informed by assessment findings, assessment processes can devolve into sterile bookkeeping and data-archiving activities. The following three approaches to curriculum design and use of assessment findings promise to keep assessment focused on how we might improve student learning: Decoding the Disciplines, the scholarship of teaching and learning, and transparency and backward design.

Decoding the Disciplines: An Interdisciplinary Approach to Solving Bottlenecks

Every discipline can identify bottlenecks, or points in the curriculum where students struggle to make progress (Middendorf & Pace, 2004). Students who get stuck on a bottleneck concept may find themselves delayed or completely derailed in their academic progress. For example, students in psychology encounter a variety of conceptual obstacles around research methods. Some students do not embrace psychology as an empirical science. They might resist the need to learn research methods, arguing that they believe psychology is primarily about helping people with their problems and that they can do this without learning about the science of behavior. This obstacle may have an affective component if students dislike science or have anxiety about mathematics. A more conceptual bottleneck is based on simplistic assumptions about experimental control. Many students learn about the scientific method and experimental control as the use of a no-treatment group. Students may struggle with the concept of experimental control as a strategy that enables researchers to eliminate rival hypotheses. Students may struggle to create comparison conditions that formally evaluate the merit of competing explanations.

The program Decoding the Disciplines (Pace, 2017) represents a process by which faculty engage in guided reflection on a disciplinary bottleneck. Faculty identify the bottleneck, describe the difficulties students experience when they encounter the bottleneck, and discover alternative strategies to explain the concept to students. The decoding process is driven by discussions with faculty in multiple disciplines, who can pose thoughtful questions about the challenges that puzzle novices. These discussions help disciplinary experts articulate the tacit aspects of their expertise. Assessment findings play a role in decoding processes because assessment findings can pinpoint content and cognitive skills that challenge students and create obstacles to making progress in a discipline.

The "curse of expertise" refers to the difficulties experts experience when they attempt to explain their discipline to novices. Expert knowledge can become tacit knowledge, which interferes with experts' ability to understand why novices find bottleneck concepts so difficult or even recognize why difficulties with learning a bottleneck concept impede further disciplinary learning. Experts may underestimate the value of concrete explanations when they instruct novices about domain-specific knowledge and procedures (Hinds, 1999; Hinds et al., 2001). The collaborative process associated with decoding enables faculty experts to discover steps they might skip, minimize, or overlook when they explain a process.

Scholarship of Teaching and Learning

Not all scholarly insights to improve teaching and learning emerge from a process such as Decoding the Disciplines. However, assessment findings provide the data required to evaluate the impact of changes faculty make to curriculum or teaching strategies. Assessment findings from courses in which faculty implement these new approaches can allow faculty to evaluate and document the success of a revised explanation, teaching strategy, or assignment. Thus, assessment, when coupled with initiatives to improve student performance, provides the core elements for a scholarly peer-reviewed publication on teaching and learning. Teaching and learning center personnel can help faculty shape their efforts to improve student learning as scholarship of teaching and learning. Institutions should adopt policies that recognize and value this work as evidence of scholarship for annual evaluations and tenure and promotion decisions. Thus, engagement with assessment can help faculty achieve professional goals for scholarship and achieve recognition for their emerging excellence in teaching as well as for their scholarly publications. See Chapter 1 in this volume for more information about the scholarship of teaching and learning.

Transparency and Backward Design

Sometimes students perform poorly on an assignment or assessment task because they did not fully understand the expectations for the task or how the instructor would evaluate their work. Winkelmes and colleagues (2016) described a collaborative assignment design initiative that helps faculty create assignments, assignment instructions, and grading rubrics that align with learning goals. A transparent assignment communicates the purpose of the assignment, how it supports important course learning outcomes, expectations for the quality of work students produce, and how the work will be evaluated (Transparency in Learning and Teaching Project, n.d.; Winkelmes et al., 2016). Instructions for transparent assignments articulate the purpose and expectations for tasks students must complete. What are the learning outcomes that students will practice? What steps must students take to fully complete the assignment? What are the expectations for the work students produce? How will this work be evaluated? What components will be evaluated (elements in a rubric), and what counts as high-quality work (descriptions of levels of quality for rubric elements)? Well-designed assignments use the principles of backward design (Fink, 2013) to align learning outcomes, tasks and learning activities that constitute an assignment, and the criteria the instructor will use to evaluate and assess learning. In a backward design model, faculty start with the learning objectives and then build out course activities to support and scaffold those objectives. Handouts and rubrics for transparent assignments clearly communicate this alignment to students, describe the task completely, and describe expectations for high-quality work. Increased transparency of assignments can improve the students' mastery of targeted learning outcomes and contribute to their academic confidence and sense of belonging (Winkelmes et al., 2016). Staff of centers for teaching and learning can promote the development of transparent assignments and projects (Transparency in Learning and Teaching Project, n.d.).

INFRASTRUCTURE TO SUPPORT EFFECTIVE ASSESSMENT AND IMPROVEMENT

Institutional cultures are established and sustained through multiple mechanisms (Bolman & Deal, 2017). A culture of assessment means that faculty have the requisite skills with assessment. It also means that the institution values this work and supports it in multiple ways—through policies, organizational structures, resources (time, money, space, and access to expertise), professional development, and appropriate public recognition of the value of this work. Institutional leaders should consider the following strategies and structures to promote meaningful assessment work on their campus.

Policies

Policies serve as institutional long-term memory. They create continuity for structures and processes in the face of administrative and faculty turnover. Institutional memories are short, especially when resistance to engagement with assessment motivates selectively forgetting past decisions. Policies establish expectations and provide guidelines for assessment procedures that support institutional memory and keep assessment processes on track. Policies establish the rationale for faculty governance entities (e.g., a curriculum approval committee, governance of general education, assessment councils or committees).

Faculty Governance

In the United States, as in many other countries, faculty own the curriculum and, as such, have responsibility for governance related to the curriculum. Faculty governance in the United States also extends to the assessment of student learning for program improvement. Traditionally, faculty governance related to the curriculum focused on faculty review and approval of changes such as revisions to courses and academic programs, proposals for new courses and new degree programs, and deletion of existing courses and programs. Increasingly, curriculum review includes expectations about the articulation of measurable learning outcomes and explicit plans to assess student learning. Faculty members participate in regular program review and serve on site teams for departmental program reviews, which include an evaluation of the currency and quality of the curriculum. Charges to curriculum committees within departments now commonly include expectations to monitor and implement processes to assess student learning. Similarly, U.S. colleges and universities now include standing committees charged to oversee the assessment of student learning as a component of the faculty governance structure.

Reporting Expectations

It is important to establish guidelines for the content and audience of department assessment reports to improve their quality and completeness. When departments view assessment reporting as simply a box to be checked off and believe that reports fall into a bureaucratic abyss, where they are filed away and never read, they spend little time on the clarity of report narratives. Good assessment reports tell the story of credible collection of tangible evidence about student learning, collective faculty reflection on the meaning of the assessment observations, and compelling evidence that these findings informed decisions and instigated implementation of concrete actions and initiatives intended to improve student performance. Too often, filing the assessment report (turning an indicator in an assessment database from red to green) becomes the final step of a program's assessment process, with no subsequent action (Fulcher et al., 2014).

Resources

Assessment should be part of business as usual in departmental work, but it does represent a set of expectations that require resources. Institutions can promote the development of meaningful assessment practices by providing resources for professional development and support projects for assessment initiatives and curriculum improvements. Resources might include access to support from individuals in an assessment office or center for teaching and learning who have expertise with rubric development, data analysis, or pedagogy. Fundable projects might include travel funds to attend an assessment conference to develop knowledge and skills with assessment, to bring an external consultant to campus for professional development, to help faculty plan a specific assessment initiative, or to support faculty as they implement a specific curriculum improvement project. For example, an institution might offer funding awards to support the design of assignments and rubrics to serve as embedded assessments of specific learning outcomes and improve the transparency of assignments and rubrics. Some institutions fund assessment projects that train raters and organize a process for independent scoring of student artifacts.

Recognition and Rewards for Faculty Contributions to Assessment and Curriculum Improvement

Institutional leaders send a strong message about what they value when they honor contributions to program-level assessment as valid evidence supporting a tenure decision. Policies related to tenure and promotion, including college and departmental bylaws and criteria for tenure and promotion, should articulate when and how assessment activities serve as evidence of teaching effectiveness, institutional service, and disciplinary scholarship. These guidelines contribute to meaningful assessment when they successfully establish concrete expectations about how reviewing committees should formally recognize faculty contributions to assessment processes. Meaningful assessment can support empirical research about teaching and learning when assessments focus on the impact of a new initiative for teaching and learning improvement. Assessment processes can generate evidence that informs the need to modify the curriculum or inspires initiatives to deploy new teaching practices. Subsequent assessments document the impact of changes faculty implement to improve student learning. Thus, faculty who collect, reflect on, and use assessment evidence to inform decisions about teaching and curriculum structure are in a position to share their insights through peer-reviewed scholarship of teaching and learning.

OPPORTUNITIES FOR PSYCHOLOGISTS IN OTHER ACADEMIC DISCIPLINES

Psychologists' expertise with research design, measurement, and data analysis positions them to offer leadership across campus to support meaningful and effective assessment processes and guide efforts to improve curriculum, instruction, and student learning. Psychology's commitment to operational definitions of concepts to manipulate and measure complex variables enables psychologists to provide leadership and guidance to developing assessment efforts. Many faculty need assistance learning to write student learning outcomes in measurable language. Faculty outside the social sciences may have difficulty drafting learning outcomes that reflect the shift from abstract academic language (*know*, *understand*, *appreciate*) to descriptions of student learning that are grounded in concrete terms (behaviors and quality of products; Adelman, 2015; Stanny, 2015, 2016). Similarly, faculty need assistance developing direct measures of learning, especially measures of outcomes that describe complex concepts such as creativity, critical thinking, artistry in expression (for the performing arts), or a commitment to social justice.

Faculty outside the social sciences may need assistance with data analysis. Faculty in the arts and humanities, for example, may resist the notion that student learning can be quantified. They may be unfamiliar with the analysis of qualitative findings. Some science, technology, engineering, and math disciplines seldom have to interpret findings that produce the level of variability observed in assessment data. Psychologists can provide leadership and guidance to assessment efforts because these issues are familiar problems in psychological research.

Measurement and Methodology

Psychologists bring disciplinary skills with measurement and research design that support effective assessment of student learning. The research paradigm of psychology, founded in methodological behaviorism, supports efforts to write measurable student learning outcomes and create direct measures for abstract concepts. Psychology has a long tradition of measuring "unmeasurable" concepts (Webb et al., 1966). Researchers articulate operational definitions and design multiple measures that converge on these challenging concepts. Potentially ambiguous constructs such as absent-mindedness (Broadbent et al., 1982; Reason & Lucas, 1984; Wallace et al., 2002), creativity (Batey, 2012), pace of life (Levine & Norenzayan, 1999; Lowin et al., 1971), expertise (Weiss & Shanteau, 2003), and love (Hatfield & Sprecher, 1986) have all been examined by psychologists using empirical measures based on direct observation of behaviors and products of behavior. Similarly, psychologists are well-versed with the challenges of collecting credible data to evaluate the impact of an intervention, such as implementing a new teaching strategy or modifying course requirements in an academic curriculum.

Deep Knowledge of the Research Literature on Cognition and Learning

Laboratory research on memory, cognition, the representation of complex knowledge, and the development of expertise provides the foundation for research-based instructional strategies faculty might implement to improve the quality of student learning. The laboratory research from psychology now finds a ready audience among institutions, teachers, and researchers who want to apply these findings to the practical problems of improving curricula, teaching, and student learning. In the United States, psychologists frequently take on leadership roles in centers for teaching and learning and disseminate the laboratory findings to faculty in multiple disciplines. Recent works address the translation of laboratory findings to instructional strategies and the design of assignments and curricula (e.g., Ambrose et al., 2010; Benassi et al., 2014; Brown et al., 2014; Doyle & Zakrajsek, 2013; National Academies of Sciences, Engineering, and Medicine, 2018; National Research Council, 2000; Nilson, 2003) and suggest strategies to motivate students to engage with the curriculum, guide students as they develop metacognitive skills, and encourage students to adopt effective study practices (McGuire, 2015; Nilson, 2013).

CONCLUSION

Institutions that make the most of assessment recognize that meaningful assessment entails more than just gathering, reporting, and archiving assessment evidence. Assessment done in the right way for the right reasons is driven by a sense of "positive restlessness," a combination of curiosity about alternative approaches to helping students learn and a chronic feeling that things could always be done a bit better (Kuh et al., 2011). This attitude contributes to a "culture of improvement" (Suskie, 2015, 2018). Leaders who endorse assessment give this work meaning when they provide tangible support that encourages and rewards faculty engagement. Nothing says "marginalized" louder than a task that is delegated to a few (often junior) faculty or to an obscure, skeletally staffed office. Institutions with strong commitments to assessment and improvement formally recognize and honor significant contributions to meaningful assessment work. Assessment evidence informs decisions about multiple institutional operations, not just decisions about curriculum and student learning.

REFERENCES

Adelman, C. (2015). *To imagine a verb: The language and syntax of learning outcomes statements* (Occasional Paper No. 24). University of Illinois and Indiana University, National Institute for Learning Outcomes Assessment. https://www.learningoutcomesassessment.org/wp-content/uploads/2019/02/OccasionalPaper24.pdf

Ambrose, S. A., Bridges, M. W., DiPietro, M., Lovett, M. C., & Norman, M. K. (2010). *How learning works: Seven research-based principles for smart teaching.* Jossey-Bass. https://firstliteracy.org/wp-content/uploads/2015/07/How-Learning-Works.pdf

American Association of University Professors. (1940). *Statement of principles on academic freedom and tenure.* https://www.aaup.org/file/1940%20Statement.pdf

Batey, M. (2012). The measurement of creativity: From definitional consensus to the introduction of a new heuristic framework. *Creativity Research Journal, 24*(1), 55–65. https://doi.org/10.1080/10400419.2012.649181

Benassi, V. A., Overson, C. E., & Hakala, C. M. (Eds.). (2014). *Applying science of learning in education: Infusing psychological science into the curriculum.* Society for the Teaching of Psychology. http://teachpsych.org/ebooks/asle2014/index.php

Bolman, L. G., & Deal, T. E. (2017). *Reframing organizations: Artistry, choice, and leadership.* John Wiley & Sons. https://doi.org/10.1002/9781119281856

Broadbent, D. E., Cooper, P. F., FitzGerald, P., & Parkes, K. R. (1982). The cognitive failures questionnaire (CFQ) and its correlates. *British Journal of Clinical Psychology, 21*(1), 1–16. https://doi.org/10.1111/j.2044-8260.1982.tb01421.x

Brown, P. C., Roediger, H. L., III, & McDaniel, M. A. (2014). *Make it stick: The science of successful learning.* Harvard University Press. https://doi.org/10.4159/9780674419377

Condon, W., Iverson, E. R., Manduca, C. A., Rutz, C., & Willett, G. (2016). *Faculty development and student learning: Assessing the connections.* Indiana University Press.

Doyle, T., & Zakrajsek, T. (2013). *The new science of learning: How to learn in harmony with your brain.* Stylus.

Ericsson, K. A., Krampe, R. T., & Tesch-Römer, C. (1993). The role of deliberate practice in the acquisition of expert performance. *Psychological Review, 100*(3), 363–406. https://doi.org/10.1037/0033-295X.100.3.363

Fink, L. D. (2013). *Creating significant learning experiences: Revised and updated.* Jossey-Bass.

Fulcher, K. H., Good, M. R., Coleman, C. M., & Smith, K. L. (2014). *A simple model for learning improvement: Weigh pig, feed pig, weigh pig.* (Occasional Paper No. 23). University of Illinois and Indiana University, National Institute for Learning Outcomes Assessment. https://www.learningoutcomesassessment.org/wp-content/uploads/2019/02/OccasionalPaper23.pdf

Gawande, A. (2004, December 6). The bell curve: What happens when patients find out how good their doctors really are? *The New Yorker.* https://www.newyorker.com/magazine/2004/12/06/the-bell-curve

Gilbert, E. (2018, January 12). An insider's take on assessment: It may be worse than you thought. *The Chronicle of Higher Education.* https://www.chronicle.com/section/Commentary/44

Gold, L., Rhoades, G., Smith, M., & Kuh, G. (2011). *What faculty unions say about student learning outcomes assessment* (Occasional Paper No. 9). University of Illinois and Indiana University, National Institute for Learning Outcomes Assessment. http://www.learningoutcomesassessment.org/documents/OccasionalPaper9.pdf

Hatfield, E., & Sprecher, S. (1986). Measuring passionate love in intimate relationships. *Journal of Adolescence, 9,* 383–410. https://doi.org/10.1016/S0140-1971(86)80043-4

Hinds, P. J. (1999). The curse of expertise: The effects of expertise and debiasing methods on prediction of novice performance. *Journal of Experimental Psychology: Applied, 5*(2), 205–221. https://doi.org/10.1037/1076-898X.5.2.205

Hinds, P. J., Patterson, M., & Pfeffer, J. (2001). Bothered by abstraction: The effect of expertise on knowledge transfer and subsequent novice performance. *Journal of Applied Psychology, 86,* 1232–1243. https://doi.org/10.1037/0021-9010.86.6.1232

Isabella, M., & McGovern, H. (2018). Identify, values, and reflection: Shaping (and being shaped) through assessment. *New Directions for Teaching and Learning, 2018*(155), 89–96. https://doi.org/10.1002/tl.20307

Kuh, G. D., Ikenberry, S. O., Jankkowski, N. A., Cain, T. R., Ewell, P. T., Hutchings, P., & Kinzie, J. (2015). *Using evidence of student learning to improve higher education.* Jossey-Bass.

Kuh, G. D., Kinzie, J., Schuh, J. H., & Whitt, E. J. (2011). Fostering student success in hard times. *Change: The Magazine of Higher Learning, 43*(4), 13–19. https://doi.org/10.1080/00091383.2011.585311

Latuca, L. R., Terenzini, P. T., & Volkwein, J. F. (2006). *Engineering change: A study of the impact of EC 2000—Executive summary.* Accreditation Board for Engineering and Technology. https://www.abet.org/wp-content/uploads/2015/04/EngineeringChange-executive-summary.pdf

Levine, R. V., & Norenzayan, A. (1999). The pace of life in 31 countries. *Journal of Cross-Cultural Psychology, 30*(2), 178–205. https://doi.org/10.1177/0022022199030002003

Lowin, A., Hottes, J. H., Sandler, B. E., & Bornstein, M. (1971). The pace of life and sensitivity to time in urban and rural settings. A preliminary study. *The Journal of Social Psychology, 83,* 247–253. https://doi.org/10.1080/00224545.1971.9922469

Magruder, J., McManis, M. A., & Young, C. C. (1997). The right idea at the right time: Development of a transformational assessment culture. *New Directions for Higher Education, 1997*(100), 17–29. https://doi.org/10.1002/he.10002

Maki, P. L. (2010a). *Assessing for learning* (2nd ed.). Stylus.

Maki, P. L. (2010b). *Coming to terms with student outcomes assessment.* Stylus.

McConnell, K. D. (2018, March 1). Assessment isn't about bureaucracy but about teaching and learning (opinion). *Inside Higher Education.*

McGuire, S. Y. (2015). *Teach students how to learn.* Stylus.

Meyer, J. H. F., & Land, R. (2005). Threshold concepts and troublesome knowledge (2): Epistemological considerations and a conceptual framework for teaching and learning. *Higher Education, 49,* 373–388. https://doi.org/10.1007/s10734-004-6779-5

Middendorf, J., & Pace, D. (2004). Decoding the disciplines: A model for helping students learn disciplinary ways of thinking. *New Directions for Teaching and Learning, 2004*(98), 1–12. https://doi.org/10.1002/tl.142

National Academies of Sciences, Engineering, and Medicine. (2018). *How people learn II: Learners, contexts, and cultures.* The National Academies Press. https://doi.org/10.17226/24783

National Institute for Learning Outcomes Assessment. (2016). *Higher education quality: Why documenting learning matters* [Policy statement]. University of Illinois and Indiana University, National Institute for Learning Outcomes Assessment. https://www.learningoutcomesassessment.org/documents/NILOA_policy_statement.pdf

National Research Council. (2000). *How people learn: Brain, mind, experience, and school: Expanded edition.* National Academies Press.

Nilson, L. B. (2003). *Teaching at its best* (2nd ed.). Anker/Jossey-Bass.

Nilson, L. B. (2013). *Creating self-regulated learners.* Stylus.

O'Neill, M., Slater, A., & Sapp, D. G. (2018). Writing and the undergraduate curriculum: Using assessment evidence to create a model for institutional change. *New Directions for Teaching and Learning, 2018*(155), 97–104. https://doi.org/10.1002/tl.20308

Pace, D. (2017). *The decoding the disciplines paradigm: Seven steps to increased student learning.* Indiana University Press. https://doi.org/10.2307/j.ctt2005z1w

Reason, J., & Lucas, D. (1984). Absent-mindedness in shops: Its incidence, correlates and consequences. *British Journal of Clinical Psychology, 23,* 121–131. https://doi.org/10.1111/j.2044-8260.1984.tb00635.x

Stanny, C. J. (2015). Assessing learning in psychology: A primer for faculty and administrators. In D. S. Dunn (Ed.), *The Oxford handbook of undergraduate psychology education* (pp. 813–831). Oxford University Press.

Stanny, C. J. (2016). Reevaluating Bloom's taxonomy: What measurable verbs can and cannot say about student learning. *Education in Science, 6*(4), 37. https://doi.org/10.3390/educsci6040037

Stanny, C. J. (2018). Putting assessment into action: Evolving from a culture of assessment to a culture of improvement. *New Directions for Teaching and Learning, 2018*(155), 113–116. https://doi.org/10.1002/tl.20310

Stanny, C. J., & Halonen, J. S. (2011). Accreditation, accountability, and assessment: Addressing multiple agendas. In L. Stefani (Ed.), *Evaluating the effectiveness of academic development: A professional guide* (pp. 169–181). Routledge.

Stanny, C. J., Stone, E., & Cook, A. (2018). Evidence-based discussions of learning facilitated through a peer review of assessment. *New Directions for Teaching and Learning, 2018*(155), 31–38. https://doi.org/10.1002/tl.20300

Suskie, L. (2015). *Five dimensions of quality: A common sense guide to accreditation and accountability.* Jossey-Bass.

Suskie, L. (2018). *Assessing student learning: A common sense guide* (3rd ed.). Jossey-Bass.

Transparency in Learning and Teaching Project (TILT) Higher Ed. (n.d.). *TILT Higher Ed Examples and Resources.* https://tilthighered.com/tiltexamplesandresources

U.S. Department of Education. (2006). *A test of leadership: Charting the future of U.S. higher education (A report of the commission appointed by Secretary of Education Margaret Spellings).* https://www2.ed.gov/about/bdscomm/list/hiedfuture/reports/pre-pub-report.pdf

Venkatraman, S. (2007). A framework for implementing TQM in higher education programs. *Quality Assurance in Education, 15*(1), 92–112. https://doi.org/10.1108/09684880710723052

Wallace, J. C., Kass, S. J., & Stanny, C. J. (2002). The cognitive failures questionnaire revisited: Dimensions and correlates. *The Journal of General Psychology, 129*, 238–256. https://doi.org/10.1080/00221300209602098

Webb, E. J., Campbell, D. T., Schwartz, R. D., & Sechrest, L. (1966). *Unobtrusive measures: Nonreactive research in the social sciences.* Rand McNally.

Weiss, D. J., & Shanteau, J. (2003). Empirical assessment of expertise. *Human Factors, 45*, 104–116. https://doi.org/10.1518/hfes.45.1.104.27233

Winkelmes, M., Bernacki, M., Butler, J., Zochowski, M., Golanics, J., & Weavil, K. H. (2016). A teaching intervention that increases underserved college students' success. *Peer Review: Emerging Trends and Key Debates in Undergraduate Education, 18*(1/2), 31–36. https://www.aacu.org/peerreview/2016/winter-spring/Winkelmes

Worthen, M. (2018, February 22). The misguided drive to measure 'learning outcomes.' *The New York Times.* https://www.nytimes.com/2018/02/23/opinion/sunday/colleges-measure-learning-outcomes.html

7

Backward Design, the Science of Learning, and the Assessment of Student Learning

Catherine E. Overson and Victor A. Benassi

In most academic courses, teachers use a variety of assessments to both evaluate student learning (summative assessments) and inform future teaching (formative assessments). Whether and how well they link these assessments to course learning outcomes and instructional activities vary widely. Some teachers intentionally define the outcomes they want students to manifest, thoughtfully consider the type of evidence (assessment) that speaks to students' acquisition of the outcomes, and carefully implement instructional activities that are intended to help students achieve the outcomes. Other teachers may consider what outcomes they have for their course and then implement instructional activities to help students achieve them. For these teachers, assessments may be an afterthought—something required to assign grades and provide students with summative feedback. Consideration of any linking between student learning outcomes (SLOs), assessment of student learning of the outcomes, and instructional activities designed to promote learning of the outcomes is often missing. As colleagues in a university teaching and learning center, we focus our work on the former approach, informed by a method of course design generally referred to as backward design (Wiggins & McTighe, 2006) or integrative course design (Fink, 2013) and by the science of learning (e.g., Benassi, Overson, & Hakala, 2014).

In backward design, the teacher begins with developing course learning goals or, in the language of assessment, SLOs. Next, the teacher considers evidence that might be gathered to addresses whether and to what extent

https://doi.org/10.1037/0000183-008
Assessing Undergraduate Learning in Psychology: Strategies for Measuring and Improving Student Performance, S. A. Nolan, C. M. Hakala, and R. E. Landrum (Editors)

students achieve the SLOs. The teacher then prepares assessments that are directly related to the SLOs. In preparing these assessments, the teacher asks, "Do my assessments provide the kind of evidence that will allow me to decide whether students have obtained my SLOs?" After the SLOs and assessments are developed, the teacher decides on specific instructional activities designed to help students to achieve course SLOs. Consider this example. A teacher has as a course SLO that students will be able to integrate concepts from multiple sources of information covered in the course. They develop a set of assessments that asks students to write essays that compare and contrast viewpoints represented in reading material and to relate what they learned to what they already know about the topic. To assist students in acquiring the SLO, the teacher creates a series of homework assignments that provides students with practice in comparing and contrasting material from different sources and in relating what they are reading to what they already know about the topic. After reading the submitted assignments, the teacher provides each student with feedback and suggestions for improvements. They might also have students discuss their homework responses with other students during class.

OUR APPROACH TO ASSESSMENT OF STUDENT LEARNING

At the University of New Hampshire's Center for Excellence and Innovation in Teaching and Learning, we have worked for more than a decade with course instructors (faculty and graduate students) from across the university to assist them in designing their courses in a manner consistent with the background design approach. When we meet with instructors, we begin by asking them to identify a learning issue that they would like to address in their course. With their assistance, we work to develop SLOs that directly address their learning issue. For example, a teacher of an introductory statistics course may say that students in the course often have difficulty identifying the correct statistical inference test to apply to a specific research design. That issue may be turned into an SLO: By the end of the course, students should be able to select the appropriate statistical inference test for the eight research designs covered in the course. Next, we suggest an instructional intervention, informed by the science of learning (e.g., Carpenter, 2014; Kang, 2017) that provides students with practice designed to help them decide which statistical test is applicable to a particular research design.

We describe three projects in which we worked with instructors who wanted to address a learning issue that they had identified for a course they teach. This work focused on SLOs and assessments related to three domains described by Fink (2013): foundational knowledge, application, and integration. Our approach is also applicable to other types of SLOs (cf. Barkley & Major, 2016; Fink, 2013). For example, if a teacher identifies an SLO that, by the end of the course, students give a persuasive oral presentation that addresses some controversial topic covered in the course, we could design an appropriate assessment and a set of instructional activities intended to help students acquire that skill.

We follow the same format for each of the examples described later. First, we describe the learning issue addressed in the project. Second, we frame that learning issue into an SLO. Third, we describe our approach to assess the SLO. Fourth, we discuss the instructional activities that the instructors implemented to promote students' acquisition of the SLO. Fifth, we present results that address assessment of the SLO. Finally, we describe the feedback we provided to the course instructor(s) at the end of the term.

Foundational Knowledge Learning Goal: Assessing the Impact of Quizzing on Exam Performance in a Large Enrollment Course

Assessing students' foundational knowledge in academic courses is important because the results of such assessments can be used by course instructors to gauge their students' learning of key course-related facts and concepts and to make changes, if needed, to their course design. The material described in this section is based on work that appears in Benassi, Tappin, et al. (2014).

Learning Issue

An instructor of a large-enrollment course (around 150–165 students) on human stress from the department of occupational therapy was interested in using weekly online quizzes as an instructional tool to improve her students' learning of key concepts in the course, as measured on major course exams. Although she knew about the potential benefits of such quizzing to strengthen student learning (Roediger & Karpicke, 2006), doing so required her to dedicate considerable time to create, score, and manage these online quizzes. She wanted to assess whether the time and effort (for her and her students) actually benefitted student learning.

Student Learning Outcome

The SLO was related to students' knowledge of the core foundational facts and concepts in the field of human stress. The instructor had taught this course many times prior to working with us, and she had a deep understanding of the facts and concepts she wanted her students to know. Because the instructor was a member of a department that had a well-developed curricular map for the major offered in her department, her overall SLO for the course was aligned with knowledge and skills in other courses offered by the department.

Assessment of the Student Learning Outcome

Prior to working with us, the instructor had written exam items that measured factual knowledge of course material, understanding of course concepts, and discrimination among concepts (comparison and contrast). In line with our backward design approach, we worked with the instructor to prepare quiz questions and pair them with exam questions that tapped a desired SLO for her course. For example, the instructor had a desired SLO that her students would learn key concepts and facts related to human stress responses. She wrote and administered weekly practice quizzes that tapped these concepts and facts. On the basis of research on the testing effect (Roediger & Karpicke, 2006), when coupled with quiz performance feedback, we would expect learning of these concepts to be strengthened. A final assessment—an exam—included items that tapped the same concepts and facts on which students were previously quizzed. For two examples of linked quiz and exam questions used in this project, refer to Benassi, Tappin, et al. (2014). Some instructors are good at creating quiz and exam questions that are aligned with each other and with learning goals to be assessed on their exams. Other instructors may require assistance and practice, but we find that they consistently learn the skill. Our office provides resources, including individual mentoring, to help faculty acquire this skill.

Activities to Promote Student Learning

The learning activity we developed was informed by research showing that quizzing of previously studied material can improve learning and retention of that material on a subsequent test (assessment). The testing effect has been well documented in laboratory and applied settings (Dunlosky et al., 2013; Roediger & Karpicke, 2006). The act of retrieving an answer to the questions has a positive effect on improving retention of the answer to the question on a subsequent final test, including when the final test question is related to, but different from, the quiz question.

We designed a learning activity in which students completed five weekly online quizzes leading up to a major course exam (Benassi, Tappin, et al., 2014, Study 2). Once weekly, by an assigned date, students completed a quiz on the course learning management site, Blackboard, in which they encountered two types of item presentations. For one type of presented item, students received a question that required them to type an answer to a question (e.g., "Cortisol is regulated in large part by what kind of mechanism?"). After students typed an answer, or typed that they did not know the answer, they submitted their response. A multiple-choice question on the same topic then appeared. They selected from among four multiple-choice alternatives.

For the second type of presented item, students received a statement (e.g., "Cortisol is regulated in large part by a negative feedback loop, meaning that when levels get too high, the system shuts down production"). They read the statement and submitted a response that they had read it. A multiple-choice question then appeared, which included among the four alternatives the answer that appeared in the statement they had just read. Students made their selection and moved on to the next quiz item. We used this second type of question to control for students' amount of exposure to the quizzed material. In this condition, students were completely exposed to the material, but they did not retrieve it from memory. After a quiz was closed at the end of a weekly quizzing period, we made available in Blackboard correct answers to all items.

For the exam, we randomly selected a subset of the questions from the two types of item presentations on the online quizzes and, for these, selected the corresponding multiple-choice exam questions that the instructor had prepared. These questions assessed the same concepts tested on the quiz questions, but they were different questions. We were interested in whether students performed better on the exam questions that were paired with recall and multiple-choice quizzing than they did on exam questions that were paired with quiz questions to which students were given a correct statement before answering the associated multiple-choice question.

Assessment Results

Students scored higher on exam questions for which they had received recall/multiple-choice quiz items ($M = 84\%$, $SD = 11$) than they did on material in the control condition ($M = 77\%$, $SD = 13$), $\eta_p^2 = .32$. For full details on this study and two related studies, refer to Benassi, Tappin, et al. (2014).

We have some additional evidence that including the recall question just prior to a parallel multiple-choice question is beneficial. Benassi, Tappin, et al. (2014, Study 3) found that students scored higher on major exam questions for which they had received recall/multiple-choice quiz items ($M = 91\%$, $SD = 10$) than they did on questions for which they had received multiple-choice-only quiz items ($M = 87\%$, $SD = 15$), $\eta_p^2 = .09$. We also found that the boost afforded by the recall/multiple-choice quizzing over multiple-choice quizzing alone was greater, on average, for students who scored lower, overall, on the exam than for their higher-performing peers (Benassi, Tappin, et al., 2014, Figure 2). Among the lower-performing students, exam scores were 12 percentage points higher, on average, for the items for which they completed recall/multiple-choice quiz questions than for multiple-choice–only items.

Feedback to the Course Instructor

Once our project was completed, the instructor of the human stress course concluded, on the basis of the results that we showed her, that the use of online quizzing leading up to her major course exams had a positive effect on her students' learning. She continued to assign online quizzes composed of recall questions with follow-up multiple-choice questions. In this way, she could score the multiple-choice questions automatically in the course management system without having to manually score a large number of open-ended recall questions.

Application Learning Goal: Assessing the Impact of Interleaved Study on Selecting Appropriate Statistical Tests for Research Designs

As with foundational knowledge, assessing students' skill at applying academic material to specific contexts or situations is important because the results can be used to make changes, if needed, to an instructor's course design. The project described next was completed with the assistance of four instructors of an introductory statistics course.

Learning Issue

A common application learning goal in introductory statistics courses in psychology is that, by the end of the term, students will be able to select the appropriate statistical tests for the various research designs covered in the course. With students' enrollment in the subsequent research methods course, required for all undergraduate majors in the psychology program, faculty in our university's psychology department had long observed that most students had little success in achieving this learning goal. To investigate these anecdotal accounts, we developed and administered a 24-item test during the first week of the semester to students in all sections of the research methods course offered during one semester in the department. The test included three research designs for each of eight statistical tests covered in the department's introductory statistics course. The mean score on the test was 27%. This was a troubling result because one of the major learning goals in the introductory statistics course in this department is that students are able to select an appropriate statistical test for a given research design (cf. McDonald, 2014). If students scored not much above chance after completing the course, one may wonder whether students forgot how to apply the skill of selecting the appropriate statistical test by the time they enrolled in the research methods course or whether they ever learned the skill at all.

Student Learning Outcome

We have worked with a number of faculty teaching introductory statistics courses who were interested in whether students in their course were learning the skill of selecting the appropriate statistical test for research designs. We summarize our work with four of those instructors whose SLO included that, for a given research design, students would be able to select the appropriate statistical test for the eight statistical tests covered in the course.

Assessment of the Student Learning Outcome

During the last week of the semester, students in all four sections completed the in-class 24-item test described previously as an assessment of their skill in selecting the appropriate statistical analysis for a given scenario. Although students received feedback on their performance after the test, it was ungraded; however, students were told that taking the test would help prepare them for the final course exam.

Here is a sample question:

> Two sleep researchers tested their hypotheses that exam performance declines, on average, when students have an inadequate night's sleep the night before an exam than when they do not. The researchers asked 55 students to sleep for 5 hours the night prior to taking an SAT prep-test the following day. The mean score on the SAT prep-test for students in the general population is 1012 with a standard deviation of 115. The average SAT prep-test score for the sleep-deprived sample was 950. The population distribution is approximately normal. The scale of measurement is considered interval/scale. Assume all test assumptions have been met.

The answer choices for each test question were as follows:

- *z*-test (correct answer); Single Sample *t*-test (*t*-test for population mean)
- *t*-test for independent (or Uncorrelated) Means (AKA: Two Independent Samples *t*-test)
- *t*-test for Matched Pairs (AKA: Dependent; Repeated; Correlated Means)
- One-way between groups ANOVA; correlation; regression chi-square for independence

Activities to Promote Student Learning

We decided that an ideal strategy to address this learning issue was to implement an interleaved program of study. We know from laboratory experiments (e.g., Cepeda et al., 2008) and experiments done in authentic classroom settings (e.g., Sobel et al., 2011) that spacing—or distributing study over time and allowing for study sessions to be separated by a study gap—benefits learning (Carpenter, 2014; Dunlosky et al., 2013). When an academic subject involves a number of subtopics, such as a statistics course in which a number of statistical analyses must be learned and appropriately applied, interleaved study, a special case of spacing, is particularly effective.

Interleaved study can be contrasted with blocked study, in which students learn elements of a given subtopic before moving on to the next subtopic. Interleaving of study has been demonstrated to produce better learning outcomes than does blocking of study in achieving a variety of both academic and motor skills (Carpenter, 2014; Dunlosky et al., 2013; Kang, 2017). In a statistics example of blocking, students would review material on the *z*-test, practice computations and applications for the *z*-test, and then move on to the next statistical analysis, repeating the process until all analyses have been covered. With interleaving, prior subtopics are revisited during study with each new to-be-learned subtopic. In our statistics example, students studying analysis of variance would alternate their study with a mixture of previously learned statistical analyses. This strategy necessarily involves elements of spacing. It is notable that, with interleaving, the added element of juxtaposition of new material with a variety of statistical analyses during study may provide the occasion for discriminatory inspection, facilitating the identification of distinguishing characteristics (Rohrer, 2012).

To examine the learning benefits of interleaving on students' performance on the SLO for the introductory statistics course, we randomly assigned the four instructors' courses to one of two conditions in this project. All four instructors taught their courses as usual, with no instruction from us. For two of the instructors' courses, after the unit in which each statistical test was covered, students completed in Blackboard an online review of the statistical test covered in that unit, which included material that detailed the conditions that must be met for that test to be appropriate to analyze data from a research design. Following the review, students completed an online quiz that included questions that asked students to select the correct statistical test for a research design described in the question or to decide whether a particular statistical test was or was not appropriate for a research design described in the question. After completing a quiz, students were given access in Blackboard to the correct answers. On each subsequent online quiz, questions covered statistical tests from that unit as well as statistical tests covered in all previous online reviews. Thus, the eighth online review included an eight-item quiz, with one question on each of the eight statistical tests covered in the course. At the end of the semester, we administered the 24-item exam.

Assessment Results

The assessment results are shown in Figure 7.1. Students in the two courses that included the online review quizzes (interleaving condition) scored considerably higher than chance on the 24-item "choosing statistical tests" final exam. They also scored higher than did the students who did not complete the online review quizzes (control). Note that the students in the two control courses scored similarly to students in the research methods courses who took the 24-item test after completing the introductory statistics course (27%).

Feedback to Course Instructors

The results from this assessment and instructional design project were enlightening. Discussions with faculty uncovered a critical learning issue, leading to the development of a central SLO. Through the development and administration of a "choosing statistical tests" assessment, we determined that most students did not achieve the SLO, as measured at the end of their statistics course or at the beginning of their subsequent research methods course. Although instructors of the statistics courses would agree that the SLO was important, we learned from discussions that the instructional activities provided by the

FIGURE 7.1. Mean Percentage Correct on Final Exam on Choosing the Appropriate Statistical Test in Control and Interleaving Courses

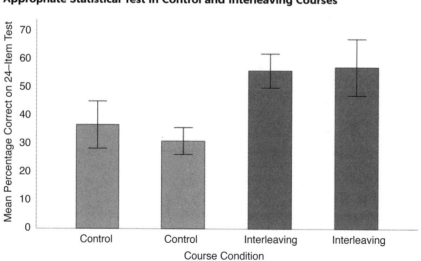

instructors did not support the learning of the identified SLO. Informed by research in the science of learning, we developed and implemented an instructional intervention that involved the interleaving of the practice of selecting the statistical test appropriate for eight research designs covered in the introductory statistics course. This assessment project provided some evidence that students could score better on the "choosing statistical tests" exam than what we had previously observed. To be sure, many factors could be at play in our work. Since this initial effort, we have used improved research designs to demonstrate that it is the interleaving of practice that promotes the learning of the SLO. Our recommendation to instructors of the introductory statistics course is that they build into their course opportunities for students to interleave their practice of selecting the appropriate statistical test for the research designs covered in the course.

Integration Learning Goal: Using Guiding Questions to Promote Students' Learning From Assigned Readings

As with foundational knowledge and application skills, assessing students' skill at integrating academic material from different sources is important because the results can be used to make changes, if needed, to an instructor's course design. The material described in this section is based on work that appears in Stiegler-Balfour and Benassi (2015).

Learning Issue

The instructor of an upper-division undergraduate course, a professor in a department of psychology at a private university in the northeastern United States, had noticed that although her students were generally successful in learning the content of individual course reading assignments (foundational knowledge), some of them (especially those with relatively poor reading comprehension skills) performed poorly on exam questions that assessed how well they were able to integrate the material from separate readings. In discussions with the instructor, we decided that a backward design approach to this issue might be helpful. We established what we wanted students to be able to do (integrate material from different course readings), decided on assessments that would measure the extent to which students met the SLO, and developed an instructional intervention that might promote the achievement of the SLO.

Student Learning Outcome

We were interested in students' performance on essay questions that asked them to write answers that integrated material from multiple reading assignments. This type of integration was a major overall student SLO in this upper-division undergraduate course. Whereas in lower-division gateway courses SLOs often focus on measures of foundational knowledge and concept acquisition, SLOs related to integration of course material are typical for instructors in upper-division courses.

Assessment of the Student Learning Outcome

Our assessment of the extent to which students successfully integrated course material was based on their performance on three essay exams administered during the semester. Exam questions were related to the material included in guiding questions that students completed leading up to an exam (more details about these activities later). These questions were intended to measure students' skill in applying the material included in the assigned readings to novel situations. Examples of essay exam questions as well as details on exam scoring are provided in Stiegler-Balfour and Benassi (2015).

Activities to Promote Student Learning

Details on the learning activities assignments are provided in Stiegler-Balfour and Benassi (2015). Each week leading up to an exam, students completed a set of reading assignments. Starting with the first week, about half of the class completed and submitted guiding questions related to the assignment. During the next week, the other half of the class completed and submitted the guiding questions, and so on. On weeks that students submitted guiding questions, the course instructor scored their responses. These questions were designed to activate prior knowledge and to guide them in connecting information covered in different parts of the weekly reading assignment.

Assessment Results

Across two sections of the course that were offered, students scored higher on essay exam questions for which they had completed and submitted answers to guiding questions ($M = 89\%$, $SD = 9$) than they did on exam questions for which they did not submit guiding questions ($M = 82\%$, $SD = 14$). Thus, having students submit responses to guiding questions prior to high-stakes exams is associated with better performance on questions designed to tap their skill in integrating academic performance (compared with their performance on exam questions not linked to guiding questions).

Prior research and theory provide a strong basis for predicting that the completion of guiding questions may be particularly beneficial to students with relatively low reading comprehension skills and less so for students with relatively high reading comprehension skills (Stiegler-Balfour & Benassi, 2015). We administered the Gates–MacGinitie Reading Test (MacGinitie et al., 2007) to the students in the two sections of the course at the beginning of the term. Figure 7.2 shows exam performance results for students with relatively low and high reading comprehension scores when they did and did not submit answers to guiding questions leading up to a major exam. Low-skill readers scored 10 percentage points higher, on average, on essay exam questions for which they had submitted answers to guiding questions than they did on exam questions for which they did not submit guiding questions. In contrast, there was little difference with this comparison for high-skill readers (3 percentage points). Stiegler-Balfour and Benassi (2015) reported the details of this analysis and discussed the significance of their findings.

FIGURE 7.2. Mean Percentage on Essay Exam Questions for Relatively Low Skilled and Relatively High Skilled Readers (Based on Gates–MacGinitie Reading Test Scores) When They Did Not Complete the Guiding Questions Versus When They Did

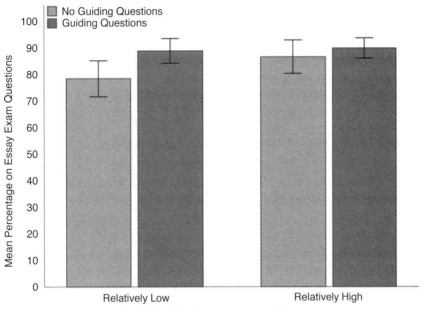

Note. Adapted from "Guiding Questions Promote Learning of Expository Text for Less-Skilled Readers," by J. J. Stiegler-Balfour and V. A. Benassi, 2015, *Scholarship of Teaching and Learning in Psychology*, *1*(4), p. 318 (https://doi.org/10.1037/stl0000044). Copyright 2015 by the American Psychological Association.

Feedback to Course Instructor

The course instructor was the lead collaborator on this project. She had considerable expertise in the area of reading comprehension that she wanted to bring to bear on addressing a practical problem that she observed in the courses she taught—namely, that many students had difficulty integrating course material on essay exam questions. Her findings, from two offerings of the course, provided good evidence that creating assignments that included guiding questions was an effective instructional activity that promoted acquisition of a course SLO. Most important, she found that this activity was particularly effective for students with relatively low reading comprehension skills. Her project, as well as other research (described in Stiegler-Balfour & Benassi, 2015), has informed her subsequent offerings of this course. Because the learning issue addressed in this project is common in most teachers' courses, the use of guiding question assignments may have wide applicability.

CONCLUSION

We described three examples of our work, as professionals working in a university teaching and learning center, with course instructors who wanted to assess student learning in their courses. We use a well-established approach to course design, and we work with instructors to develop, implement, and assess the impact of instructional activities informed by the science of learning. Ideally, the approach to assessment of course SLOs described in this chapter is best undertaken with assistance from professionals with relevant expertise (e.g., staff of teaching learning centers or assessment offices). Where that is not possible, faculty can, with time and effort, develop the skills needed to create, implement, and assess the impact of their instructional activities (e.g., Benassi, Tappin, et al., 2014; Gurung, 2014; Motz et al., 2018). Including an appropriate research design in a course allows the instructor to assess whether the particular SLO being measured is related to a particular instructional activity. In the three examples described in this chapter, we provided evidence that particular learning activities (quizzing, interleaving of practice, and guiding questions) promoted better SLOs than did comparison instruction (restudy, no interleaving, and no guiding questions). Of course, undertaking such projects may not be possible or feasible for course instructors. Still, we suggest that following the backward design approach would be helpful because it involves instructors explicitly connecting course SLOs, assessment of those outcomes, and learning activities intended to promote students' achievement of those outcomes. Recently, Jensen et al. (2017) described an approach (backward design in education research) to education research and assessment in science, technology, engineering, and mathematics that is similar to our approach—that is, it incorporates the elements of backward course design, learning science, and assessment.

In the examples we described, we used three types of SLOs: foundational knowledge, integration, and application. These outcomes are usually listed by instructors in their course syllabi and in academic program curricular maps, and they have been the focus of our work with individual faculty and with academic department curriculum committees. However, our approach is applicable to other types of SLOs that instructors and curriculum committees may want to assess (e.g., oral communication and writing skills, group collaboration).

REFERENCES

Barkley, E. F., & Major, C. H. (2016). *Learning assessment techniques: A handbook for college faculty*. Jossey Bass.

Benassi, V. A., Overson, C. E., & Hakala, C. M. (Eds.). (2014). *Applying science of learning in education: Infusing psychological science into the curriculum*. Society for the Teaching of Psychology. http://teachpsych.org/ebooks/asle2014/index.php

Benassi, V. A., Tappin, E. M., Overson, C. E., Lee, M. J., O'Brien, E. J., Prudhomme White, B., Stiegler-Balfour, J. J., & Hakala, C. M. (2014). Applying the science of learning: The cognition toolbox. In V. A. Benassi, C. E. Overson, & C. M. Hakala

(Eds.), *Applying science of learning in education: Infusing psychological science into the curriculum* (pp. 194–205). Society for the Teaching of Psychology. http://teachpsych.org/ebooks/asle2014/index.php

Carpenter, S. K. (2014). Spacing and interleaving of study and practice. In V. A. Benassi, C. E. Overson, & C. M. Hakala (Eds.), *Applying science of learning in education: Infusing psychological science into the curriculum.* Society for the Teaching of Psychology. http://teachpsych.org/ebooks/asle2014/index.php

Cepeda, N. J., Vul, E., Rohrer, D., Wixted, J. T., & Pashler, H. (2008). Spacing effects in learning: A temporal ridgeline of optimal retention. *Psychological Science, 19,* 1095–1102. https://doi.org/10.1111/j.1467-9280.2008.02209.x

Dunlosky, J., Rawson, K. A., Marsh, E. J., Nathan, M. J., & Willingham, D. T. (2013). Improving students' learning with effective learning techniques: Promising directions from cognitive and educational psychology. *Psychological Science in the Public Interest, 14,* 4–58. https://doi.org/10.1177/1529100612453266

Fink, L. D. (2013). *Creating significant learning experiences: An integrated approach to designing college courses* (2nd ed.). Jossey-Bass.

Gurung, R. A. R. (2014). Assessing the impact of instructional methods. In V. A. Benassi, C. E. Overson, & C. M. Hakala (Eds.), *Applying science of learning in education: Infusing psychological science into the curriculum.* Society for the Teaching of Psychology. http://teachpsych.org/ebooks/asle2014/index.php

Jensen, J. L., Bailey, E. G., Kummer, T. A., & Weber, K. S. (2017). Using backward design in education research: A research methods essay. *Journal of Microbiology & Biology Education, 18*(3), 1–6. https://doi.org/10.1128/jmbe.v18i3.1367

Kang, S. H. K. (2017). The benefits of interleaved practice for learning. In J. C. Horvath, J. M. Lodge, & J. Hattie (Eds.), *From the laboratory to the classroom: Translating science of learning for teachers* (pp. 79–93). Routledge.

MacGinitie, W. H., MacGinitie, R. K., Maria, K., Dreyer, L. G., & Hughes, K. E. (2007). *Gates-MacGinitie Reading Tests: Technical manual, Forms S & T* (4th ed.). Rolling Meadows.

McDonald, J. H. (2014). *Handbook of biological statistics* (3rd ed.). Sparky House.

Motz, B. A., Carvalho, P. F., de Leeuw, J. R., & Goldstone, R. L. (2018). Embedding experiments: Staking causal inference in authentic educational contexts. *Journal of Learning Analytics, 5*(2), 47–59. https://doi.org/10.18608/jla.2018.52.4

Roediger, H. L., III, & Karpicke, J. D. (2006). The power of testing memory: Basic research and implications for educational practice. *Perspectives on Psychological Science, 1,* 181–210. https://doi.org/10.1111/j.1745-6916.2006.00012.x

Rohrer, D. (2012). Interleaving helps students distinguish among similar concepts. *Educational Psychology Review, 24,* 355–367. https://doi.org/10.1007/s10648-012-9201-3

Sobel, H. S., Cepeda, N. J., & Kapler, I. V. (2011). Spacing effects in real-world classroom vocabulary learning. *Applied Cognitive Psychology, 25*(5), 763–767. https://doi.org/10.1002/acp.1747

Stiegler-Balfour, J. J., & Benassi, V. A. (2015). Guiding questions promote learning of expository text for less-skilled readers. *Scholarship of Teaching and Learning in Psychology, 1*(4), 312–325. https://doi.org/10.1037/stl0000044

Wiggins, G., & McTighe, J. (2006). *Understanding by design: A framework for effecting curricular development and assessment* (2nd ed.). Association for Supervision and Curriculum Development.

II

INDIVIDUAL APPROACHES

8

Assessment as a Pedagogical Science

A Stealthy Approach to Studying Effective Teaching

Bridgette Martin Hard

I pursued a doctoral degree in psychology because I wanted to be both a scientist and a teacher—to make new discoveries about human mind and behavior, and to share my field with students. In graduate school, I learned primarily to be a scientist, specifically, a cognitive and developmental psychologist. I was enculturated to insist on data to evaluate an idea, dive eagerly into the research literature, identify gaps in knowledge, and generate novel research questions and studies to test them. I was trained to think critically about everything, most especially about my own work. In graduate school, I also learned about being a teacher, although those lessons were more implicit. I shadowed faculty as their teaching assistant (TA), led my own discussion sections, and taught courses over the summer.

In the early years of my career, these two valued roles of scientist and teacher felt extremely separate. They were roles I enjoyed but that had little in common besides some overlapping content. I certainly did not consider teaching as a scientific endeavor or myself as "experimenting" with pedagogy. I did not view what my students produced, such as tests and assignments, as "data." I am confident that my view of teaching as distinct from science was not unique. As one of my friends and favorite psychology teachers, Stephen Chew (2018), said during a presentation on teaching, psychologists often "research like scientists and teach like dummies."

Today, my perspective on science and teaching could not be more different. I have learned to harness my skills as a scientist to achieve two important

https://doi.org/10.1037/0000183-009
Assessing Undergraduate Learning in Psychology: Strategies for Measuring and Improving Student Performance, S. A. Nolan, C. M. Hakala, and R. E. Landrum (Editors)

goals: to discover whether I am achieving my pedagogical goals and to test broader beliefs and assumptions about effective pedagogy. In this chapter, I share with you how my teaching became more data driven when I developed a practice of *assessment*, that is, using data to evaluate whether I was meeting my instructional goals. I also share how my practice of assessment evolved into a scientific research program that draws on the theories and methods of psychology. Along the way, I describe tools in my assessment tool kit in the hope of providing fresh ideas to inspire your own assessment practices.

DISCOVERING ASSESSMENT TO IMPROVE PERSONAL PEDAGOGY

Like many of my peers in graduate school, my early approach to teaching drew primarily from my experiences as a student, meaning that I emulated my own professors. I viewed assignments and exams as serving the function of "earning grades" because that what they did in my own student life. This perspective shifted when, after finishing a postdoctoral fellowship, I was hired to lead the program at Stanford University known as the Psychology One Program. The university created this program as part of its greater effort to improve some of its largest and most impactful "gateway" courses in the sciences, including in psychology. My role was to manage the curriculum for introductory psychology, a large, single-section lecture course accompanied by small weekly discussion sections. I collaborated with a team of faculty to develop and continuously improve the lectures, learning activities, assignments, and exams. I also trained and mentored an instructional team of graduate and undergraduate students whose training in teaching was far more explicit than my own had been. They received direct training in pedagogy and worked collaboratively to design and refine active learning experiences to lead in their weekly discussion sections.

For the first time, I was teaching nearly 300 students in a class, and in such high numbers, grades looked different—like data. Suddenly, I saw my students' grades as providing valuable information. They were a means of evaluating how well students were accomplishing the learning objectives of the course and how well we were achieving our goals as an instructional team. Even better, student grades could inform changes to our teaching methods. I had stumbled on a process for evaluating and improving teaching: assessment.

Using Grade Data to Inform Better Teaching

The first way I learned to use assessment was to measure how well students were accomplishing specific learning objectives. One of the key objectives we had in introductory psychology was that students should learn how concepts and theories fit together to reveal deeper insights into the human experience, which we called *integrative themes* (see Nordmeyer, Hard, & Gross, 2016, for a summary). Students completed an in-class essay assignment at the end of the term to assess their accomplishment of this objective, as shown in Exhibit 8.1. The average scores were high, but given how much my instructional team valued this objective, we wondered how we could adjust our pedagogy to ensure that as many students as possible could master the objective well enough to earn an "A" on the essay.

Undergraduate and graduate teaching fellows worked together to refine our teaching practices. We added an explicit mention of integrative themes to the lesson plans for the weekly 50-minute discussion sections in the course. To give the students practice writing about integrative themes, we provided them with a written-answer question on an earlier midterm that was similar in spirit and format to the final essay. We gave students explicit instruction in their weekly discussion section on how to think about integrative themes and how to approach the essay successfully. Compared with when I first started teaching the course 10 years ago, my students now perform at least 2 percentage points higher on that final essay ($M = 92.9$ vs. 90.3), $t(514) = 4.31$, $p < .001$, $d = .38$, CI_{diff} [1.43, 3.82]. Grade distributions in Figure 8.1 reveal that more students now master the learning objective, as measured by the essay, than they did 10 years ago.

Once I realized the power of using course assignments as measures of pedagogical effectiveness, I started to examine my course assignments more carefully to ensure that all of my learning objectives were being assessed.

EXHIBIT 8.1

Sample Integrative Essay Question on Final Exam

One of the core themes in this class has been that malfunctions, or breakdowns in thinking, feeling, and behavior, reveal how psychological systems work. Discuss this idea by considering four examples of how thinking, feeling, and behavior "go wrong" in predictable ways that reveal useful insights about how our psychology works.

Your essay requires an **introduction**, discussion of **four examples**, and a **conclusion**. All four of your examples should come from DIFFERENT categories of psychology (as listed below), and two must come from the first half of the course and two from the second half of the course:

FIRST HALF
(Choose TWO examples from this section)
• the brain and nervous system
• sensation/perception
• memory and learning
• thinking and language
• intelligence
• motivation and emotion

SECOND HALF
(Choose TWO examples from this section)
• social psychology
• development
• personality
• clinical psychology
• health and happiness

Your essay should include a discussion of the general theme through clear and detailed discussions of each example. Each example should describe specific evidence (studies, theories, or observations from lecture, the text, or your section). Use diverse, *nonoverlapping* examples that represent different topics from the course, but be sure to draw connections between your examples.

FIGURE 8.1. Distribution of Scores on the Integrative Essay Assessment at Two Time Points

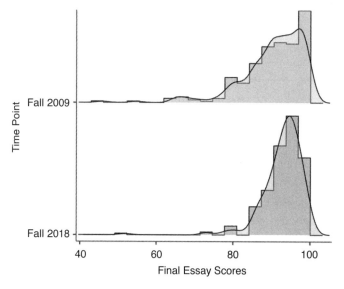

Note. Over the course of 10 years, numerous pedagogical adjustments were made to improve students' ability to discuss course topics according to deeper integrative themes.

As a new faculty member at Duke University, I created a curriculum map for my introductory psychology course. I outlined all of my course learning goals for introductory psychology and all of my formal graded assessments, and then I mapped their alignment. The results of this process are shown in Table 8.1.

Examination of my curriculum map revealed two glaring weaknesses in my assessments. First, collaborative thinking skills, in the context of weekly discussion sections, were an important learning objective, but I was not assessing those skills meaningfully. TAs were assigning a subjective participation score at the end of the term, but I was not confident that these scores reflected what students were learning, and neither were the students. Each term, we received a few emails from students who were confused about the score received. A gap in my assessments motivated me to change my pedagogy. I tasked a pair of advanced doctoral students[1] with developing a list of concrete objectives that would define the effective use of collaborative thinking skills in a weekly discussion section (see Exhibit 8.2). Each week, TAs would assign a score based on how well each student met the objectives. A "check" meant that the student had met all objectives. A "check-minus" meant that some objectives needed work, and a "check-plus" meant that the student had exceeded expectations.

---

[1]Special thanks to Brenda Yang and Paula Yust for their work developing the participation rubric for introductory psychology.

TABLE 8.1. Curriculum Map of an Introductory Psychology Course to Identify Assessment Gaps

Learning goals	Formal graded assessments					
	Weekly quizzes	Exams: Multiple choice	Exams: Written answer	Integrative essay	Research and writing project	Section participation
Conceptual foundations of psychology: Recognize/describe a wide range of psychological concepts, themes, and associated scientists.	X	X	X	X	X	
Application/connection: Recognize/describe the psychological dimension of everyday experience as well as important social problems (e.g., education, health care).	X	X	X			
Scientific literacy:						
• Recognize/describe various scientific methods that are used to answer scientific questions and critically evaluate their strengths and limitations.			X		X	
• Recognize/describe the basic components of an empirical research article and know how to find articles on topics of interest.						
Scientific research skills: Generate original research questions and define methods for addressing those questions.					X	
Collaborative thinking: Support others' learning in small and large groups.						X
Critical thinking: Analyze psychological claims with an open-minded yet critical stance, including those that appear in popular portrayals of psychological science (e.g., popular press).						

EXHIBIT 8.2

Section Participation Rubric for Introductory Psychology

Standards for Successful Section Participation Evaluated Each Week

✓ = met all expectations, ✓− = did not meet all expectations, ✓+ = exceeded expectations

Preparation
Student comes to section having read all of the assigned material and completed any required tasks.

In-section engagement
Student is an active participant for the entire section, both directly contributing and allowing for the contributions of others. The student's behaviors throughout section support their own learning and others' learning, such as by

- responding to a prompt/question from others
- building from other students' contributions
- asking clarification questions
- engaging nonverbally (e.g., by making eye contact, nodding, other providing other cues that indicate engaged listening)
- staying on task
- working with class member(s) in a positive and respectful way

Other forms of engagement
Student communicates thoughtfulness about course material outside of section, such as by

- attending office hours
- sharing real-world course connections with their teaching assistant
- participating in other activities that show they are engaging with the course material and their classmates

End-of-semester participation grading guidelines

Score	Description
10	Exceeded expectations; got all ✓ as well as a few ✓+ throughout the semester
9	Met expectations; got all ✓ (maybe one ✓+) throughout the entire semester, consistently meeting expectations
8	Very good participation; got almost all ✓ with perhaps one ✓− in the mix; generally was engaged to the standards on the rubric
7	Pretty good participation; generally got ✓ but had a few more ✓− in the mix; was often engaged but on several occasions was not meeting expectations
4	Fair participation; half the time they were engaged, but half the time, they did not meet expectations and received a ✓−
2	Low participation; occasionally engaged but more often than not were disengaged
1	Poor participation; very rarely engaged, often disruptive, got nearly all ✓−

Once we had a new rubric in place, it was a simple matter to give students feedback on their performance midway through each semester and to offer concrete suggestions for how they could participate more effectively. At the end of the semester, we had very clear guidelines on what type of weekly performance should lead to what participation score (see Exhibit 8.2). The TAs felt more confident in their assignment of participation grades, and students no longer sent puzzled emails about their scores.

I am currently tackling a second gap in my assessments of learning objectives. According to the course goals in my syllabus, I wanted students to learn to "analyze psychological claims with an open-minded yet critical stance, including those that appear in popular portrayals of psychological science (e.g., popular press)." But I was merely talking about this topic in class, not measuring students' ability to do it. To remedy this gap, that same pair of graduate students who revised my participation rubric are now working to develop activities and assessments of these critical thinking skills to use in the weekly discussion sections. Of course, the challenges in developing such activities include keeping examples relevant for introductory-level students as well as having the appropriate level of desirable difficulty that is challenging enough yet not impossible to solve.

Going Beyond Grades: The Value of Survey Data

Student grades can provide a wealth of information to inform teaching, but so can surveys. As one example, I have found it extremely valuable to design and implement my own course evaluation at the end of the term. This "in-house" evaluation asks students many more details about the course than does my institutional evaluation. Do students believe that lecture overlapped too little with the textbook? Too much? Do they perceive the teaching staff as available when they needed help? Do they find the level of challenge appropriate? Do they struggle to afford the textbook? How tempted were they to multitask with their laptops and cell phones in class? Surveys also allow me to capture detailed demographic information to learn about my students: their gender, race, parental education, whether they are athletes, and even where they sit in the lecture hall. Such questions allow me to explore whether my class is serving different groups of students equally. Critically, if delivered online, surveys can capture information about student identity that allows me to link student responses to other course data, such as grades. Thus, I can learn how student attitudes and characteristics are related to course performance.[2]

Using surveys has offered me numerous insights into my students and my introductory psychology course. For example, I've learned that students

---

[2]I assure students that their survey responses are viewed as anonymous. Once student responses are connected to other aspects of their course performance, I de-identify the responses, replacing names with an ID number created just for the course. I analyze the data only after the course is complete and final grades are posted.

who took Advanced Placement psychology before my course (~15%–20%) perform just as well as students with no psychology background. They are also just as satisfied with the course, suggesting that the course is not perceived as redundant or useless for them. I've also learned that self-reported multitasking with laptops is associated with worse performance in my class, a point that has led to course policy changes.

USING ASSESSMENT FOR PEDAGOGICAL SCIENCE

Understanding the process and value of assessment shifted me into a "scientific mind-set" about my teaching in that I was formulating research questions and collecting data to answer those questions. Importantly, once I adopted a scientific mind-set about my teaching, I also started to feel frustrated about the many ways my assessment approach was decidedly *un*scientific. First, I struggled to define what criteria to use in determining whether I was meeting my pedagogical goals. How good was good enough? Was I succeeding if my students scored a "B average" or an "A"? I was setting an arbitrary bar and felt motivated to set that bar at a level I was sure to jump over, especially if I wanted to share my assessment data with department chairs and others who needed convincing of my teaching effectiveness. Second, I could not fully understand which practices were (or were not) leading to improvement for my students. I was changing my pedagogy based on assessment data, but I was often changing many practices at once. As I tracked changes to my students' performance across different semesters, I could only guess at which change (if any) contributed to their improvement.

At the same time that I was confronting the flaws in my assessment approach, I was inspired by departmental colleagues who had moved beyond their labs to develop and rigorously test psychological interventions in the field, especially educational interventions. Carol Dweck and her collaborators were testing interventions to teach students a *growth mind-set*—the belief that intelligence is malleable and can develop—to great effect on academic performance (e.g., Paunesku et al., 2015). Greg Walton and his collaborators were testing interventions to reduce school suspensions (Okonofua et al., 2016), boost student motivation (Yeager et al., 2014), and reduce achievement gaps in higher education (Yeager et al., 2016). Their work, in the tradition of social psychologist Kurt Lewin (e.g., Lewin, 1952), sought to hone scientific theories by rigorously testing them in the real world and also to combat important social problems by being wise to their underlying psychology. These interventions were thus dubbed "wise" interventions (Walton, 2014; Walton & Crum, 2019; Yeager & Walton, 2011).

Could I not adopt a similar approach in my own classroom? I could start by working to understand the psychological dimension of some classroom problem. Why do students "psych themselves out" on exams? Why do students multitask on their laptops in class, even when they have learned that multitasking harms their grades? I could design studies—descriptive or correlational—to test these hypotheses in my own and other classrooms. These studies could even be experimental: I could design wise interventions rooted in psychological theory and then test them against a control group. Not only could such research help me understand how to serve my own students more effectively, it could also inform theories of how education works, more broadly. Suddenly, assessment becomes *pedagogical science*.

Taking a "Stealthy" Approach to Pedagogical Science

My approach to assessment has evolved into what I call "stealthy" pedagogical science. The gist of this approach is that research is so intertwined with the pedagogy as to be virtually undetectable. My students know that research is going on in the class, thanks to a statement in the syllabus and a consent form that requests permission to analyze their data, but they are not made to feel like research participants. The research approach is stealthy for at least three reasons. First, my primary role in my course is to be the instructor, not a researcher, and I do not want my research to detract from a focus on learning. Second, I want to understand natural student behavior and avoid demand characteristics coloring the nature of my findings. Third, researchers who design psychosocially "wise" interventions have argued that the delivery of these interventions needs to be surreptitious to be successful; that is, they need to allow participants to believe that any positive changes in achievement, health, and well-being are the result of their own autonomous choices rather than the result of experimental manipulation (Robinson, 2010; Yeager & Walton, 2011). Indeed, research on a well-supported intervention to reduce achievement gaps in education, the *values affirmation* intervention, finds that participants benefited less from the intervention the more aware they were of it (Sherman et al., 2009).

Stealthy pedagogical science is accomplished in several ways in my course. First, I collect measures from students that serve as research data but that also have immediate pedagogical value, such as to illustrate course concepts. Students may see their own data used in lectures to illustrate errors in memory, growth and fixed mind-sets, the relationship between their anxiety and performance, or the association between multitasking and course grades. Second, my measures and experimental manipulations are fully integrated with my curriculum so that everything students complete is relevant to the course (see Table 8.2).

My research measures include not only grades but also students' responses to brief surveys that, as mentioned, collect data to illustrate course concepts or that assess academic behaviors, assess attitudes, or request feedback on the curriculum. In addition to the in-house course evaluation described earlier, I offer students several surveys online across the semester. These surveys are for extra credit but do not have to be. I have found that once my students understand how I use their data to illustrate concepts (and to be a better teacher),

TABLE 8.2. Stealthy Pedagogical Tool Kit

Experimental manipulations embedded in:	Research measures embedded in:
Extra credit surveys (paper or online)	Extra credit surveys (paper or online)
Course evaluations (paper or online)	Course evaluations (paper or online)
Weekly low-stakes quizzes (paper or online)	Weekly low-stakes quizzes (paper or online)
Optional surveys (survey items appended to exams or other course materials)	Optional surveys (survey items appended to exams or other course materials)
Written activities	Written activities
Classroom activities	Classroom activities
Electronic communications (e.g., emails)	Course grades

they are curious to see what I am up to and motivated to be helpful. They will answer survey questions as long as they are convenient, such as in the form of ungraded questions in a weekly online quiz or on a paper survey appended to the back of an in-class exam.

Students must consent to allow any of these data to be used for research purposes (as opposed to course improvement purposes). A remarkable 97% agree to do so. Critically, students' grades and ability to earn extra credit do not depend on whether they consent to allow their data to be analyzed for research. As explained to students, their consent is never examined until after the term is complete and final grades are posted.

Conducting Stealthy Classroom Experiments

My approach to pedagogical science sometimes includes experimental manipulations.[3] In one study, Shannon Brady, James Gross, and I were interested in whether the commonsense advice to "calm down" before a test was helpful. Lab researchers were suggesting that a better way to handle test anxiety was to reinterpret it as neutral or even beneficial (Jamieson et al., 2010). Extending from these lab findings, we manipulated an email to students the night before the first exam (Brady et al., 2018). For half the students, the email contained the standard exam reminders. For the other half, the email contained an extra paragraph telling them that their anxiety would not necessarily hurt their performance on the exam and might even help. Via a paper survey appended to the end of the exam packet, we measured students' performance on their exam the next day and how anxious and worried they felt during the exam. We found that first-year students who received the extra paragraph, but not upper-year students, were significantly less worried, on average, during the exam and also performed significantly better, on average ($d = 32$ for both effects).

---

[3]My research is approved by my institutional review board (IRB). I manipulate minor communications to students or small, optional activities, comparing something new to standard "best" practices.

In another study, Cayce Hook, Greg Walton, and I were concerned with the potentially problematic role of technology in a large, lecture-based course. Over the course of several terms, I surveyed my students on their technology use in class and found consistent negative correlations between their off-task technology use (technology "multitasking") and their academic performance, consistent with a growing body of evidence (Gingerich & Lineweaver, 2014; Ravizza et al., 2017; Sana et al., 2013; Zhang, 2015). Drawing from the literature on self-regulation, my collaborators and I manipulated ungraded writing exercises in a weekly quiz (Hook, Hard, & Walton, 2020). All students were asked to share their plan for how they would use technology in class that semester. Half the students, before completing their plan, learned how multitasking with technology creates *distraction pollution*, making it harder for nearby students to concentrate (e.g., Sana et al., 2013). This same group of students also learned a strategy for self-regulation called *situation modification*, which involves changing your situation in advance to avoid temptations that interfere with your goals, such as setting your cell phone to silent mode and putting it away (Duckworth, Gendler, & Gross, 2016; Duckworth, White, et al., 2016). Later in the term, we gave students survey questions asking about their temptation to multitask in class and their actual multitasking behavior. We found that teaching students about distraction pollution and situation modification reduced their multitasking with cell phones in class, at least for a few weeks, but the effects of the intervention wore off quickly and had no effect on grades.

In both of these experimental studies, a new pedagogical practice—an email message to students or a writing exercise in a quiz—was contrasted with standard practice in the class, allowing our research team to assess within a single course whether a new pedagogical practice could enhance student experience and performance. This approach eliminates many of the third-variable problems that arise when comparing students taught in different academic terms or in different sections of a course. Because we embedded experimental manipulations within electronic communications to students, we could randomly assign students to conditions with little effort and without student awareness.

Using Stealthy Policy Evaluation

In addition to conducting experiments, I have also used stealthy pedagogical science to evaluate classroom policies and anchor my policy decisions in psychology theory. Given data from my class suggesting that technology multitasking was associated with worse grades, I considered whether allowing technology in class was doing students a disservice. My concern deepened after learning of several studies that found students perform better in classrooms where technology is not permitted (Carter et al., 2017; Patterson & Patterson, 2017).

Along with my colleagues Cayce Hook and Greg Walton, I developed a social psychological hypothesis that was relevant to this problem. We were curious about the ways that social norms change the need to self-regulate behavior. We hypothesized that when there is a clear social norm against a behavior, people experience less temptation to engage in it. For example, I feel tempted to take a cookie from a communal plate but would not feel tempted to take a cookie from a stranger's plate. The social norm to not take someone else's food may even prevent the tempting behavior from coming to mind. We wondered if a clear social norm against multitasking, via a no-technology policy in class, would reduce temptation to multitask for students.

We decided to test this idea by surveying students about their temptations to multitask and then examining the effects of implementing a no-technology policy (Hook et al., 2019, 2020). We predicted that with a clear policy prohibiting technology, students would not be tempted to multitask in class. That prediction was confirmed. More surprisingly, from other survey data, we found that students' predictions of and experiences with a no-technology policy were different. In an in-house course evaluation, students who were *allowed* to use technology were pessimistic about the benefits of a no-technology policy. Nearly 40% of students one semester predicted that a no-technology would be "not beneficial at all" (the lowest possible rating), and only 12% predicted that it would be "extremely beneficial" (the highest rating). But, among students who experienced a *no-technology policy*, only 3% reported that a no-technology policy was "not beneficial at all," and 56% reported that it was "extremely beneficial." Importantly, students experiencing the no-technology policy were significantly more engaged in class and did significantly better on exams than those who had been allowed to use technology.

This research was valuable on multiple dimensions. From a teacher perspective, I had clear evidence that a no-technology policy was beneficial to my students, and I could share this evidence with colleagues who taught similarly large, lecture-based classes. I also had a deeper understanding of the psychological reasons that the policy was helpful: The shift in the social norms about whether multitasking was acceptable put temptations out of mind for my students, allowing them to engage more fully in the class. From a researcher perspective, this research allowed testing of a new theory about the role of social norms in shaping self-regulation in a messy, natural context.

GETTING STARTED WITH PEDAGOGICAL SCIENCE

I hope that my approach to using assessment as pedagogical science will inspire other instructors to harness the hidden laboratory in their own classroom. What are some simple ways to get started?

Reflect on What You Want to Know

The classroom is such a rich environment filled with cognition, emotion, and social interaction to be studied. What do you really want to know about teaching and learning? How will the answers to your questions benefit your students? How will the answers help instructors learn about effective pedagogy? For ideas and inspiration, read research articles on teaching and learning, such as those in *Scholarship of Teaching and Learning in Psychology* or *Teaching of Psychology*. Teaching conferences also provide a wellspring of research inspiration.

Check With Your Institutional Review Board

Different institutions treat classroom research differently. Some consider it exempt from IRB review, and a few have strict prohibitions on instructors ever doing research with their own students. Different institutions also have different interpretations of the laws that govern how student grades are protected (i.e., the Family Educational Rights and Privacy Act, 1974). If you plan on conducting classroom research, you need to coordinate with your IRB to develop ethical procedures that will protect your students' autonomy and privacy. Reach out to colleagues (including me) for sample IRB protocols and best practices to guide your own.

Evaluate Your Existing "Data"

Everything students produce in your course can be a form of data. What are you already collecting in your course and what questions could these data be used to answer? How large are your "samples" (i.e., class size)? For instructors of smaller courses, aggregating data across sections, terms, and years of a course will increase your sample size and ability to derive meaningful conclusions. Consider collaborating with other instructors who teach the same course at your institution or collaborate with instructors at other institutions.

Examine Your Course for Ways to Integrate New Measures and Even Manipulations

Consider the wide array of opportunities described in Table 8.1 for incorporating experimental manipulations and data collection into a class. What are the opportunities in your own course design to incorporate these approaches or something similar? Every course is different, and a stealthy approach integrates research into the natural flow of a course so that teaching and learning remain the priorities.

CONCLUSION

For me, assessment is a process that unites the two valued identities that motivated me to pursue psychology. When I introduce myself to my students on the first day of class, I now explain that I am both a *scientist* and a *teacher*, and moreover, I am a scientist who studies teaching and learning. I aim to discover new facts and principles about human behavior and mental processes that are relevant to enhancing the scholarly and personal development of my students. I insist on data to evaluate whether my personal pedagogical goals are being met. Moreover, I approach problems and challenges in my classroom by diving eagerly into the psychology research literature, drawing concepts and methods, identifying gaps in our knowledge, and generating novel research questions and studies to test them. Anyone can become a pedagogical scientist by simply reflecting on the educational questions that interest them and looking for convenient (and sometimes creative) ways to address these questions within the context of our courses.

REFERENCES

Brady, S. T., Hard, B. M., & Gross, J. J. (2018). Reappraising test anxiety increases academic performance of first-year college students. *Journal of Educational Psychology, 110*(3), 395–406. https://doi.org/10.1037/edu0000219

Carter, S. P., Greenberg, K., & Walker, M. S. (2017). The impact of computer usage on academic performance: Evidence from a randomized trial at the United States Military Academy. *Economics of Education Review, 56*, 118–132. https://doi.org/10.1016/j.econedurev.2016.12.005

Chew, S. L. (2018, August). *Why do psychologists do research like scientists but teach like dummies?* [Paper presentation, Charles L. Brewer special address]. American Psychological Association, 126th Annual Convention, San Francisco, CA, United States.

Duckworth, A. L., Gendler, T. S., & Gross, J. J. (2016). Situational strategies for self-control. *Perspectives on Psychological Science, 11*(1), 35–55. https://doi.org/10.1177/1745691615623247

Duckworth, A. L., White, R. E., Matteucci, A. J., Shearer, A., & Gross, J. J. (2016). A stitch in time: Strategic self-control in high school and college students. *Journal of Educational Psychology, 108*(3), 329–341. https://doi.org/10.1037/edu0000062

Family Educational Rights and Privacy Act of 1974, Pub. L. 93–380, 20 U.S.C. § 1232g; 34 C.F.R. Part 99. https://www.govinfo.gov/content/pkg/USCODE-2011-title20/pdf/USCODE-2011-title20-chap31-subchapIII-part4-sec1232g.pdf

Gingerich, A. C., & Lineweaver, T. T. (2014). OMG! Texting in class = U fail: Empirical evidence that text messaging during class disrupts comprehension. *Teaching of Psychology, 41*(1), 44–51. https://doi.org/10.1177/0098628313514177

Hook, C. J., Hard, B. M., & Walton, G. M. (2019, February). *Social norms shape experiences of temptation* [Data blitz]. Society for Social and Personality Psychology, Annual Meeting, Motivation Science Preconference, Portland, OR, United States.

Hook, C. J., Hard, B. M., & Walton, G. M. (2020). *Everyday norms offload burdens of self-control* [Manuscript submitted for publication]. Department of Psychology, Stanford University.

Jamieson, J. P., Mendes, W. B., Blackstock, E., & Schmader, T. (2010). Turning the knots in your stomach into bows: Reappraising arousal improves performance on the GRE. *Journal of Experimental Social Psychology, 46*(1), 208–212. https://doi.org/10.1016/j.jesp.2009.08.015

Lewin, K. (1952). Group decision and social change. In G. E. Swanson, T. M. Newcomb, & E. L. Hartley (Eds.), *Readings in social psychology* (Rev. ed., pp. 459–473). Holt.

Nordmeyer, A., Hard, B. M., & Gross, J. J. (2016). Using integrative concepts as a theme in introductory psychology. In D. S. Dunn & B. M. Hard (Eds.), *Thematic approaches for teaching introductory psychology* (pp. 79–92). Cengage Learning.

Okonofua, J. A., Paunesku, D., & Walton, G. M. (2016). Brief intervention to encourage empathic discipline cuts suspension rates in half among adolescents. *Proceedings of the National Academy of Sciences of the United States of America, 113*(19), 5221–5226. https://doi.org/10.1073/pnas.1523698113

Patterson, R. W., & Patterson, R. M. (2017). Computers and productivity: Evidence from laptop use in the college classroom. *Economics of Education Review, 57,* 66–79. https://doi.org/10.1016/j.econedurev.2017.02.004

Paunesku, D., Walton, G. M., Romero, C., Smith, E. N., Yeager, D. S., & Dweck, C. S. (2015). Mind-set interventions are a scalable treatment for academic underachievement. *Psychological Science, 26*(6), 784–793. https://doi.org/10.1177/0956797615571017

Ravizza, S. M., Uitvlugt, M. G., & Fenn, K. M. (2017). Logged in and zoned out: How laptop internet use relates to classroom learning. *Psychological Science, 28*(2), 171–180. https://doi.org/10.1177/0956797616677314

Robinson, T. N. (2010). Stealth interventions for obesity prevention and control: Motivating behavior change. In L. Dubé, A. Bechara, A. Dagher, A. Drewnowski, J. LeBel, P. James, & R. Y. Yada (Eds.), *Obesity prevention* (pp. 319–327). Academic Press. https://doi.org/10.1016/B978-0-12-374387-9.00025-8

Sana, F., Weston, T., & Cepeda, N. J. (2013). Laptop multitasking hinders classroom learning for both users and nearby peers. *Computers & Education, 62,* 24–31. https://doi.org/10.1016/j.compedu.2012.10.003

Sherman, D. K., Cohen, G. L., Nelson, L. D., Nussbaum, A. D., Bunyan, D. P., & Garcia, J. (2009). Affirmed yet unaware: Exploring the role of awareness in the process of self-affirmation. *Journal of Personality and Social Psychology, 97*(5), 745–764. https://doi.org/10.1037/a0015451

Walton, G. M. (2014). The new science of wise psychological interventions. *Current Directions in Psychological Science, 23*(1), 73–82. https://doi.org/10.1177/0963721413512856 (Erratum published 2014, *Current Directions in Psychological Science, 23,* p. 154. https://doi.org/10.1177/0963721414525908)

Walton, G. M., & Crum, A. J. (2019). *Handbook of wise interventions: How social-psychological insights can help solve problems.* Guilford Press.

Yeager, D. S., Henderson, M. D., Paunesku, D., Walton, G. M., D'Mello, S., Spitzer, B. J., & Duckworth, A. L. (2014). Boring but important: A self-transcendent purpose for learning fosters academic self-regulation. *Journal of Personality and Social Psychology, 107*(4), 559–580. https://doi.org/10.1037/a0037637

Yeager, D. S., & Walton, G. M. (2011). Social-psychological interventions in education: They're not magic. *Review of Educational Research, 81*(2), 267–301. https://doi.org/10.3102/0034654311405999

Yeager, D. S., Walton, G. M., Brady, S. T., Akcinar, E. N., Paunesku, D., & Keane, L., Kamentz, D., Ritter, G., Duckworth, A. L., Urstein, R., Gomez, E. M., Markus, H. R., Cohen, G. L., & Dweck, C. S. (2016). Teaching a lay theory before college narrows achievement gaps at scale. *Proceedings of the National Academy of Sciences, 113*(24), E3341–E3348. https://doi.org/10.1073/pnas.1524360113

Zhang, W. (2015). Learning variables, in-class laptop multitasking and academic performance: A path analysis. *Computers & Education, 81,* 82–88. https://doi.org/10.1016/j.compedu.2014.09.012

Evidence-Based Teaching and Course Design

Using Data to Develop, Implement, and Refine University Courses

Danae L. Hudson

For many of us in academia, the beginning of each semester or quarter is met with a sense of excitement and perhaps apprehension as we prepare for our upcoming courses. Having a job that includes the opportunity to refine our work multiple times each year can be both a blessing and a curse. For those truly interested in teaching and learning, the design and execution of a quality university course involves continuous improvement (Bernstein et al., 2010; Matulich et al., 2008). Until we are confident all students have learned the concepts and developed the skills associated with our course, we can never check the "done" box. Furthermore, even as our teaching and our students' performance progress, our field is continually evolving, prompting us to evaluate those changes and adapt where appropriate. Although this reality is unsatisfying at times, it is an important realization that drives us toward continuous improvement. Innovation in all fields requires a commitment to continuous improvement. Thankfully, a foundation of scientific research exists in education to help guide course development and revision decisions.

The evolution of evidence-based practice began in the 1990s in medicine and clinical psychology. The impetus for evidence-based medicine stemmed from a general dissatisfaction with subpar clinical practices that negatively impacted the quality and cost of patient care (Sur & Dahm, 2011). Informed by this paradigm shift in medicine, in 1993, the Division of Clinical Psychology of the American Psychological Association appointed a task force on the "promotion and dissemination of psychological procedures" (Chambless &

https://doi.org/10.1037/0000183-010
Assessing Undergraduate Learning in Psychology: Strategies for Measuring and Improving Student Performance, S. A. Nolan, C. M. Hakala, and R. E. Landrum (Editors)

Ollendick, 2001, p. 686). The task force was charged with identifying empirically validated treatments for specific psychological conditions, and it developed a list of empirically supported treatments that could provide guidance to practitioners, patients, and third-party payers (O'Donohue et al., 2000). Assembling this list required task force members to determine the important ingredients in effective treatments and agree on a method to assess whether individual treatments met the standards proposed. This lofty endeavor was not without controversy but did eventually produce an initial list of empirically supported treatments (Chambless & Ollendick, 2001). More important, the process established a new set of values for clinical psychology that emphasized the assessment and development of evidence-based treatments.

Teaching shares many of the same characteristics with the fields of medicine and clinical psychology. All three fields include professionals who have the opportunity to significantly shape an individual's future. Furthermore, despite strong historical roots, these fields must be willing to adapt to the population of patients, clients, and students and their respective environments. Chew and colleagues (2018) discussed that as experts in the field of psychology, we have a unique skill set that perfectly situates us to model continuous improvement in teaching and learning. They urged psychology instructors to not only use evidence-based principles of teaching and learning but to also rigorously assess the efficacy of their teaching practices. Not all practitioners or psychology instructors are experts in research design and have the ability to conduct ongoing research. However, educators can and should use their skills to seek out empirical literature to guide their practices. That is, educators should use their scientific literacy skills to guide decisions regarding course design, implementation, and refinement.

A MODEL FOR EVIDENCE-BASED COURSE DESIGN

Course design refers to the development of a new course or, in many cases, involves the "redesign" of an existing course that you or other colleague has previously taught. When faced with developing or making major changes to a course, it is easy to get caught up in the latest teaching fad or enamored by a new educational technology tool discussed on social media. Some have even referred to this tendency as succumbing to the "cult" of teaching and learning (Daniel, 2019). Commitment to continuous improvement is not the same as merely introducing novel ideas into a course. Some of the most beneficial changes may involve implementing core principles that have been part of educational theory for decades. But how do you know which avenue to pursue? And then how do you know what approach to take? Informed by the scientific literature and our specific course goals, my colleagues and I developed a model to guide the process of course redesign we began at Missouri State University in 2011. Figure 9.1 presents this basic model, which outlines the steps of evidence-based course design.

FIGURE 9.1. An Approach to Evidence-Based Teaching and Course Design

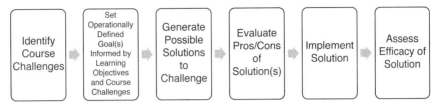

According to our model, the most important place to start with course design is with an overall assessment of your course. How did events go this past semester? What seemed to work, or not? Did the students achieve the learning objectives associated with the course? Were the students happy? Were *you* happy?[1] Ideally, you will have some objective data to answer these questions. But if you do not, a subjective analysis is an acceptable place to start (and then maybe one of your goals will be to collect objective data in the near future). Make notes of strategies or techniques that worked well and then shift your focus to the questions you have and challenges you identified. This is also a good time to reflect on the learning objectives for your course. Are the current learning goals appropriate, well defined, and authentically tied to the content of your course? Sometimes course difficulties arise from a mismatch among learning objectives, the content provided, and how the learning is assessed (Paolini, 2015; Wiggins & McTighe, 2005). As you begin to plan, how you frame these early stages of course design/redesign is important. Rather than viewing challenges as failures, it is helpful to see them as opportunities—opportunities to learn and to make meaningful changes that could impact student learning, and a chance to conduct research in your own classroom.

Identifying the challenges you experienced or anticipating the ones you will encounter should be what drives goal setting and ultimately course design decisions. Oftentimes, faculty members are quick to identify a new teaching technique they want to incorporate in the future semester. However, these instructors often also struggle to answer the question, What problem are you hoping that solution will solve? Setting goals from specific challenges helps shine a spotlight on a smaller group of possible solutions, which is helpful when trying to choose one to implement. Imagine you are creating a road map for your course. Your commitment to evidence-based teaching is the starting point. Your goals, which you have articulated by identifying your challenges, are where you want to go, and the strategies or solutions are the roads that will take you to your destination. Deciding which road to take can be a daunting process; just because you've identified the problem doesn't

---

[1]If you are new to teaching and preparing to teach your first course, consider seeking out a mentor and asking them these questions about the courses they are teaching. Establishing a mentoring relationship with a teacher you respect will be one of the most beneficial early-career decisions you can make.

TABLE 9.1. Online Teaching Resources

Source	Title
Society for the Teaching of Psychology (APA Division 2; n.d.-a)	*Resources for Teachers of Psychology*
Society for the Teaching of Psychology (APA Division 2; n.d.-b)	*STP E-Books*
APA (n.d.-b)	*Resources for Teachers*
APA (n.d.-a)	*Office of Precollege and Undergraduate Education*
Association for Psychological Science (n.d.-a)	*Classroom Resources*
Association for Psychological Science (n.d.-b)	*Reinventing Introductory Psychology*
Hub for Intro Psych & Pedagogical Research (n.d.)	*Literature Central*

Note. APA = American Psychological Association.

mean you know how to remedy it. Seeking evidence-based teaching strategies should involve many avenues of inquiry. Thanks to the internet, social media, journals, and the numerous centers for teaching and learning at academic institutions, gaining access to possible solutions is easier now.

When seeking potential course design solutions, it can be helpful to initially cast a broad net and then begin to narrow down your choices. Table 9.1 presents a list of online teaching resources, many of which focus specifically on psychology. In addition to these general resources, many subdisciplines of psychology have organizations (e.g., Society for Personality and Social Psychology) that maintain their own websites and include teaching resources. These resources can be broad, which is why it is helpful if you begin your search with the goal in mind.

In our current hyperconnected world, the potential richness of social media, podcasts, and personal networking should not be overlooked. I have found Twitter (particularly #academictwitter) to be a robust source of professional development. If you follow like-minded colleagues and organizations or companies that share your pedagogical values, you will be exposed to a steady stream of creative ideas and suggestions. It has never been easier to instantly contact someone by sending an email or direct message to a person who posted, tweeted, or blogged about an interesting topic. Academics who communicate their work through social media tend to be extremely open to sharing information and resources with those who ask. You should view contacting someone about their work as a compliment, not as a bother.

If you have a clear goal in mind, then it is easier to search for a person who or institution that has already successfully implemented the strategy of interest. For example, the National Center for Academic Transformation (NCAT; http://www.thencat.org) maintains a large list of institutions that have successfully completed course redesign projects in various departments.[2]

---

[2]NCAT is no longer participating in new course redesign projects. The website includes an archive of all NCAT course redesign projects through 2013.

NCAT also created the Redesign Scholars Program (https://www.thencat.org/RedesignAlliance/ScholarsProgram.htm), which includes a list of individual faculty members who have been involved in course redesign and are available to serve as consultants or mentors for colleagues. It is almost always the case that any course design or redesign results in "lessons learned," and it is wise to take advantage of the experience and knowledge others have gained through their process to avoid similar pitfalls in your own course transformation (Hudson et al., 2015).

Once you have narrowed down your list of potential solutions, consult the scientific literature and investigate the empirical work conducted with the identified pedagogical strategies. Although you are unlikely to find complete consensus regarding the efficacy and implementation of a particular strategy, you should be generally interested in whether the preponderance of evidence supports the use of this strategy in the way you intend to implement it in your class. It is possible, however, that no published research exists related to your proposed strategies. In this case, you have the opportunity to conduct your own research. Thinking through research methodology will also help to ensure you have a strong implementation plan. Course design is a labor-intensive process; therefore, it behooves you to spend the time beforehand to ensure you have made wise and sustainable decisions.

EVIDENCE-BASED IMPLEMENTATION STRATEGIES

Before implementing any significant course changes, it is prudent to understand the idiosyncratic features of your institution and students. Whereas many full-time, tenured faculty members enjoy the freedom to independently develop their courses, others, particularly adjunct—especially those who teach online—and some untenured faculty are given a prescriptive "course in a box" and have less flexibility in course design. In addition to understanding the external, environmental conditions, we should appreciate the numerous student variables that can moderate the effects of good teaching. In his Charles L. Brewer Distinguished Teaching of Psychology Award address at the 2018 American Psychological Association convention, Stephen Chew (2018) highlighted nine cognitive factors empirically related to learning (e.g., student mental mind-set, metacognition and self-regulation, prior knowledge, misconceptions) and discussed how they also create challenges for teaching because of their interactive nature. He argued that effective teaching involves creating an environment that addresses a dynamic nine-way interaction of cognitive factors, many of which are not under our control. Of course, there are additional emotional and sociocultural factors to also consider. One reaction to this daunting picture is to conclude that the endeavor to apply evidence-based practices to your specific course is hopeless; however, a growth mind-set would involve challenging yourself to identify the factors relevant to your institution and student population, and systematically addressing those factors over time (Gurung & Hackathorn, 2018). When engaging in course design/ redesign it is easy to fall into the trap of wanting to change everything at one time. Reining yourself in and focusing on just a few key changes will not only help you maintain your sanity during the implementation semester, but it will also create an environment more conducive to the scholarship of teaching and learning (SoTL).

If you are engaging in the redesign of an existing course in your department and that course involves a number of different sections, I strongly encourage you to conduct a "pilot semester." Implement the new course in only one section, ideally, your section. This approach has pros and cons. Implementing anything new requires a culture change on behalf of the institution and the students (Hudson et al., 2015). The pilot section will be compared with the traditional sections, and, unfortunately, students tend to talk about the amount of work required. One section taught differently from the other sections can spark course drift, which involves students' dropping out of the pilot section in favor of one of the traditional sections. This behavior not only impacts the narrative around the redesigned course but can negatively impact the withdrawal rate of the pilot section (which is often used as a measure of course efficacy). Despite these potential downsides of conducting a pilot section, the lessons learned during this semester far outweigh the impact on course drift and withdrawal rates. A pilot section is like a test drive: It is an opportunity to implement your changes in the context of a real class. You will likely discover many logistical, technological, and even pedagogical issues you had not considered during the course development. Conducting the pilot class during the spring semester is ideal because you then likely have the summer semester to make any necessary changes to the structure or content of the course.

Another aspect of evidence-based implementation occurs during the class itself. Using student data both inside and outside the classroom can provide a rich source of understanding and pedagogical guidance. Having your students complete assignments before coming to class provides an opportunity to assess their understanding of the content. This approach, often referred to as *just in time teaching*, allows you to determine how you might best serve your students in that class (Novak, 2011; Novak et al., 1999). Which concepts appear to be difficult for them to grasp? Are there any predictable or consistent misconceptions in their understanding of a topic? Professors sometimes say things like, "Educational technology is going to work me out of a job." I see it differently. Technology can help you pinpoint exactly where you are most needed. It can help you to provide students with instruction in topics or areas that are less easily communicated through a written narrative or interactive activity. Using student performance data from homework assignments affords you the opportunity to tailor the class time into a targeted and personalized experience for your students.

Engaging students in class via polling questions, short writing assignments, or group activities are ways to collect real-time data. Polling questions, whether high-tech (e.g., clickers [audience response systems], smartphones), low-tech (e.g., Plickers[3]), or no-tech (e.g., raising hands), are an efficient and effective way to determine if your students currently understand a concept that was identified as problematic in their preclass homework (DeLozier & Rhodes, 2017; O'Flaherty & Phillips, 2015). These strategies elicit in vivo data that provide some evidence of student learning. However, what about the broader impact of the course design/redesign decisions? How do you know if all of your hard work had the hypothesized positive impact on your students? Continually assessing and refining components of the course are inherent and important parts of the continuous improvement model.

EVIDENCE-BASED COURSE REFINEMENT: ASSESS THE EFFICACY OF THE SOLUTION

Psychology instructors are in the unique position to wear two hats in the classroom: teacher and scientist. The majority of doctoral students spend most of their training learning how to be good researchers and little time learning how to teach. As a result, the two identities are often seen as separate (Hudson & Whisenhunt, 2017; Richmond et al., 2016). Blending the teacher and researcher identities opens the door to a new world of empirical teaching that has direct implications for your students. An evidenced-based teacher is not just one who looks to the empirical literature to inform teaching practices but is also a teacher who asks empirical questions of their own pedagogical practices. Many instructors experience thoughts such as, "I wonder if this technique helped students achieve the learning outcomes of the course? Did the students think it was helpful? Was the gain in student learning worth the time and energy it took me to implement this new strategy?" Evidence-based instructors not only ask these questions, but they design classroom or lab studies to obtain some empirical answers to them.

Because students and their environments are so varied, commitment to continuous improvement in teaching should involve the assessment of your own students. The type of assessment method you choose should flow logically from the research question you pose (Aslam & Emmanuel, 2010; Suskie, 2018). If your question involves how much your students are learning, then you should choose an assessment strategy that will yield that information. If you plan to measure student learning in your course, then it is important to gather

---

[3]Plickers is a free assessment system that can be used in the classroom for polling and retrieval practice. Students are provided cards printed with a QR (quick response) code that indicates their answer (i.e., "A," "B," "C," or "D") based on the orientation by which they are holding the card. Only the instructor uses the Plickers app on their smartphone to scan the cards, which displays the results on the instructor's phone and, if a presentation is projected, on the screen. Go to http://www.plickers.com for more information about Plickers.

baseline data at the beginning of the course.[4] Baseline data can involve the measurement of topical knowledge, relevant skills, or both.

If you choose not to use a validated measure, or a validated measure of the construct does not exist, you will need to create one. Assessment development is an entire field of its own, but if you want to feel confident in the data you collect, it pays to put in the time to ensure you are working with a reliable and valid instrument. For example, if you are creating a knowledge pretest for your course, you should write or choose questions that appear to closely measure the learning objectives of your course (Richmond et al., 2016). Then, administer this measure to a group of students who are representative of the population you will be studying. Conducting an item analysis (e.g., difficulty level and discrimination index) will provide information regarding the appropriateness and quality of the items in the assessment. If you have already been using another learning assessment in your course, examining group means and correlating the scores between the two measures will give you a general sense if they are comparable.

It is best to gather these assessment data in an objective way early on in the course. Then, you administer the same assessment at the end of the course, and the difference between pretest and posttest can serve as a decent proxy of learning. Of course, learning can be assessed in a variety of ways (e.g., cumulative exams, writing assignments, course projects); however, the more subjective the assessment, the greater threat there is to the internal validity of your study. Subjective measures of learning can provide interesting information but are best used as a complement to more objective measures (Gosen & Washbush, 2004).

One example of a subjective yet important form of assessment is student evaluations of teaching. I am not referring to the standard university student evaluations of teaching that professors are required to administer at the end of the course that have been shown to lack validity, are inherently biased against female instructors, and tend to be misinterpreted by faculty (Boring, 2017; Boring et al., 2016; Boysen, 2015). Instead, I am suggesting a thoughtfully created measure of student perceptions of the key components of a course. Although there may be some value for someone to examine data about the students' beliefs about the professor's knowledge or availability, these items provide little pedagogical feedback. A specific evaluation that targets key course components or pedagogical interventions can provide you with meaningful feedback to guide evidence-based course revision decisions (Carini et al., 2006) and can increase the extent to which students value and enjoy the learning process (Shaw et al., 2019). A useful tip in designing this type of assessment is to be sure to ask not only whether or not the students "liked" a particular

---

[4]Although each academic institution is different, it is advisable to obtain approval from your institutional review board to conduct SoTL research. Although you may initially think these data are only for your professional development, your results may be of interest to others and be well suited to a poster, a presentation, or even publication. Any of these activities typically requires institutional review board approval.

aspect of the course, but whether or not they believed that component "helped them learn." The evidence-based teacher recognizes the limits of student opinion data, so the next empirical question might involve determining if that pedagogical strategy predicts objectively measured learning.

Posing the overarching question of "Did my students learn?" can be an overwhelming place to start. Just as we teach students to operationally define variables and break large goals into smaller ones, we need to step back and identify the results that would indicate learning has occurred in our courses. Articulating the end goal can help you work backward to identify the pedagogical components chosen with the intention of creating an environment conducive to learning, which is a form of backward design (Wiggins & McTighe, 1998). Perhaps you want to start by researching the efficacy of just one of those components? Or, if you already have data supporting the use of that strategy, maybe you want to examine the additive effect of several course components. Alternatively, if you are interested in examining all pedagogical components and determining the relative efficacy of each part, a research approach used in clinical psychology could be helpful. Clinical researchers often conduct *dismantling studies*, which attempt to not only identify the active ingredients in an efficacious psychotherapy but also determine the relative magnitude of change attributable to each component (Papa & Follette, 2015). An example of a powerful pedagogical dismantling study would be one that attempts to distill the most active and powerful study skills that improve learning. For example, when students are taught evidence-based study skills (e.g., retrieval practice, concept map-making, deep processing of information via note-taking, interleaved practice), which one is responsible for the most improvement in learning? Or, could it be the synergistic effect of the different study strategies responsible for significant improvements in exam performance? A pedagogical dismantling study would be a more advanced SoTL project but is discussed here to demonstrate the range of opportunities for empirical work within your own classes.

CASE STUDY OF EVIDENCE-BASED TEACHING

My colleagues and I had been teaching Introductory Psychology at Missouri State University for a number of years and were starting to grow disillusioned with the lack of student engagement and accompanying modest reflections of learning as measured by our departmental pre- and postcourse assessments. We discovered on a 30-item multiple choice test that students were, on average, improving their scores by only three questions by the end of a 16-week semester. This embarrassing realization happened to coincide with an initiative in course redesign led by the governor of Missouri. All public, 4-year institutions in the state were invited to apply to work with the NCAT to redesign one high-enrollment course. My colleagues and I thought this was a good opportunity to tackle the full-scale redesign of our Introductory Psychology program.

In hindsight, the most important step we took was our collective commitment to take an evidence-based approach to the redesign and our agreement to always work as a team. The pathway to our redesigned course was not always clear—and not always smooth—but the mutual respect we had for each other led us to accomplish a significant overhaul of our course. We have published papers elsewhere detailing our specific process (Drab-Hudson et al., 2012), short-term results (Hudson et al., 2014), and longer term outcomes (Hudson et al., 2015). Despite the enormous amount of work and excitement, not all of our results were immediately positive. Although a significant improvement in learning was immediately evident, several semesters passed before our DFW rate (percentage of "Ds," "Fs," and withdrawals) decreased substantially. In the 10 semesters since we reported our first five semesters of data (Hudson et al., 2015), the improvement in learning as measured by a pretest and a posttest assessment continues to be high (average = 71% improvement) and our DFW rate remains at least 10% lower than it was before our redesign (average DFW rate = 15%).

Although our outcome measures have yielded relatively stable results over time, this does not mean our course has not changed since 2012. Our team is committed to continuous improvement, and we follow the process outlined in Figure 9.1. One example has been our attempt to find a way for students in this large class (typically 330 students per section) to interact with each other in smaller groups. One of our goals for Introductory Psychology has been to implement strategies to attempt to make our big classes feel small, and our data suggest that we have made significant progress even if we have not completely caught up to the expectations held by students in small classes (Whisenhunt et al., 2019).

Our initial attempt to promote group interaction was to have students work on shared wiki projects throughout the semester. They would contribute to various sections of the wiki and receive one group grade. Partway into the semester, it became clear this was a terrible idea. Rather than promoting group cohesiveness, students were angry at certain group members and at us for creating an assignment that was above a desirable level of difficulty and did not use best practices for group work (Barkley et al., 2005; Fink, 2004). The students confirmed our hypothesis about their perception of the effectiveness of this course component by a mean rating of 2.78 ($SD = 1.64$) on a 7-point scale (1 = *ineffective* to 7 = *extremely effective*). By the next semester, we had thrown out the wikis and introduced discussion boards. Although the students' perception ratings increased ($M = 3.73$; $SD = 1.74$), they were still not at a place that was acceptable for us.

By fall 2013, we completely revamped our small group aspect of the class again. This time, instead of wikis or discussion boards, students were required to attend one small group study session before each exam. These study sessions were led by our trained undergraduate learning assistants (ULAs) and focused on the most difficult concepts from each chapter. Retrieval practice was incorporated into the study sessions by having students answer multiple choice questions representative of those included on the exams. Student perception data from that semester suggested we were moving in the right direction ($M = 4.80$; $SD = 1.85$).

Since 2013, we have continued to make small adjustments to the structure of the study sessions. For example, many of the rooms used for study sessions across campus were not equipped with technology, so we were unable to have the students use their electronic-device clickers to answer questions. We initially had students hold up paper-based cards with a large "A," "B," "C," or "D" to provide their answer for the retrieval practice portion of the study session. Although this strategy enabled the ULA to visually scan to see if students were generally understanding the concept, it was not anonymous, which made some students hesitant to provide an answer. We were then introduced to Plickers at a teaching conference, and in fall 2017, we replaced the cardstock answer cards with laminated Plickers cards, which not only allows students to respond anonymously (they hold up a QR code that the ULA scans with their smartphone) but provides the ULA with real-time data regarding student understanding. Our most recent analysis allowed us to conclude that most students are happy with the study sessions and believe in their efficacy (spring 2018: $M = 5.26$, $SD = 1.74$).

Evidence-based teaching encompasses a broad range of theoretical ideas and strategies. Our process of course redesign began in 2010 and, as outlined in this chapter, continues today. Being evidence-based involves a mind-set focused on continuous improvement, a commitment to following the data (in the literature and in your own class), and the tenacity to follow through with strategies to improve the learning environment for your students.

CONCLUSION

The primary goal of this chapter was to demystify the process of evaluating and incorporating evidence-based teaching into university courses. However, the secondary goal was to inspire and encourage you to become a principal investigator in your own class. As university instructors, we can bring so much more than the content from our discipline to the classrooms. With the guiding principles and specific steps discussed in this chapter, you can focus on continuous improvement in your courses. Over time, you will notice how this approach maintains your own enthusiasm for teaching and creates an environment conducive to successful student learning.

REFERENCES

American Psychological Association. (n.d.-a). *Office of Precollege and Undergraduate Education.* https://www.apa.org/ed/precollege/index.aspx

American Psychological Association. (n.d.-b). *Resources for teachers.* https://www.apa.org/action/resources/teachers/index.aspx

Aslam, S., & Emmanuel, P. (2010). Formulating a researchable question: A critical step for facilitating good clinical research. *Indian Journal of Sexually Transmitted Diseases and AIDS, 31,* 47–50. https://doi.org/10.4103/0253-7184.69003

Association for Psychological Science. (n.d.-a). *Classroom resources.* https://www.psychologicalscience.org/members/teaching/classroom-resources

Association for Psychological Science. (n.d.-b). *Reinventing introductory psychology.* https://www.psychologicalscience.org/members/teaching-psychology/reinventing-introductory-psychology

Barkley, E. F., Cross, K. P., & Major, C. H. (2005). *Collaborative learning techniques: A handbook for college faculty.* Jossey-Bass.

Bernstein, D. J., Addison, W., Altman, C., Hollister, D., Komarraju, M., Prieto, L., Rocheleau, C. A., & Shore, C. (2010). Toward a scientist–educator model of teaching psychology. In D. F. Halpern (Ed.), *Undergraduate education in psychology: A blueprint for the future of the discipline* (pp. 29–45). American Psychological Association. https://doi.org/10.1037/12063-002

Boring, A. (2017). Gender biases in student evaluations of teaching. *Journal of Public Economics, 145,* 27–41. https://doi.org/10.1016/j.jpubeco.2016.11.006

Boring, A., Ottoboni, K., & Stark, P. B. (2016). Student evaluations of teaching (mostly) do not measure teaching effectiveness. *ScienceOpen Research.* Advance online publication. https://doi.org/10.14293/S2199-1006.1.SOR-EDU.AETBZC.v1

Boysen, G. A. (2015). Uses and misuses of student evaluations of teaching: The interpretation of differences in teaching evaluation means irrespective of statistical information. *Teaching of Psychology, 42*(2), 109–118. https://doi.org/10.1177/0098628315569922

Carini, R. M., Kuh, G. D., & Klein, S. P. (2006). Student engagement and student learning: Testing the linkages. *Research in Higher Education, 47,* 1–32. https://doi.org/10.1007/s11162-005-8150-9

Chambless, D. L., & Ollendick, T. H. (2001). Empirically supported psychological interventions: Controversies and evidence. *Annual Review of Psychology, 52,* 685–716. https://doi.org/10.1146/annurev.psych.52.1.685

Chew, S. (2018, August). *Why do psychologists do research like scientists but teach like dummies?* [Paper presentation]. American Psychological Association, 126th Annual Convention, San Francisco, CA, United States.

Chew, S. L., Halonen, J. S., McCarthy, M. A., Gurung, R. A., Beers, M. J., McEntarffer, R., & Landrum, R. E. (2018). Practice what we teach: Improving teaching and learning in psychology. *Teaching of Psychology, 45*(3), 239–245. https://doi.org/10.1177/0098628318779264

Daniel, D. B. (2019, January). *Faith-based or evidence-based teaching: Are you a zealot, infidel or gnostic?* [Paper presentation]. 41st Annual National Institute on the Teaching of Psychology, St. Pete Beach, FL, United States.

DeLozier, S. J., & Rhodes, M. G. (2017). Flipped classrooms: A review of key ideas and recommendations for practice. *Educational Psychology Review, 29,* 141–151. https://doi.org/10.1007/s10648-015-9356-9

Drab-Hudson, D. L., Whisenhunt, B. L., Shoptaugh, C. F., Newman, M. C., Rost, A., & Fondren-Happel, R. N. (2012). Transforming introductory psychology: A systematic approach to course redesign. *Psychology Learning & Teaching, 11*(2), 146–157. https://doi.org/10.2304/plat.2012.11.2.146

Fink, L. D. (2004). Beyond small groups: Harnessing the extraordinary power of learning teams. In L. K. Michaelsen, A. B. Knight, & L. D. Fink (Eds.), *Team-based learning: A transformative use of small groups* (pp. 3–26). Stylus.

Gosen, J., & Washbush, J. (2004). A review of scholarship on assessing experiential learning effectiveness. *Simulation & Gaming, 35*(2), 270–293. https://doi.org/10.1177/1046878104263544

Gurung, R. A. R., & Hackathorn, J. (2018). Ramp it up: A call for more research in introductory psychology. *Teaching of Psychology, 45*(4), 302–311. https://doi.org/10.1177/0098628318796413

Hub for Intro Psych & Pedagogical Research. (n.d.). *Literature central.* http://hippr. oregonstate.edu/literature-central/

Hudson, D. L., & Whisenhunt, B. L. (2017, May). *Following the data: Improving student learning (and your CV)* [Paper presentation]. 29th Annual Convention for the Association for Psychological Science, Boston, MA, United States.

Hudson, D. L., Whisenhunt, B. L., Shoptaugh, C. F., Rost, A., & Fondren-Happel, R. N. (2014). Redesigning a large enrollment course: The impact on academic performance, course completion and student perceptions in introductory psychology. *Psychology Learning & Teaching, 13*(2), 107–119. https://doi.org/10.2304/plat.2014.13.2.107

Hudson, D. L., Whisenhunt, B. L., Shoptaugh, C. F., Visio, M. E., Cathey, C., & Rost, A. D. (2015). Change takes time: Understanding and responding to culture change in course redesign. *Scholarship of Teaching and Learning in Psychology, 1*(4), 255–268. https://doi.org/10.1037/stl0000043

Matulich, E., Papp, R., & Haytko, D. L. (2008). Continuous improvement through teaching innovations: A requirement for today's learners. *Marketing Education Review, 18*(1), 1–7. https://doi.org/10.1080/10528008.2008.11489017

Novak, G. M. (2011). Just-in-time teaching [Special issue]. *New Directions for Teaching and Learning, 2011,* 63–73. https://doi.org/10.1002/tl.469

Novak, G. M., Patterson, E. T., Gavrin, A. D., & Christian, W. (1999). *Just in time teaching.* Prentice-Hall. https://doi.org/10.1119/1.19159

O'Donohue, W., Buchanan, J. A., & Fisher, J. E. (2000). Characteristics of empirically supported treatments. *Journal of Psychotherapy Practice and Research, 9*(2), 69–74.

O'Flaherty, J., & Phillips, C. (2015). The use of flipped classrooms in higher education: A scoping review. *The Internet and Higher Education, 25,* 85–95. https://doi.org/ 10.1016/j.iheduc.2015.02.002 (Corrigendum published 2015, *The Internet and Higher Education, 27,* p. 90)

Paolini, A. (2015). Enhancing teaching effectiveness and student learning outcomes. *Journal of Effective Teaching, 15*(1), 20–33.

Papa, A., & Follette, W. C. (2015). Dismantling studies of psychotherapy. In R. L. Cautin & S. O. Lilienfeld (Eds.), *The encyclopedia of clinical psychology* (pp. 1–6). Wiley-Blackwell. https://doi.org/10.1002/9781118625392.wbecp523

Richmond, A. S., Boysen, G. A., & Gurung, R. A. R. (2016). *An evidence-based guide to college and university teaching.* Routledge. https://doi.org/10.4324/9781315642529

Shaw, T. J., Yang, S., Nash, T. R., Pigg, R. M., & Grim, J. M. (2019). Knowing is half the battle: Assessments of both student perception and performance are necessary to successfully evaluate curricular transformation. *PLoS One, 14,* e0210030. https:// doi.org/10.1371/journal.pone.0210030

Society for the Teaching of Psychology. (n.d.-a). *Resources for teachers of psychology.* http://teachpsych.org/page-1603066#

Society for the Teaching of Psychology. (n.d.-b). *STP e-books.* http://teachpsych.org/ ebooks/index.php

Sur, R. L., & Dahm, P. (2011). History of evidence-based medicine. *Indian Journal of Urology, 27*(4), 487–489. https://doi.org/10.4103/0970-1591.91438

Suskie, L. (2018). *Assessing student learning: A common sense guide* (3rd ed.). Wiley.

Whisenhunt, B. L., Cathey, C., Visio, M. E., Hudson, D. L., Shoptaugh, C. F., & Rost, A. D. (2019). Strategies to address challenges with large classes: Can we exceed student expectations for large class experiences? *Scholarship of Teaching and Learning in Psychology, 5,* 121–127. Advance online publication. https://doi.org/10.1037/ stl0000135

Wiggins, G., & McTighe, J. (1998). *Understanding by design.* Association for Supervision and Curriculum Development.

Wiggins, G., & McTighe, J. (2005). *Understanding by design* (2nd ed.). Association for Supervision and Curriculum Development.

10

A Taxonomy for Assessing Educational Change in Psychology

Raymond J. Shaw

In early 2018, Molly Worthen, a history professor at the University of North Carolina at Chapel Hill, raised concerns about assessment in an essay published in *The New York Times*. Her concerns boiled down to a characterization of assessment practices at many institutions that seems all too familiar. Because assessment of learning is required by accreditors, administrators at many institutions take the lead, and faculty in that context consequently often feel no ownership of assessment and register little understanding of the merits of assessment work. Furthermore, faculty (and administrators) often feel that the goal is just busywork to satisfy accreditors (e.g., Blaich & Wise, 2018). As Davidson (2017a) wrote,

> Just the other day, a friend of mine . . . was railing against her university's imposition of a requirement that every faculty member provide "learning outcomes" for their courses. It was the end of the semester, and she'd worked hard to provide a meaningful class for her students, and it felt cynical to then tack on a bunch of meaningless outcomes. Who hasn't felt anger at this increasingly frequent, seemingly cynical tendency of institutions to reduce the complexity of learning to a metric, productivity and outcomes? (para. 1)

As an example of the administrative/accreditation "purpose" for assessment, the *APA Guidelines for the Undergraduate Psychology Major: Version 2.0* (*APA Guidelines 2.0*; American Psychological Association [APA], 2013) state that

> Faculty in undergraduate psychology programs should be eager to document their success and use their successes to create persuasive arguments for more

https://doi.org/10.1037/0000183-011
Assessing Undergraduate Learning in Psychology: Strategies for Measuring and Improving Student Performance, S. A. Nolan, C. M. Hakala, and R. E. Landrum (Editors)

141

resources and confer protection during periods of resource competition and reallocation. The task force believes that the proposed framework will be helpful to departments as they *respond to accountability demands.* (p. 3; emphasis added)

Also supporting the faculty concern that assessment is administrative busywork, perhaps, is that hands-on assessment work often includes a focus on rigid adherence to using the "right verbs" (e.g., "Bloom's Revised Taxonomy"; Colorado College, n.d.) based on a canonical list of verbs tied to Bloom's taxonomy (Anderson & Krathwohl, 2001; Bloom et al., 1956). As they debate which verbs are correct for use in writing learning outcome statements (e.g., Adelman, 2015; Shireman, 2016), assessment scholars have focused on measurability and relevance to what students learn. As with many examples in the literature, the *APA Guidelines 2.0* (APA, 2013) recommend "the use of action verbs to support measurable aspects of student learning" (p. 4). Shireman (2016) went so far as to characterize the focus on which verbs are acceptable as "a bizarre system of verb-choice rules" (para. 8). Such recommendations often conflict with the tendency of faculty members to be interested in developing in their students more abstract outcomes like "understanding," "awareness," and "appreciation." As a result, when I examine the learning outcomes my colleagues have listed for their courses, I see a tendency to satisfy the requirement by prepending those outcomes with the action verb "demonstrate," as in "demonstrate an understanding," "demonstrate an awareness," and "demonstrate an appreciation." Furthermore, the strong advice from assessment professionals is to limit assessment to measurable outcomes only (e.g., Adelman, 2015; Suskie, 2018), and accreditors demand evidence of learning based on measured outcomes.

In the face of these demands and constraints, the easy path is to assess the low-hanging fruit of student learning: Did they learn this content and acquire those skills? Academics can easily and quickly generate measures of knowledge and skills. But, like Worthen, my interest in student learning extends beyond such easily measured outcomes.

I teach statistics to psychology majors. On its face, there is probably no more straightforward course in the major to assess. Students should learn the various relevant statistical techniques, when to use them, how to do them, and the logic of null hypothesis testing and concerns about that approach (e.g., Cumming, 2012). Measuring those is as simple as it gets; all can be evaluated with questions on exams or with assignments that require students to use particular skills. So, I can satisfy the dean's desire that I assess learning by just assessing these skills and knowledge. Over the years, I have used the results of such assessment to enhance the likelihood that students will know when to use a *t*-test versus an analysis of variance. But is that the goal? My students are unlikely to remember most of that by the time the next semester starts, and the next time they need to do statistics, there are websites and online calculators.

Do students understand why psychologists value statistical methods, that is, do they understand the limitations of null hypothesis significance testing?

Can they reflect on the inadequacy of statistical models—that when observations (human beings) are not described well by the model (e.g., outliers), it is a weakness of the model and not a legitimate assertion of abnormality, marginalization, or measurement error for those human beings? I try to move students to an understanding of these larger issues, but how can I measure that? What are the verbs approved in Bloom's taxonomy (Anderson & Krathwohl, 2001; Bloom et al., 1956) for determining that my students have achieved the learning outcome of becoming "woke" when evaluating statistical models?

Over the years of teaching the statistics course, I have encountered anecdotal evidence that at least some of the students have achieved those more abstract learning outcomes. For example, occasionally a student might tell me individually that "outlier sounds kind of insulting" or ask me, "What do researchers do about people who do not fit the model?" One approach to acquiring more systematic evidence of such outcomes is to use a focus group (e.g., Suskie, 2018). Although that time-intensive strategy might be useful for assessing more abstract outcomes for a major program, the work would be prohibitive to assessing a single semester of a course. Perhaps I should just be satisfied that some students occasionally get there and hope that more do. Given the challenge of measuring outcomes that matter and the administrative pressure to assess something, the prudent approach might be to limit my assessment efforts to easily measured skills and content knowledge using those "right verbs" (Adelman, 2015) aligned with Bloom's taxonomy (Anderson & Krathwohl, 2001; Bloom et al., 1956). The dean would be satisfied that I am "doing assessment."

Two factors mitigate against forgoing the assessment of the more meaningful but difficult-to-measure outcomes. First, on a personal level, not exploring whether my students "get" those meaningful outcomes would be unsatisfying, and it means that my time engaged in assessment of learning really is just busywork to make my department chair and dean happy. But the whole point of assessment is to improve teaching and learning. If the work is "just busywork," am I actually going to act on the data I collect and try to improve student learning (Blaich & Wise, 2018)? If I am measuring outcomes in which I am not invested, will I follow up and change my teaching to improve student achievement of those outcomes?

Second, there is a larger issue beyond individual courses and programs. Accreditors are now requiring (e.g., New England Commission of Higher Education, 2016) that institutions publish both learning goals and "verifiable" evidence of student achievement of those goals based on "valid" measures. Furthermore, institutions in New England at least are expected to have "readily available valid documentation for any statements and promises regarding . . . learning outcomes" (New England Commission of Higher Education, 2016, Standard 9.16). This means that faculty members must assess—with valid and verifiable measures—whatever student learning they identify as goals, and that evidence of student learning is to be published for the public.

The implication is that what professors identify and assess becomes a defining statement to the public of the educational purposes of higher education (Shaw, 2017a). At a time when the value of higher education is losing public confidence, the public image of how students are changed by their education matters. The easiest outcomes to measure are those that show evidence of the acquisition of skills or content knowledge. But if a college education is just about skills and content, is it worth it? One critic of assessment noted that "the object of education is not a set of contents or even a skill but rather a praxis that cannot be measured by any test" (Champagne, 2011, p. 2). Worthen (2018) wrote that

> if we describe college courses as mainly delivery mechanisms for skills to please a future employer, if we imply that history, literature and linguistics are more or less interchangeable "content" that convey the same mental tools, we oversimplify the intellectual complexity that makes a university education worthwhile in the first place. (para. 20)

Suskie (2018) wrote, "Some learning goals are promises we can't keep" (p. 274) and that it may be best to focus on the assessable learning goals rather than the difficult ones. She acknowledged that some people are concerned that higher education is becoming just about career preparation and that assessing only outcomes related to that would push aside outcomes like "thoughtful appreciation of works of art or compassion for others" (p. 276). She noted that "a world where such traits are a rarity would be a dismal place. So continue to acknowledge and value difficult-to-assess goals even if you're not assessing them" (p. 276). But Shavelson (2007) and Shaw (2017a) argued that we cannot just value such goals. As Shavelson wrote, "If we do not measure [personal and social responsibility] skills, they will drop from sight as accountability pressures force campuses to focus on a more restricted subset of learning outputs that can be more easily and less expensively measured" (p. 1). And the consequence of focusing on the easily measured is that "then we stand the risk of narrowing the mission and diversity of the American system of higher education, as well as the subject matter taught" (p. 3). In short, not assessing them, Shavelson argued, will mean that faculty members will likely stop teaching them.

If higher education faculty members collectively claim that all that is accomplished with student learning is the acquisition of content and skills, then the current model of higher education has substantially less expensive and viable alternatives. After all, the internet provides a vast multitude of opportunities to acquire those same skills and content knowledge for free. Professors are therefore obligated to articulate what really matters for student learning (Shaw, 2017a) and, most significantly, to assess it. The call for education to be understood as being deeper than skills and content knowledge can be found throughout the higher education press and in the *APA Guidelines 2.0* (APA, 2013), among many examples. As Davidson (2017b) wrote, "Students today need a new education that emphasizes creativity, collaboration, and adaptability over expertise in a single, often abstract discipline" (para. 6).

Identifying and assessing richer outcomes is difficult work because what really matters is often intangible and, perhaps most problematic for psychologists, may have a multitude of operational definitions. For example, if I asked seven randomly selected psychologists to define *critical thinking*, I suspect I would collect 14 different definitions. When I talk with colleagues outside of psychology, I hear a substantially larger number of definitions. A colleague in the English department asked how it was possible to engage in critical thinking without a text, and a colleague in Computer Science wondered how anyone could engage in critical thinking outside of writing code. However, conceptualizing learning as change, and then measuring change, is a natural activity for psychology. Wisdom is intangible and complex (Baltes & Smith, 1990), depressive symptoms are intangible and complex (Beck, 1972), character strengths are intangible and complex (e.g., Peterson & Seligman, 2004), yet measures have been developed for all of them. The same can be done for intangible and complex aspects of learning and the changes brought about by higher education experiences.

A TAXONOMY OF EDUCATIONAL CHANGE

I conceptualize learning outcomes as falling into four categories: performance, affective, intangible, and transformational (Shaw, 2017b). There are several existing taxonomies, and Bloom's taxonomy (Anderson & Krathwohl, 2001; Bloom et al., 1956) is the most well-known (see also Fink, 2013). Bloom's taxonomy (as revised; Anderson & Krathwohl, 2001) categorizes cognitive processes (there are separate taxonomies for affective and for psychomotor domains) in an ordered list from simple (factual remembering) to increasingly complex, ranging from understanding, to applying, to analyzing, evaluating, and creating. Within each category are multiple processes (e.g., the "Apply" category includes executing and implementing; the "Analyze" category includes differentiating, organizing, and attributing). One can find numerous examples of lists of verbs to use in creating learning objectives or outcome statements (e.g., "Bloom's Revised Taxonomy"; Colorado College, n.d.). Assessment practitioners recommend the use of that taxonomy both to ensure that student learning covers a broader range of learning and that learning objectives are written in a way that leads to a greater likelihood of measurability.

The present conceptualization, however, captures some more recent work on higher level outcomes and is connected to several resources and examples that might be useful in identifying ways to measure the more complex and difficult-to-assess outcomes. I use the broader term "change" instead of "learning" because the term "learning" is too associated with just the cognitive domain (Bloom et al., 1956). In brief, the category *performance* refers to content and skills; *affective*, to interests, attitudes, and personal characteristics—ways of being; *intangible*, to morals, ethics, social justice, and lifelong learning—skills and activities; and *transformational*, to deep, long-lasting changes in perspective.

Performance Outcomes

Performance outcomes are those that measure skills and content knowledge that students acquire from their learning experiences. Bloom's taxonomy (Anderson & Krathwohl, 2001; Bloom et al., 1956) includes a variety of ways of describing and conceptualizing content knowledge but is ultimately limited to deeper levels of knowledge and understanding. The knowledge part of the performance category is captured in the various action verbs recommended for stating measurable learning outcomes (Anderson & Krathwohl, 2001). The term "performance" is used to reflect the notion that the verbs derived from and associated with the levels in Bloom's taxonomy are all used to create measures of learning based on student performance on exams, assignments, papers, projects, and the like.

The other aspect of the performance category are the skills that students acquire, consistent with what Anderson and Krathwohl (2001) called "procedural knowledge" in the revised taxonomy (p. 27). As psychology majors, students may, for example, learn how to perform statistical analyses, dissect a sheep's brain, and design an experiment. One way of thinking about the performance category is that it represents the combination of semantic and procedural memory (Tulving, 1985) as a cognitive psychologist might describe those memory systems, or perhaps it represents crystallized intelligence (Cattell, 1963; see also Shavelson & Huang, 2003). Having students demonstrate this knowledge may involve complex skills (think of the higher levels in Bloom's taxonomy; Anderson & Krathwohl, 2001; Bloom et al., 1956). But ultimately, the purpose of all of Bloom's levels is that they are used to demonstrate the richness of knowledge and abilities, not to demonstrate the ability to engage in the activities themselves. In short, learning outcomes in the performance category are aimed at uncovering what students remember from their educational experiences as long as remembering is understood in the broad way that cognitive psychologists might think of it.

Thus, when learning goals are constrained to the verbs in Bloom's taxonomy (Anderson & Krathwohl, 2001; Bloom et al., 1956), the underlying conceptualization of how education changes students is limited to what they know, albeit in potentially complex forms of demonstrating that knowledge. From "remembering" and "understanding" to "evaluating" and "creating," Bloom's levels provide a way to demonstrate that students have learned content knowledge and skills. In my statistics course, performance outcomes include knowing how to conduct various statistical tests, knowing which statistical tests to use in different contexts, and being able to evaluate a statistical result and reach an appropriate conclusion. Assessing these is built into exams, assignments, and course projects. For example, 15 items on my final exam assess the extent to which students can identify the appropriate statistical test when given a brief description of a study. Given that students rarely, if ever, collect their final exams, I use the same items every year to track changes over time in response to changes in the way that I organize and present that information in the course.

However, relatively early dissatisfaction (e.g., Shavelson, 2007) with performance outcomes as the sole type of change produced by higher education has led to the development of measures of more complex outcomes. Shavelson (2007) emphasized the importance of personal and social responsibility skills. Two groups—the Wabash Study (e.g., Pascarella & Blaich, 2013; Pascarella et al., 2005) and the Valid Assessment of Learning in Undergraduate Education (VALUE) project of the Association of American Colleges & Universities (AAC&U; McConnell & Rhodes, 2017; Rhodes, 2010)—produced sets of measures of skills that go beyond performance outcomes. Those sets of measures form the basis for the next two categories: affective and intangible outcomes.

Affective Outcomes

Affective learning outcomes are about attitudes, beliefs about the self, and personal interests. Broadly, one might refer to them as "ways of being." For my statistics course, affective learning outcomes would be that students develop a positive attitude toward the importance of statistical analysis, an interest in learning more about statistical analysis, and an interest in the scientific aspects of psychology. The following are examples:

- interest in engaging intellectually challenging work
- interest in political and social involvement
- well-being
- positive attitude toward literacy
- interest in contributing to the arts
- interest in contributing to the sciences
- openness to engaging new ideas and diverse people
- orientation toward interacting with diverse people
- academic motivation (see list at Center of Inquiry at Wabash College, n.d.)

In the larger scope, I would like students to come to develop an interest in contributing to research after taking the course. To assess outcomes like these, one can give brief surveys at the beginning and end of the semester. These surveys should be anonymous so that students will not just give the socially desirable answers (Edwards, 1953). Anonymity, of course, means that the results are about group changes only, but for assessment of learning outcomes, that is usually the goal rather than tracking changes in individual students.

Intangible Outcomes

Intangible learning outcomes are hard to measure and generally represent or require complex intellectual and social skills. There is overlap with the affective category in that an interest in behaving a particular way or interacting with a particular group underlies the ability to do so effectively. Interest in outcomes like these pervades higher education. The AAC&U, in collaboration with many institutions across the country, developed the Liberal Education and America's Promise initiative that led to the development of 16 "essential outcomes" for a liberal education (AAC&U, 2008). They subsequently developed the VALUE rubrics (McConnell & Rhodes, 2017; Rhodes, 2010) for measuring these complex skills. Recently, McConnell and Rhodes (2017) reported on evidence from a large number of institutions on the successful use of the VALUE rubrics for evaluating student artifacts (for examples of how to use the rubrics for assessment, see AAC&U, n.d.-b). Some outcomes from the Liberal Education and America's Promise initiative that illustrate the intangible category are as follows:

- personal and social responsibility:
  - "Civic Knowledge and Engagement—Local and Global"
  - "Intercultural Knowledge and Competence"
  - "Ethical Reasoning and Action"
  - "Foundations and Skills for Lifelong Learning"
  - "Global Learning"

- integrative and applied learning:
  - "Integrative Learning"

- intellectual and practical skills:
  - "Inquiry and Analysis"
  - "Critical Thinking"
  - "Creative Thinking"
  - "Teamwork"
  - "Problem Solving" (see lists at AAC&U, n.d.-a)

Critical thinking represents the archetype of intangible outcomes. As Worthen (2018) wrote, "Consider that holy grail of learning outcomes, critical thinking—what the philosopher John Dewey called the ability 'to maintain the state of doubt and to carry on systematic and protracted inquiry'" (para. 23). It is difficult to define critical thinking in a readily measurable way. The *APA Guidelines 2.0* (APA, 2013) include "Scientific Inquiry and Critical Thinking" as one of the broad outcomes of the major. Those guidelines include a description of assessing critical thinking both in a general sense and in the context of research experiences. They also list 13 different instruments for measuring critical thinking (pp. 24–25), more than for any of the other four outcomes. Clearly, critical thinking is a concept that has challenged scholars in finding a consensus definition, which illustrates its intangible nature.

In brief, though, intangible outcomes are complex skills and activity that require bringing to bear multiple sources of information. The other outcomes mentioned earlier are additional examples of such skill sets. Another example of an intangible outcome was identified by Dibartolo et al. (2016) as they developed a method for assessing "thinking like a psychologist" in their students. They described "thinking like a psychologist" as "a complex learning goal that is more than a collection of discrete skills" (p. 193). For example, they wrote, "Thinking like a psychologist involves applying . . . ideas flexibly where the weight or even applicability of any particular idea is a matter of context" (p. 193).

In my statistics course, I hope for students to develop enhanced critical thinking skills in the context of interpreting the results of statistical analysis and reasoning about the meaning of their work in a logical manner. In an ideal situation, they would "think like psychologists" about the results of a research project in the sense of Dibartolo and colleagues (2016). They asked students to evaluate a collection of research results and reach a conclusion using their knowledge of statistics and research methods to make a recommendation based on those results. Although their work was aimed at evaluating the entire psychology curriculum, such an assignment could easily be part of a course on statistics or research methods as well.

Transformational Outcomes

The fourth category is *transformational outcomes*, which represent deep, long-lasting changes in perspective or ways of seeing the world. I previously described several transformational experiences that occurred in my under-graduate classes (Shaw, 2017a). These transformational experiences were the result of classroom experiences that led to changed perspectives on life. Such outcomes are difficult (at best) to identify and conceptualize and may happen only rarely. Suskie (2018) identified learning outcomes as goals that all students should achieve, and if those goals are not going to be achieved by all students, then professors should neither identify nor try to assess them. However, if faculty members value outcomes like these, then they should identify them and potentially try to measure if they happen, even if only to a few students.

The primary challenge with assessing transformational outcomes that might occur in some students is that it is unclear whether those outcomes will be long lasting. For example, in my first year of college, in a required Religious Studies course, the professor said one day that the purpose of the course was to make one's midlife crisis easier to manage. At the time, the comment was memorable but mysterious. Thirty years later, the comment and the lessons of the course were hugely impactful (Shaw, 2017a). Although one could not have known at the end of the semester that I would have a subsequent midlife experience, it may be possible to identify the antecedent components of lifelong perspective change. The course from my first year of college was ultimately about Christian existentialism, and a philosopher once pointed out to me that my understanding of that perspective was key to my midlife experience, so measuring students' understanding of that philosophy at the time of the course is an example of assessing the antecedents for the longer lasting transformational outcome. Likewise, in my statistics course, as described earlier, I want my students to understand that statistical analyses provide a clarified window on the nature of the world but, at the same time, that statistical models are limited in scope. This can be done by providing real-world examples for which an answer can be derived, but that does not necessarily solve the actual real-world problem. When individuals are not accurately included in a statistical model, it represents a problem with the model, not the individuals. Placing human values before data is a radical (and transformational) notion in a time when data analytics are at the center of social and business life. Asking students to evaluate a data set that has an identifiable group of individuals described as outliers provides a window into the possibility of this change in perspective.

EXAMPLES OF STUDENT ATTRIBUTES AND OUTCOMES IN THE *APA GUIDELINES 2.0*

The *APA Guidelines 2.0* (APA, 2013) include, for each of the comprehensive learning outcomes, "the kinds of attributes associated with strong performance in each of the learning goals" (p. 17). For example, the "attributes inferred from successful demonstration" of Goal 1, "Knowledge Base in Psychology" are the following:

- capable of coping with complexity and ambiguity
- conversant about psychological phenomena
- curious
- flexible in thinking
- knowledgeable about psychology
- motivated
- open minded
- prepared
- psychologically literate (p. 19)

The authors noted that "these adjectives typically surface in letters of recommendation of students for future employment or graduate school. As such, they reflect the kinds of implicit judgments faculty have always crafted in response to student requests of this type" (p. 17). These are the kind of attributes of successful students that faculty members value.

Across the five learning outcomes in the *APA Guidelines 2.0* (APA, 2013) is a total of 54 different attributes (some are repeated across outcomes). Exhibit 10.1 organizes those outcomes according to the taxonomy just described. Particular items could be placed differently, depending on the context or definition of each term, but the table demonstrates that what professors value in students can be understood as fitting well with the taxonomy of outcomes. It is also not clear that these are outcomes that can be taught, enabled, or developed in college students, but that is an empirical question. The authors of *APA Guidelines 2.0* noted that they wanted to make an explicit connection between these attributes and learning outcomes; at the very least, they are correlated with educational achievement and worth exploring further. The table serves to help elucidate what each category includes.

EXHIBIT 10.1

Desirable Attributes of Students Who Achieve APA-Recommended Learning Outcomes

Performance outcomes (knowledge and basic skills)
Comprehensible
Conversant about psychological phenomena
Knowledgeable about psychology
Prepared
Psychologically literate

Affective outcomes (ways of being)

Adaptable	Intentional
Attentive	Intuitive
Confident	Motivated
Conscientious	Open minded
Conventional	Persistent
Courageous	Reflective
Curious	Reliable
Dependable	Resilient
Efficient	Respectful
Fair minded	Responsible
Flexible	Self-starting
Flexible in thinking	Sensitive
Generous	Trustworthy
Industrious	

Intangible outcomes (complex skills)

Amiably skeptical	Ethical
Beneficent	Inventive
Capable of coping with complexity and ambiguity	Investigative
Careful	Logical
Civically engaged	Moral
Collaborative	Precise
Community involved	Resourceful
Constructively critical	Systematic
Creative	Tolerant
Directed	Tolerant of ambiguity

The question of measurement of these attributes remains. The performance outcomes are easily measured by examining student work. The affective attributes can be measured by observing student behavior (e.g., attentive, generous, sensitive) or by developing instruments to measure them (e.g., curiosity; Mussel, 2013), and the intangible attributes can be measured with the VALUE rubrics (McConnell & Rhodes, 2017) by observing behavior or by responses on carefully crafted assessments (e.g., Dibartolo et al., 2016).

The attributes listed in the *APA Guidelines 2.0* (APA, 2013) do not include transformative outcomes because they are attributes of college students, and it is hard to know whether any changes will be long lasting. But students may nevertheless have experiences both in the curriculum and outside of the classroom that can create some of the attributes in the affective and intangible categories in a transformative way. For example, students may experience an epiphany that permanently shifts their thinking toward an ethical or tolerant mind-set or a lifetime of civic engagement.

ASSESSMENT EXAMPLES

Conversations with my colleagues generated three outcomes that they identify as hard to measure: curiosity, self-efficacy, and a broadening of worldview. What follows is a description of each followed by an illustration of how they might be assessed with the hope of increasing the likelihood of their achievement among students.

One colleague requires his students to generate curiosity questions on a frequent basis in the hope that the students will develop a sense of curiosity. He then has students discuss and work out ways to possibly answer those questions. For example, after a class on attention theories, a student posted the following question on the course website: "How does Broadbent's filter model or any theories about attention relate to someone who has [attention-deficit/hyperactivity disorder] and has difficulties focusing on one thing?" In the following class meeting, the professor put the question on the screen and had students, in teams of three or four, discuss how they could use the scientific method to investigate the question. He asked them to consider potential independent and dependent variables, and the design of a study. After group discussion, the class as a whole discussed possibilities, leading to discussion of experimental and quasiexperimental designs, measurement of attention-deficit/hyperactivity disorder, follow-up experiments, limitations of research to the larger question, and so on (M. J. Stroud, personal communication, April 2, 2019). By engaging students, he hopes to show them that curiosity can be the basis for meaningful learning.

Another colleague and I talk about helping students become confident that they can do challenging activities and helping them develop a stronger sense of self-efficacy in important activities. One of my hopes for students in my statistics course, for example, is that they come to believe that they can do mathematics and statistical analysis. I teach the course in a flipped pedagogy, and class time is spent working on doing statistics; I act more as a cheerleader for their success than as an evaluator of performance during class.

Another colleague shared with me that she hopes that students will come to see that their own particular view of the world—of reality—is not the same as everyone else's and that other people have other experiences and perspectives. She works on this, for example, by emphasizing the constructed nature of perception and the reconstructed nature of memory in her Introductory Psychology class.

These goals are hard to measure, and each of us has generally relied on the ancient practice of hoping that students "get it" by using our intuition to sense that at least some do and continuing to encourage these changes in students by modifying our teaching as we continue in our careers. But it could be possible to assess these desirable affective changes and perhaps provide ourselves with evidence that we could use for a more systematic method for improvement.

One approach to assessment of affective change is to use existing measures. For example, one could use or adapt measures of curiosity developed by Mussel (2013) and by Kashdan et al. (2009), who defined *curiosity* as "recognizing, embracing, and seeking out knowledge and new experiences" (p. 988). They found that their measure "includes empirical support for two dimensions of curiosity: being motivated to seek knowledge and new experiences (*Stretching*; five items) and a general willingness to embrace the novel, uncertain, and unpredictable nature of everyday life (*Embracing*; five items)" (p. 995). It is not clear that the "Embracing" factor is as relevant to the intellectual curiosity that drives learning as the "Stretching" factor is, and Kashdan and colleagues also noted that "an important direction of future research will be modifying and adapting the items to fit particular domains of interest. This includes curiosity in school, work, relationships, or any other activity or context" (p. 996). Thus, professors interested in cultivating intellectual curiosity in students could adapt Kashdan and colleagues' instrument to the particulars of their class, administer the survey (with anonymous responding) to students at the beginning and end of the semester, and look for change at perhaps even the level of individual items as a source of ideas for changing the course.

The professor who wants students to see the world from the perspective of others is potentially confronting the natural egocentrism of adolescents. However, the development and encouragement of perspective taking (e.g., Batson, 2009) is a well-studied behavior. The importance of perspective taking was identified by the AAC&U in their Core Commitments project (Dey et al., 2010) and the subsequent development of the "Intercultural Knowledge and Competence" VALUE rubric (AAC&U, 2009). A term that captures perspective taking is *empathy*. This VALUE rubric, paraphrasing Bennett (1998), defines *empathy* as imagining another person's perspective and thus participating in both the intellectual and emotional dimensions of that person's experience. It also includes the concept of *openness*, which involves

> [suspending] judgment in valuing their interactions with culturally different others: Postpones assessment or evaluation (positive or negative) of interactions with people culturally different from one self. Disconnecting from the process of automatic judgment and taking time to reflect on possibly multiple meanings. (AAC&U, 2009, p. 1)

Although that instrument is aimed at intercultural perspective taking, it can be adapted to measure general interpersonal perspective taking.

Another tool that could be adapted to evaluate the degree to which students engage in perspective taking is the Interpersonal Reactivity Index (Davis, 1983), which includes seven items specifically measuring a *perspective-taking factor*, which Davis (1983) defined as "the tendency to spontaneously adopt the psychological point of view of others" (pp. 113–114). As with assessing curiosity development, by administering those items in a survey at the beginning and end of the semester, and then conducting an item analysis to determine areas for improvement, a professor could alter the course to improve the development of perspective taking in students.

A common desire for our students is that they develop confidence in their ability to do the particular work, for example, the belief that they can actually do statistics; this is *self-efficacy* (Bandura, 1977). Measuring self-efficacy beliefs is straightforward and potentially quite useful for assessment purposes at the course level. Bandura (2006), noting that self-efficacy is "not a global trait but a differentiated set of self-beliefs linked to distinct realms of functioning" (p. 307), provided a guide for creating context-specific measurement scales. A self-efficacy scale can list the behaviors required to perform well in the domain; respondents rate how confident they are that they can accomplish each behavior or task. Thus, a statistical self-efficacy scale could be constructed by listing a variety of skills needed to do statistical analysis (e.g., "I can translate a formula into the steps needed to complete the analysis," "I can identify the independent variable in an experiment"). Having students complete the scale at the end of the semester would provide evidence of their self-efficacy for statistics.

A self-efficacy scale of this sort has a side benefit as well. By examining average ratings of individual items, a professor could then determine what skills need further development the next time the course is taught. That is, a statistical self-efficacy skill could be constructed from a list of the component skills involved in doing statistical analyses. In effect, these would be a list of the low-level performance learning goals for the course. Student responses then would be a guide for modifying the course to improve student achievement of those goals. The instrument would therefore provide both a detailed indirect assessment measure for the course at the same time that it would provide evidence about the achievement of the intangible goal of increased self-efficacy beliefs in the domain.

SUMMARY AND IMPLICATIONS

By thinking of learning objectives in terms of the taxonomy described in this chapter, professors can identify and value their more abstract, less well-defined goals for their students. Furthermore, by identifying learning goals as being about memory (performance goals), ways of being (affective goals), complex skills (intangible goals), and transformational outcomes (lifetime goals), methods of assessment become clearer. The achievement of performance goals is measurable by examining performance on assignments, exams, and the like; affective goals are measurable primarily with surveys and questionnaires; and intangible goals are measured by identifying either existing measures of complex skills or by developing essays, projects, or other assignments that require the use of those skills (e.g., as Dibartolo et al., 2016, did).

Recognizing that affective and intangible outcomes can be measured in the ways that psychologists have always measured ways of being and skills in research contexts means that one can measure the more elusive, hard-to-measure outcomes for our courses in meaningful ways. By doing so, one is less likely to feel constrained by rewriting those meaningful and desirable outcomes to be sure to use approved action verbs. And as a result, faculty members might find assessment personally meaningful rather than simply an administrative task to satisfy deans and accrediting agencies.

One of the potential barriers to developing measures of affective and intangible outcomes, particularly for researchers in psychology, is the issue of reliability and validity of the measures. Twing and O'Malley (2017), for example, noted that "the concepts of validity and reliability are fundamental to the field of measurement" (p. 78) and argued that concerns about validity and reliability of measures are—and will continue to be—paramount in the assessment of student learning outcomes. Should that also apply to assessing student change in affective and intangible ways? Twing and O'Malley raised the issue of *consequential validity*, which is concerned with the uses of assessment results. How are the scores to be used? Are such uses valid with reference to what and how an outcome was measured? In that context, it is worth noting that many assessment scholars have argued for a different perspective on evaluating assessment measures—what may be described as a "usefulness criterion." For example, Suskie (2018) defined *effective assessment practices* as those that "yield evidence of student learning that is used to inform meaningful, substantive changes to teaching and learning" (p. 25). Given that, she wrote, "If you are comfortable using your evidence to inform meaningful decisions, your assessment practices are good enough, period" (p. 25). My view is that for course-level assessment in which the consequences are changes in a single course, that criterion is best. For program-level change or institutional-level change, a more compelling or psychometrically rigorous approach might be preferable.

How should performance, affective, intangible, and transformational outcomes appear on a syllabus to avoid the critique that one is not using the right verbs? My syllabus (see Appendix 10.1) has performance outcomes with the Bloom's taxonomy (Anderson & Krathwohl, 2001; Bloom et al., 1956) verbs for the cognitive domain fully in place. That list is then followed by a list titled "Also by the end of the semester, I hope to encourage the following perspectives, interests, and beliefs" for affective outcomes, and then there is a list of intangible outcomes titled "Further, during the course, students can plan to improve or develop the following complex skills." My dream (i.e., transformational goal) that students will become aware of the limitations of statistical models to accurately characterize all groups of people is then stated at the end of those lists. By including all of the goals, even the loftiest, on my syllabus, I communicate to students targets for them to strive to achieve.

Davidson (2017a) also argued that faculty should include "aspirational learning outcomes" on their syllabi to ensure that professors do not forget the difficult-to-assess but important goals of education. She listed 10 different examples, including the following:

In this course I hope that we will . . .

- Learn to respect intellectual life and education as a precious gift that no one can steal from us.
- Learn to absorb and transfer knowledge and wisdom from lectures, readings and class discussion into [one's] own cogent thinking and writing.
- Form an appreciation of the importance of critical and creative thinking and problem-solving and use these to guide my future life and work.
- Gain the highest respect for intellectual rigor, including self-respect . . .
- Learn to masterfully control chaos whenever we are faced with a complex web of ideas and results. . . . (para. 9)

Listing our aspirations as professors allows us to reclaim all the learning goals we have for our students, from acquiring knowledge and skills, to enabling ways of being, to encouraging the development of complex skills, and ultimately to inspiring the potential for transformative, life-long change.

APPENDIX 10.1
SYLLABUS: LEARNING OBJECTIVES FOR PSY 2110 STATISTICAL METHODS IN PSYCHOLOGY

By the end of the semester, students should be able to

- interpret statistical information encountered in the world,
- calculate a variety of statistics for modeling psychological phenomena,
- choose the appropriate statistical analyses to answer a variety of research questions, and
- evaluate the results of data analysis in research reports and reach an appropriate conclusion.

Also by the end of the semester, I hope to encourage the following perspectives, interests, and beliefs:

- a positive attitude toward the importance of statistical analysis
- statistical self-efficacy: a belief that you can actually "do statistics"
- an interest in learning more about statistical analysis
- an interest in the scientific aspects of psychology
- an interest in contributing to research after taking the course

Furthermore, during the course, students can plan to improve or develop the following complex skills:

- critical thinking skills in the context of interpreting the results of statistical analysis
- reasoning about the meaning of their work in a logical manner
- "thinking like psychologists" about the results of a research project

Finally, my hope is that students will also come to realize that although statistical analysis is a means for clarifying and objectively describing human behavior, the resulting models of psychological functioning and human characteristics can fail to capture all the nuances and individual differences that make psychology a rich and meaningful discipline for understanding the human condition. When there are individuals who are not accurately included in a statistical model, it represents a problem with the model, not the individuals.

Note. "PSY 2110" refers to the psychology course for which this syllabus was created.

REFERENCES

Adelman, C. (2015, February). *To imagine a verb: The language and syntax of learning outcome statements* (NILOA Occasional Paper No. 24). University of Illinois and Indiana University, National Institute for Learning Outcomes Assessment.

American Psychological Association. (2013). *APA guidelines for the undergraduate psychology major: Version 2.0.* https://www.apa.org/ed/precollege/about/psymajor-guidelines.pdf

Anderson, L. W., & Krathwohl, D. R. (2001). *A taxonomy for learning, teaching, and assessing: A revision of Bloom's taxonomy of educational objectives.* Longman.

Association of American Colleges & Universities. (2008). *College learning for the new global century.*

Association of American Colleges & Universities. (2009). *Intercultural knowledge and competence VALUE rubric.* http://www.aacu.org/value/rubrics/intercultural-knowledge

Association of American Colleges & Universities. (n.d.-a). *VALUE rubrics.* https://www.aacu.org/value-rubrics

Association of American Colleges & Universities. (n.d.-b). *VALUE rubrics case studies.* https://www.aacu.org/value/casestudies

Baltes, P. B., & Smith, J. (1990). Toward a psychology of wisdom and its ontogenesis. In R. J. Sternberg (Ed.), *Wisdom, its nature, origins and development* (pp. 87–120). Cambridge University Press. https://doi.org/10.1017/CBO9781139173704.006

Bandura, A. (1977). Self-efficacy: Toward a unifying theory of behavioral change. *Psychological Review, 84*(2), 191–215. https://doi.org/10.1037/0033-295X.84.2.191

Bandura, A. (2006). Guide for constructing self-efficacy scales. In F. Pajares & T. Urdan (Eds.), *Self-efficacy beliefs of adolescents* (pp. 307–337). Information Age.

Batson, C. D. (2009). Two forms of perspective taking: Imagining how another feels and imagining how you would feel. In K. D. Markman, W. M. P. Klein, & J. A. Suhr (Eds.), *Handbook of imagination and mental simulation* (pp. 267–279). Psychology Press.

Beck, A. T. (1972). *Depression: Causes and treatment.* University of Pennsylvania Press.

Bennett, J. (1998). Transition shock: Putting culture shock in perspective. In M. J. Bennet (Ed.), *Basic concepts of intercultural communication* (pp. 215–224). Intercultural Press.

Blaich, C., & Wise, K. (2018). Scope, cost, or speed: Choose two—the iron triangle of assessment. *Change: The Magazine of Higher Learning, 50*(3–4), 73–77. https://doi.org/ 10.1080/00091383.2018.1509606

Bloom, B. S., Englehart, M. D., Furst, E. J., Hill, W. H., & Krathwohl, D. R. (1956). *Taxonomy of educational objectives: Handbook I: Cognitive domain.* David McKay.

Cattell, R. B. (1963). Theory of fluid and crystallized intelligence: A critical experiment. *Journal of Educational Psychology, 54*(1), 1–22. https://doi.org/10.1037/h0046743

Center of Inquiry at Wabash College. (n.d.). *Wabash National Study instruments.* https:// centerofinquiry.org/wabash-national-study-instruments-investigate-liberal-arts- education/

Champagne, J. (2011). Teaching in the corporate university: Assessment as a labor issue. *Journal of Academic Freedom, 2,* 1–26.

Colorado College. (n.d.). *Bloom's revised taxonomy.* https://www.coloradocollege.edu/ other/assessment/how-to-assess-learning/learning-outcomes/blooms-revised- taxonomy.html

Cumming, G. (2012). *Understanding the new statistics: Effect sizes, confidence intervals, and meta-analysis.* Routledge.

Davidson, C. N. (2017a, August 28). Design learning outcomes to change the world. *Inside Higher Ed.* http://www.insidehighered.com/views/2017/08/28/learning- outcomes-help-students-translate-classroom-learning-life-tools-essay

Davidson, C. N. (2017b, October 22). A newer education for our era. *Chronicle of Higher Education.* https://www.chronicle.com/article/Commentary-A-Newer-Education/ 241313

Davis, M. H. (1983). Measuring individual differences in empathy: Evidence for a multidimensional approach. *Journal of Personality and Social Psychology, 44*(1), 113–126. https://doi.org/10.1037/0022-3514.44.1.113

Dey, E. L., Ott, M. C., Antonaros, M., Barnhardt, C. L., & Holsapple, M. A. (2010). *Engaging diverse viewpoints: What is the campus climate for perspective-taking?* Association of American Colleges and Universities.

Dibartolo, P. M., Rudnitsky, A. M., Duncan, L. E., & Ly, M. (2016). Using a "messy" problem as a departmental assessment of undergraduates' ability to think like psychologists. *Journal of Assessment and Institutional Effectiveness, 6*(2), 191–211. https://doi.org/10.5325/jasseinsteffe.6.2.0191

Edwards, A. (1953). The relationship between the judged desirability of a trait and the probability that the trait will be endorsed. *Journal of Applied Psychology, 37*(2), 90–93. https://doi.org/10.1037/h0058073

Fink, D. F. (2013). *Creating significant learning experiences: An integrated approach to designing college courses.* Jossey-Bass.

Kashdan, T. B., Gallagher, M. W., Silvia, P. J., Winterstein, B. P., Breen, W. E., Terhar, D., & Steger, M. F. (2009). The curiosity and exploration inventory-II: Development, factor structure, and psychometrics. *Journal of Research in Personality, 43*(6), 987–998. https://doi.org/10.1016/j.jrp.2009.04.011

McConnell, K. D., & Rhodes, T. L. (2017). *On solid ground.* Association of American Colleges and Universities. https://www.aacu.org/OnSolidGroundVALUE

Mussel, P. (2013). Introducing the construct curiosity for predicting job performance. *Journal of Organizational Behavior, 34*(4), 453–472. https://doi.org/10.1002/job.1809

New England Commission of Higher Education. (2016). *Standards for accreditation.* http://www.neche.org/resources/standards-for-accreditation/

Pascarella, E. T., & Blaich, C. (2013). Lessons from the Wabash National Study of Liberal Arts Education. *Change: The Magazine of Higher Learning, 45*(2), 6–15. https://doi.org/10.1080/00091383.2013.764257

Pascarella, E. T., Wolniak, G. C., Seifert, T. A. D., Cruce, T. M., & Blaich, C. F. (2005). Liberal arts colleges and liberal arts education: New evidence on impacts. *ASHE Higher Education Report, 31*(3), 1–148.

Peterson, C., & Seligman, M. E. P. (2004). *Character strengths and virtues: A handbook and classification.* American Psychological Association.

Rhodes, T. (2010). *Assessing outcomes and improving achievement: Tips and tools for using rubrics.* Association of American Colleges and Universities.

Shavelson, R. J. (2007). *A brief history of student learning assessment: How we got where we are and a proposal for where to go next.* Association of American Colleges and Universities.

Shavelson, R. J., & Huang, L. (2003). Responding responsibly to the frenzy to assess learning in higher education. *Change, 35*(1), 10–19. https://doi.org/10.1080/00091380309604739

Shaw, R. J. (2017a). Assessing the intangible in our students. *Chronicle of Higher Education.* https://www.chronicle.com/article/Assessing-the-Intangible-in/240744

Shaw, R. J. (2017b). *Dreams of learning: Ineffable learning outcomes* [Workshop]. 2017 New England Educational Assessment Network Fall Forum, Worcester, MA, United States.

Shireman, R. (2016, April 7). SLO madness. *Inside Higher Ed.* http://www.insidehighered.com/views/2016/04/07/essay-how-fixation-inane-student-learning-outcomes-fails-ensure-academic-quality

Suskie, L. (2018). *Assessing student learning: A common sense guide* (3rd ed.). Wiley.

Tulving, E. (1985). How many memory systems are there? *American Psychologist, 40*(4), 385–398. https://doi.org/10.1037/0003-066X.40.4.385

Twing, J. S., & O'Malley, K. J. (2017). Validity and reliability of direct assessments. In T. Cumming & M. D. Miller (Eds.), *Enhancing assessment in higher education: Putting psychometrics to work* (pp. 78–101). Stylus.

Worthen, M. (2018, February 23). The misguided drive to measure "learning outcomes." *The New York Times.* http://www.nytimes.com/2018/02/23/opinion/sunday/colleges-measure-learning-outcomes.html

11

Using Formative Self-Assessment to Improve Teaching and Learning in Educational Psychology Courses

Eva Seifried and Birgit Spinath

At universities, assessments are often used as assessments *of* teaching and learning (*summative assessment*) instead of assessments *for* teaching and learning (*formative assessment*). It is the timing and use of the assessments that distinguish these two forms from one another. Formative assessment includes "all those activities undertaken by teachers, and/or by their students, which provide information to be used as feedback to modify the teaching and learning activities in which they are engaged" (Black & Wiliam, 1998, pp. 7–8). Formative assessment comprises five key strategies: (a) having clear and shared learning intentions and success criteria, (b) using learning tasks that show whether students have understood the material, (c) providing feedback that helps learners move forward, (d) activating students "as instructional resources for one another," and (e) activating students "as the owners of their own learning" (Black & Wiliam, 2009, p. 8). Thus, both instructors and students can be involved in formative assessment. It is relevant for teachers to analyze whether students are making progress toward the intended learning objectives and to adapt one's teaching to the students' needs. However, it seems to be more compatible with the aims of higher education to also help students learn to recognize when they are not making progress and to figure out how to improve their performance. Thus, besides summative and formative assessments, formative *self-assessments* also play a critical role in university contexts.

https://doi.org/10.1037/0000183-012
Assessing Undergraduate Learning in Psychology: Strategies for Measuring and Improving Student Performance, S. A. Nolan, C. M. Hakala, and R. E. Landrum (Editors)

Educational psychology is a field in which research and teaching can be perfectly combined and even cross-fertilize when formative self-assessments are applied. In this chapter, we illustrate how we use several forms of formative self-assessments (which can be performed and analyzed by the instructor, the students, or both) to continuously improve our teaching and our students' learning in our educational psychology courses, both regarding their knowledge and their learning strategies. The latter aspect is important because self-regulated learning is crucial for success in higher education, and study techniques are an important predictor of students' academic performance (e.g., Credé & Kuncel, 2008). Researchers further indicate that the use of different strategies might be aligned with recommendations and requirements within a course (e.g., Bartoszewski & Gurung, 2015); thus, in the following, we illustrate how we try to foster the application of effective strategies.

FORMATIVE SELF-ASSESSMENT AS A MEANS TO IMPROVE ONE'S TEACHING

Faculty often stress the reliance on empirical evidence (i.e., evidence-based thinking and acting) in their discussions and in their teaching, and what they want to convey to their students. There also is a movement that emphasizes the idea of transferring research methods to one's own teaching: The goal of the scholarship of teaching and learning (SoTL; e.g., Boyer, 1990; Hutchings et al., 2011) is to investigate one's own teaching and students' learning to improve teaching and learning by sharing one's insights within the scientific community. Certainly, it is necessary to assess the outcomes of one's teaching to achieve this aim. In our courses, we apply a similar approach called *Forschendes Lehren* (Spinath & Seifried, 2012; Spinath et al., 2014, 2016), which might best be translated as "inquiry-based teaching" following the well-established concept of inquiry-based learning. However, whereas *inquiry-based learning* primarily focuses on outcomes at the learners' side, the goals of *inquiry-based teaching* are more manifold: With our approach, we want to address a range of goals for learners, instructors, and teaching quality (e.g., increases in learning and motivation and satisfaction as well as evidence-based teaching; see Spinath et al., 2014, 2016). These goals can be achieved within an iterative cycle (see Table 11.1): At first, instructors should keep up to date with the principles of good teaching and learning (Phase I), and check whether these are embedded in their own teaching. Furthermore, they should also test the effects of their current way of teaching (Phase II). Subsequently, instructors should initiate empirical studies: They should deduce hypotheses about how to improve their current teaching–learning arrangement based on theory and empirical work (Phase III) and test these hypotheses with adequate research designs (Phase IV). When a method has proven successful in practice, it should be implemented in one's course (Phase V). Moreover, instructors should contribute to theory development so that new hypotheses can be derived and

TABLE 11.1. Seven Phases to Continuously Improve One's Teaching

	Phase I	Phase II	Phase III	Phase IV	Phase V	Phase VI	Phase VII
Goals	Review of theoretical and empirical evidence	Evaluation of the output	Development of hypotheses and research designs	Hypotheses testing	Implementation	Further development of theory and empiricism	Iterative process
Summary	Take together all your knowledge about good teaching and learning.	Check how well your current teaching–learning arrangement corresponds to the knowledge about good teaching and learning and check the results that you achieve.	Derive hypotheses from theory and empirical evidence about how your teaching-learning arrangement needs to be changed to optimize results.	Check the results of your new teaching–learning arrangement with an adequate research design.	Implement the elements of your teaching–learning arrangement that have shown the desired effects.	Extend theory, derive new hypotheses, and test them.	Pass through phases IV–VI again.

Note. See also Spinath and Seifried (2012) and Spinath et al. (2014, 2016).

tested (Phase VI). Using this iterative cycle (Phase VII: repeating Phases IV–VI) is meant to continuously improve one's teaching (see also Spinath & Seifried, 2012; Spinath et al., 2014, 2016). Thus, this model is about applying an action research model to teaching (see also the scientist educator model; Bernstein et al., 2010). Again, what is needed to achieve the aim of improving one's teaching is continuous self-assessment. Implementing this process also is in line with Hattie (2009), who argued that teachers should monitor their actions with the help of empirical data. "Know thy impact" is his recommendation for teachers (Hattie, 2012, p. 169).

FORMATIVE SELF-ASSESSMENT AS A MEANS TO IMPROVE STUDENTS' LEARNING

Improving students' learning includes not only more knowledge but also better learning skills (see also Black & Wiliam, 2009). In the past decade, there has been an increase in research on students' learning at universities: There are reviews indicating which strategies are most effective empirically (e.g., Dunlosky et al., 2013) and books about their application (e.g., Benassi et al., 2014; Brown et al., 2014). However, many students do not make the best decisions about study efforts because they have incorrect ideas about the most effective learning strategies and do not apply the best learning strategies without assistance (e.g., Karpicke et al., 2009; Kornell & Bjork, 2007; McCabe, 2011). In the following, we refer to just a few of the effective strategies, namely, those that are the most important to the design of our teaching–learning format (i.e., distributed practice, practice testing, and feedback).

Distributed practice (or spaced practice) has been identified as one of two highly useful strategies by Dunlosky and colleagues (2013): Regarding long-term retention, students who distribute their learning over time typically outperform students who mass their study activities uninterruptedly (for reviews, see Carpenter et al., 2012, and Cepeda et al., 2006). *Practice testing* (or retrieval practice) is the second strategy that received a high utility assessment by Dunlosky and colleagues. Concerning later retention, learners benefit more from taking a test or some other way that encourages them to recall the information from memory than from spending the same amount of time restudying the to-be-learned material; this phenomenon is called the *testing effect* (Roediger & Karpicke, 2006; for further reviews, see also Kornell & Vaughn, 2016, and Roediger & Butler, 2011). Besides the direct effect of strengthening learning, retrieval practice can also have several indirect effects and further benefits, such as improved study effectiveness and increased metacognitive accuracy (see Roediger et al., 2011). Combining distributed and retrieval practice leads to the idea of continuous self-testing: Frequent self-assessments can both improve students' learning and help them to realize what they know and what they do not know so they can allocate their time and study efforts accordingly. The corresponding tests can be composed either by the instructor (i.e., as ready-made tests that students can take) or by the students to help them test themselves on themselves or in groups (for our implementation, see the next section); the results of these self-assessments can then be used for both improving teaching and learning. Testing itself can be fruitful, but combining it with *feedback* leads to even better results because feedback prevents the acquisition of incorrect knowledge (e.g., Butler & Roediger, 2008). In general, feedback has been identified as one of the most important strategies to enhance learning (Hattie, 2009, 2011), and it can also help to correct metacognitive errors (e.g., Butler et al., 2008). Thus, besides distributed learning and retrieval practice, providing feedback is the third general strategy that we apply in our teaching. Furthermore, using assessments as feedback for students and instructors also is at the core of formative assessment (see Black & Wiliam, 1998).

OUR IMPLEMENTATION: CONTINUOUS FORMATIVE SELF-ASSESSMENT

Based on the idea that formative self-assessment is especially important for university students, we give our students the opportunity to assess themselves in a formative way in our courses. Each semester, we have two large introductory courses in educational psychology with psychology first-year students (about $N = 150$) and preservice teachers (about $N = 200$). Both student groups receive credit points for passing an exam with forced-choice and open questions at the end of the semester. As follows, we outline a typical order of events in our courses and how these are aligned with continuous formative self-assessments (see also Table 11.2).

Pretest

We start our courses with a pretest: After the introduction, we ask our students to participate in an online survey that includes a short test on their (objective and subjective) prior knowledge and their motivation for the course as well as some further varying aspects, depending on the focus of our ongoing research to improve our teaching–learning arrangement continuously (e.g., questions about our students' expectations for the course). This survey serves several aims. First, we receive an impression about our students' prior knowledge and their motivational prerequisites, and our students receive an impression about educational psychology's research questions and methods. Thereby, we aim to avoid or reduce false expectations about what students will learn in the course. Second, we use the pretest to connect to our students in the large courses as we give students feedback on the groups' characteristics and—based on an anonymous code—on their individual prerequisites. Third, we explain some statistics (e.g., concepts like mean and standard deviation)

TABLE 11.2. Activities Embedded in Our Course and Their Aims for Instructors and Students

Activity	Aims for instructors: Instructors can . . .	Aims for students: Students can . . .
Pretest	. . . get an impression about their students' prerequisites. . . . get connected to their students, even in large courses. . . . introduce their intentions to improve the course and raise students' willingness to participate (i.e., transparency). . . . have a baseline to evaluate the effects of their teaching (pretest–posttest design).	. . . receive insights into the contents and methods of psychology (i.e., topics and statistics). . . . learn to understand and make use of the results of the upcoming formative self-assessments. . . . see that they can actively participate in the improvement of the course. . . . become acquainted with the item format of the final exam.
Session on teaching and learning at universities	. . . keep up to date with research on teaching and learning strategies. . . . adjust their course design to the current state of knowledge. . . . show their students that they "practice what they preach."	. . . gain knowledge about good learning strategies. . . . reflect and adjust their own learning strategies. . . . understand and appreciate the research conducted in the course but also recognize their own responsibility for their learning outcomes.
Learning-related tasks (i.e., assignments, CTF items)	. . . ensure constructive alignment. . . . receive feedback on what their students have understood/have not understood. . . . refute misconceptions. . . . adapt their teaching to their students' needs.	. . . practice the tasks that they will be graded on. . . . use effective learning strategies (i.e., distributed learning, retrieval practice/ testing oneself and one another). . . . engage with the contents more deeply. . . . receive individual feedback and can thereby correct misunderstandings.
Surveys	. . . continuously monitor the effects of their teaching (with data). . . . practice SoTL. . . . overcome the dichotomy of research and teaching.	. . . test themselves (and thereby learn the contents). . . . monitor their own learning and motivation. . . . actively participate in research.
Final exam	. . . fulfill the obligation to assess their students' learning. . . . evaluate the effects of their teaching.	. . . show what they have learned (and practiced). . . . attain good grades.

Note. CTF = confidence-weighted true–false; SoTL = scholarship of teaching and learning.

and thereby help our students to understand and make use of the results of the upcoming surveys. Fourth, we explain our students that we are interested in improving our teaching, their learning, and the learning conditions in the course, and hence raise their interest in an active participation in this process of active formative self-assessment. Fifth, the pretest enables us to evaluate the effects of our teaching with a pretest–posttest design. Sixth, students become acquainted with the item format of the final exam. For the objective prior knowledge test—and all further knowledge tests, including the final exam—we use confidence-weighted true–false (CTF) items with which we can assess both students' cognitive and metacognitive performance (Dutke & Barenberg, 2015). These CTF items include one-sentence statements that students are asked to evaluate as true or false while simultaneously indicating the confidence in their answer. Using this item format helps both the students and us to assess students' knowledge while also fostering students' metacognitive competencies, which are in turn essential for their regulation and learning processes. We can identify and reduce misconceptions among our students (i.e., beliefs that are held with strong confidence but are not in accordance with the current status of research). Also, by using items like these in our surveys during the semester (see the Learning-Related Tasks section and the Surveys section of this chapter), we can ascertain content that has been imparted in a way such that students feel unsure or sure about it. Subsequently, we can repeat content or teach this content in another way next time. Furthermore, our students can monitor their learning progress, identify gaps or weaknesses in their knowledge as well as overconfidence in certain aspects, and then adjust their learning accordingly.

Session on Teaching and Learning at Universities

The second lecture session is dedicated to teaching and learning at universities (see videos by Stephen Chew, n.d., for a similar approach). In this session, we present both empirical findings on effective learning strategies and our attempts to engage in SoTL, including our experiences in the past semesters and how the previous results influenced the current teaching–learning arrangement. Based on this information, we stress the importance of distributed learning and retrieval practice, and how we want to help students to apply these strategies: We invite students to attend the weekly lecture sessions and ask questions and engage in discussions. We provide detailed lecture material with references that students might consult; we also provide questions that are comparable with chapter-ending questions in books and that can be used to check whether students have understood the main aspects of a certain unit. We also encourage our students to get together in groups outside the classroom to test and assess each other. All of these offers are meant to help students learn and test themselves continuously (instead of cramming) so that they are well prepared for the final exam at the end of the semester. In general, including this session serves several aims: We keep up to date with research on teaching and learning strategies, and we might further adjust our course design to the current state of knowledge so that we can act as role models by showing our students that we "practice what we teach." Furthermore, our students not only gain knowledge about good learning strategies but they can (and should) also reflect and adjust their own learning strategies (also based on and supported by the opportunities offered in the course). Our students should thereby understand and appreciate the research conducted in the course but also recognize their own responsibility for their learning outcomes.

Learning-Related Tasks

During the semester, our students have the opportunity to continuously practice those tasks on which they will be assessed in the final exam (see constructive alignment; Biggs & Tang, 2011): Students may submit either assignments or CTF items. The first kind of task includes answering questions that refer to but also exceed the course's contents; it requires elaboration and reflection (e.g., comparing new knowledge with one's prior knowledge, applying the lecture's contents to real-life problems) in a continuous text, and thereby supports the writing-to-learn approach (see Dunn et al., 2013). For these assignments, we try to set meaningful application-oriented and challenging but attainable tasks to enhance students' motivation (see expectancy–value theory; Wigfield & Eccles, 2000). The second kind of task—which we have recently introduced to strengthen the idea of formative self-assessment in our lectures—requires students to identify key aspects of a session's content and to phrase them precisely in one-sentence statements as in the CTF items, which we use in our surveys and in the exam at the end of the semester (see the Surveys and Final Exam sections of this chapter). Furthermore, students are asked to generate a task that might be used as an assignment and to also give a short horizon of expectations for this assignment (for examples of the learning-related tasks and the items that we use for our surveys and exams, see Table 11.3). We employ trained student tutors who read the submissions and provide individual feedback to the students. Besides ensuring constructive alignment (i.e., students can practice the tasks that they will be graded on), the way we implement these learning-related tasks serves further aims. We receive feedback on what our students have or have not understood; if necessary, we can refute misconceptions (for the importance of refutational teaching, e.g., Taylor & Kowalski, 2014) and adapt our teaching to the students' needs. Our students can apply several effective learning strategies (i.e., distributed learning, retrieval practice/ testing oneself and one another) and engage more deeply with the contents. Furthermore, because they receive individual feedback, they can also correct misunderstandings and feel that their efforts are valued.

Surveys

Besides the concrete learning-related tasks, we provide several surveys that include knowledge tests, specific tasks that help to prepare for or review

TABLE 11.3. Examples of the Three Types of Tasks We Use for Formative Self-Assessments in Our Lecture

Task	Examples
Writing assignments	You are now familiar with the international large-scale studies on school achievement such as TIMSS and PISA.
	1. How do you judge the overall quality of these studies? Are there aspects that you would like to criticize?
	2. What would you say is the importance of these studies for the educational system in Germany?
	3. What are the consequences that should follow these studies?
Generating CTF items and assignment tasks	Please generate a deepening assignment task about the topic of the current session. The task should demand the respondents to expand the content of the session in order to apply it. Please also give a short comprehensible horizon of expectations for the assignment task (with 10 points as a maximum).
	Please also generate four statements about the topic of the current session. These statements should be either unambiguously true or false; please indicate the correct verisimilitude in brackets after your statements.
Answering CTF items	In a psychological experiment, the control group is the one in which diverse variables are controlled for. (false)
	There is a sex difference in general intelligence favoring men/boys. (false)
	Gifted children show considerably more behavioral disorders than average children. (false)
	Attention deficit hyperactivity disorders are often caused by sensory overload. (false)
	Intelligence can be increased via trainings. (true)

Note. The first two rows include examples for the learning-related tasks that students can submit during the semester. The third row includes examples for the tasks that are included in the learning-related part of the surveys during the semester. Both assignments and CTF items are included in the final exam at the end of the semester. TIMSS = Trends in International Mathematics and Science Study (Beaton et al., 1996); PISA = Programme for International Student Assessment (Organisation for Economic Co-operation and Development, 2014); CTF = confidence-weighted true–false.

the lecture's content (e.g., taking a self-assessment to test one's aptitude as a teacher, applying diagnostic criteria to an example case) as well as questions on students' motivation. The results of these surveys are discussed within the lecture and, as with the pretest, we provide students with their individual and their group's results so that students can assess what they do or do not know. The use of these surveys has several aims. We can continuously monitor the effects of our teaching as we receive feedback on our students' current understandings or misunderstanding and further learning-related variables. Furthermore, we can practice SoTL and thereby overcome the dichotomy of research and teaching, that is, we can combine research—which is often perceived as the most important part of university staff—and teaching—which we perceive as an equally important task. Our students can test themselves and thereby not only learn the contents but also monitor their own learning and actively participate in research.

Final Exam

By continuously offering varied tasks, we continue to monitor both students' knowledge and motivation, and we offer several alternatives for how students can distribute their learning and assess themselves without being graded. Therefore, the final exam at the end of the semester fulfills the obligation to assess students in a summative way, but it can also be used to evaluate the overall effect of one's teaching. Due to the aforementioned course of action, students can use the exam to show what they have learned (and practiced), and, consequently, they can attain good grades. In general, our approach is meant to increase both the quality of and the motivation and satisfaction for teaching on the instructors' side and the quality of learning and the motivation and satisfaction with the course on the students' side.

OUR EXPERIENCE WITH THE CONTINUOUS FORMATIVE SELF-ASSESSMENT

We have used pretests for several years in the courses for both psychology first-year students and preservice teachers, and it is a stable finding that both student groups come with little prior knowledge. They even have some misconceptions (i.e., they wrongly classify statements with high confidence) and cannot rate the level of their prior knowledge correctly (i.e., there is no correlation between students' objective and subjective knowledge). However, our students come with good motivational prerequisites, that is, with high values in terms of the expectancy–value theory by Wigfield and Eccles (2000): They are interested in the content of educational psychology and perceive it as useful and important, and this is a great motivation boost for instructors.

We have tried different versions regarding the learning opportunities. For example, we experimented with the number of obligatory tasks within our teaching–learning format. We found the assignments to be a good preparation for the final exam, but when we offered the assignments as optional learning opportunities, we learned that only some students took advantage of them (Seifried et al., 2018). We also have successfully used *latent semantic analysis* (LSA)—that is, a semantic technology with which the content of an essay can be assessed—as assistance for our tutors. LSA can be used to facilitate essay writing in large university courses and thereby help to improve learning and teaching at universities. We have applied LSA successfully to detect plagiarism (Seifried et al., 2015) and to identify poor assignments (Seifried et al., 2017). We are now testing a version with no obligatory tasks at all but with high incentives for our students to seize the learning offers, for example, by providing increasingly detailed feedback. As mentioned earlier, we also have started to include some tasks other than assignments, for example, the generation of examlike CTF items to teach students how to study effectively on their own or in groups. Our experience with this item format has been positive. Not only do our students appreciate the shorter tasks, but we also learn a lot from the student-generated items: We can see what students identify as key aspects of a unit and whether these aspects match our intended learning outcomes. When we start preparing exams, we often have difficulties finding appropriate new items. The items generated by our students can then serve as an inspiration or might even be used for the final exam. This might in turn increase students' participation in the design of the teaching–learning arrangement and the perceived fairness of the exam. Furthermore, at best, students will learn to assess themselves and generate their own feedback. By asking our students to share their items and test each other, we hope to approximate this goal.

Apposite to our engagement in SoTL and the idea of continuously assessing and improving our teaching and our students' learning in a formative fashion, we have extended both the number and the content of the surveys that accompany the lecture. Although students are not obliged to take the surveys, the high participation rates show that our students see their benefits. This engagement is also reflected in students' evaluations at the end of the term, when the vast majority of participants rate the surveys as meaningful (see Figure 11.1). Some comments from our students further add to the picture of the surveys as a successful and esteemed supplement to the lecture, for example, "As far as I'm concerned, there might have been even more practice items because I perceived it as enormously helpful to practice the format of the exam and to test my current knowledge" or "happy to have more [surveys] (e.g., one survey after each session)."

FIGURE 11.1. Students' Evaluation of the Usefulness of the Surveys

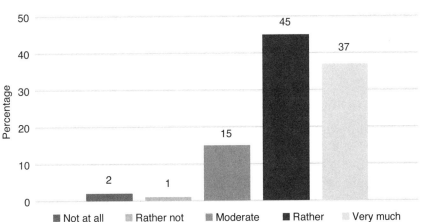

Note. Using a 5-point Likert-type scale (1 = *not at all* to 5 = *very much*), students were asked to indicate how meaningful they perceived the surveys. The data presented were collected at the end of the winter term 2017–2018 from our psychology first-year students.

Although we found evidence of improved learning gains and increased satisfaction with the learning conditions on our students' side, we found both intended and unintended effects on the metacognitive level. In general, we found that many students endorsed several misconceptions at the beginning of the term (see percentage of incorrect and confident answers in the pretest in Figure 11.2). At the end of the semester, there are few wrong replies that are given with high confidence. Students give more correct answers of which they are confident as well as fewer incorrect answers of which they are confident (see percentages of corresponding answers in the examination in Figure 11.2). In one study, we found that items relating to content on which students had submitted an assignment were answered correctly more often and with higher confidence than items relating to content on which students had not prepared an assignment. However, there also was an increase in students' (unjustified) confidence in incorrect answers (Barenberg et al., 2016). Further research is needed to disentangle the desired effects of our assignments on students' learning gains from the overconfidence that seems to come along with them. However, it is promising that the correlation between students' objective and subjective knowledge is not significant at the beginning of the semester but typically rises during the semester.

In general, monitoring students' learning and motivation during the semester provides us with information that we can use to improve the course design—both during the semester and after. We can adapt our teaching; for example, we can repeat content that many students have been struggling with or implement further learning opportunities that can be used for formative self-assessment. We have engaged in research on our teaching and its continuous improvement for more than 10 years now—and we are still keen to do so. We have learned a lot, but we also feel still a lot might be investigated.

FIGURE 11.2. Gains in Confident Correct Answers and Reduction of Misconceptions (i.e., Incorrect and Confident Answers)

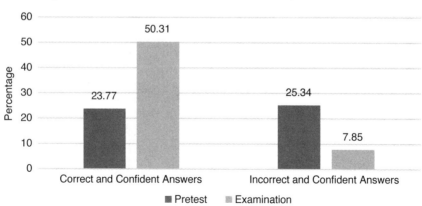

Note. Students' knowledge was tested with confidence-weighted true–false items at the beginning and at the end of the semester. The data presented were collected in the winter term 2011–2012 from our preservice teachers.

OUR FUTURE ENDEAVORS

Our current teaching–learning format includes several opportunities for our students to assess themselves continuously, but we are planning to expand these possibilities. For example, we are considering asking students to undergo a kind of reality check on their expectancies about the course before they enter the first session. We might inform students about and justify the contents of psychological courses and, hence, avoid unrealistic expectations. Furthermore, to more closely align the surveys with the topics of educational psychology and our research as well as to strengthen our idea that students learn to assess themselves, we have asked our students to list their personal intentions on how they want to prepare for the course during the semester (e.g., whether and how often they plan to attend the lecture or submit assignments). We found that students had high intentions to use several learning activities at the beginning of the semester, but the survey at the end of the semester showed that students indicated they did not implement their intentions. Thus, although we offer several learning activities to our students that should help them to deepen and assess their knowledge, and although students understand the value of these learning activities (i.e., they have high intentions to take advantage of them), students do not manage to fulfill their own standards. Hence, there is a gap between students' self-imposed goals and their performance, so there is some need to improve students' motivation-related competencies (see Schaller & Spinath, 2017). A first idea toward this goal might be to ask students to monitor their own development more explicitly, for example, by recording their personal results from our surveys in a graphic. This kind of documentation might help students to see when there is a decline in their motivation and help them to engage in corrective action. An individual graphical monitoring might also be done for students' learning results because this might make it even easier for students to recognize what they know and where they still need to adjust their learning. Such activities that use intraindividual comparisons might be another way to optimal self-assessment and improved learning gains.

RECOMMENDATIONS

We close this chapter with recommendations for college and university instructors. These suggestions are based on our research and the expertise that we have accumulated over the years: First and foremost, invest effort into continuously improving your teaching by using self-assessments. This endeavor is more than worthwhile because your students will benefit regarding both their professional knowledge and their study habits, which in turn will motivate you for your courses. Second, reveal to your students that you want to improve both your teaching and their learning. Your students will appreciate your efforts, especially when you take appropriate action based on your implemented self-assessments. Third, make use of what you know. Implement your knowledge on what makes up good learning and teaching to your own courses. Including these insights within one lecture session is not only helpful for your students but also forces you to stay up to date about current research. Fourth, starting a course with a pretest leads to a great resonance in class. Show and discuss the results, and how you want to build on these in the course later in the semester. Fifth, apply constructive alignment. Allow students to perform the tasks that they will be graded on and teach them how to do well. Sixth, make sure that both you and your students can monitor their learning progress. Learning-related tasks or surveys might be useful for your students to test themselves in a formative fashion and for you to adjust and improve your teaching. So, be curious about how students come to your lecture and how they leave, practice inquiry-based teaching to investigate the effects of your teaching, and think of ways to make students' progress visible both to you and to the students themselves. And last but not least: Enjoy your teaching, especially because it will improve continuously!

REFERENCES

Barenberg, J., Seifried, E., Spinath, B., & Dutke, S. (2016). Die Bearbeitung schriftlicher Problemaufgaben erhöht den Lernerfolg in einer Psychologie-Vorlesung [Solving written problem-related tasks increases learning achievement in a psychology lecture]. In M. Krämer, S. Preiser, & K. Brusdeylins (Eds.), *Psychologiedidaktik und Evaluation XI* [Psychology teaching and evaluation XI] (pp. 323–330). Shaker Verlag.

Bartoszewski, B. L., & Gurung, R. A. R. (2015). Comparing the relationship of learning techniques and exam score. *Scholarship of Teaching and Learning in Psychology, 1*(3), 219–228. https://doi.org/10.1037/stl0000036

Beaton, A. E., Mullis, I. V. S., Martin, M. O., Gonzalez, E. J., Kelly, D. L., & Smith, T. A. (1996). *Mathematics achievement in the middle school years: IEA's Third International Mathematics and Science Study (TIMSS).* Center for the Study of Testing, Evaluation, and Educational Policy, Boston College.

Benassi, V. A., Overson, C. E., & Hakala, C. M. (2014). *Applying science of learning in education: Infusing psychological science into the curriculum (2014).* Society for the Teaching of Psychology. http://teachpsych.org/ebooks/asle2014/index.php

Bernstein, D. J., Addison, W., Altman, C., Hollister, D., Komarraju, M., Prieto, L., Rocheleau, C. A., & Shore, C. (2010). Toward a scientist–educator model of teaching psychology. In D. F. Halpern (Ed.), *Undergraduate education in psychology: A blueprint for the future of the discipline* (pp. 29–45). American Psychological Association. https://doi.org/10.1037/12063-002

Biggs, J., & Tang, C. (2011). *Teaching for quality learning at university: What the student does* (4th ed.). Society for Research into Higher Education & Open University Press; McGraw-Hill Education.

Black, P., & Wiliam, D. (1998). Assessment and classroom learning. *Assessment in Education: Principles, Policy & Practice, 5*(1), 7–74. https://doi.org/10.1080/0969595980050102

Black, P., & Wiliam, D. (2009). Developing the theory of formative assessment. *Educational Assessment, Evaluation and Accountability, 21*, 5–31. https://doi.org/10.1007/s11092-008-9068-5

Boyer, E. L. (1990). *Scholarship reconsidered. Priorities of the professoriate.* The Carnegie Foundation for the Advancement of Teaching.

Brown, P. C., Roediger, H. L., III, & McDaniel, M. A. (2014). *Make it stick: The science of successful learning.* Harvard University Press. https://doi.org/10.4159/9780674419377

Butler, A. C., Karpicke, J. D., & Roediger, H. L., III. (2008). Correcting a metacognitive error: Feedback increases retention of low-confidence correct responses. *Journal of Experimental Psychology: Learning, Memory, and Cognition, 34*(4), 918–928. https://doi.org/10.1037/0278-7393.34.4.918

Butler, A. C., & Roediger, H. L., III. (2008). Feedback enhances the positive effects and reduces the negative effects of multiple-choice testing. *Memory & Cognition, 36,* 604–616. https://doi.org/10.3758/MC.36.3.604

Carpenter, S. K., Cepeda, N. J., Rohrer, D., Kang, S. H. K., & Pashler, H. (2012). Using spacing to enhance diverse forms of learning: Review of recent research and implications for instruction. *Educational Psychology Review, 24,* 369–378. https://doi.org/10.1007/s10648-012-9205-z

Cepeda, N. J., Pashler, H., Vul, E., Wixted, J. T., & Rohrer, D. (2006). Distributed practice in verbal recall tasks: A review and quantitative synthesis. *Psychological Bulletin, 132*(3), 354–380. https://doi.org/10.1037/0033-2909.132.3.354

Chew, S. (n.d.). *How to study.* Samford University. https://www.samford.edu/departments/academic-success-center/how-to-study

Credé, M., & Kuncel, N. R. (2008). Study habits, skills, and attitudes: The third pillar supporting collegiate academic performance. *Perspectives on Psychological Science, 3*(6), 425–453. https://doi.org/10.1111/j.1745-6924.2008.00089.x

Dunlosky, J., Rawson, K. A., Marsh, E. J., Nathan, M. J., & Willingham, D. T. (2013). Improving students' learning with effective learning techniques: Promising directions from cognitive and educational psychology. *Psychological Science in the Public Interest, 14*(1), 4–58. https://doi.org/10.1177/1529100612453266

Dunn, D. S., Saville, B. K., Baker, S. C., & Marek, P. (2013). Evidence-based teaching: Tools and techniques that promote learning in the psychology classroom. *Australian Journal of Psychology, 65*(1), 5–13. https://doi.org/10.1111/ajpy.12004

Dutke, S., & Barenberg, J. (2015). Easy and informative: Using confidence-weighted true–false items for knowledge tests in psychology courses. *Psychology Learning & Teaching, 14*(3), 250–259. https://doi.org/10.1177/1475725715605627

Hattie, J. (2009). *Visible learning: A synthesis of over 800 meta-analyses relating to achievement.* Routledge.

Hattie, J. (2011). Which strategies best enhance teaching and learning in higher education? In D. Mashek & E. Y. Hammer (Eds.), *Empirical research in teaching and learning: Contributions from social psychology* (pp. 130–142). Blackwell. https://doi.org/10.1002/9781444395341.ch8

Hattie, J. (2012). *Visible learning for teachers: Maximizing impact on learning.* Routledge. https://doi.org/10.4324/9780203181522

Hutchings, P., Huber, M. T., & Ciccone, A. (2011). *The scholarship of teaching and learning reconsidered: Institutional integration and impact.* Jossey-Bass.

Karpicke, J. D., Butler, A. C., & Roediger, H. L., III. (2009). Metacognitive strategies in student learning: Do students practise retrieval when they study on their own? *Memory, 17*(4), 471–479. https://doi.org/10.1080/09658210802647009

Kornell, N., & Bjork, R. A. (2007). The promise and perils of self-regulated study. *Psychonomic Bulletin & Review, 14,* 219–224. https://doi.org/10.3758/BF03194055

Kornell, N., & Vaughn, K. E. (2016). Chapter 5—How retrieval attempts affect learning: A review and synthesis. *Psychology of Learning and Motivation, 65,* 183–215. https://doi.org/10.1016/bs.plm.2016.03.003

McCabe, J. (2011). Metacognitive awareness of learning strategies in undergraduates. *Memory & Cognition, 39,* 462–476. https://doi.org/10.3758/s13421-010-0035-2

Organisation for Economic Co-operation and Development. (2014). *PISA 2012: What 15-year-olds know and what they can do with what they know.*

Roediger, H. L., III, & Butler, A. C. (2011). The critical role of retrieval practice in long-term retention. *Trends in Cognitive Sciences, 15*(1), 20–27. https://doi.org/10.1016/j.tics.2010.09.003

Roediger, H. L., III, & Karpicke, J. D. (2006). The power of testing memory: Basic research and implications for educational practice. *Perspectives on Psychological Science, 1*(3), 181–210. https://doi.org/10.1111/j.1745-6916.2006.00012.x

Roediger, H. L., III, Putnam, A. L., & Smith, M. A. (2011). Ten benefits of testing and their applications to educational practice. *Psychology of Learning and Motivation, 44*, 1–36. https://doi.org/10.1016/B978-0-12-387691-1.00001-6

Schaller, P., & Spinath, B. (2017). Selbstberichtskalen zur Erfassung motivationsbezogener Kompetenzen (MOBEKO) im Studium: Entwicklung und Validierung [A self-report instrument for measuring Motivation-Based Competences (MOBEKO) of students in higher education: Development and validation]. *Diagnostica, 63*(4), 229–241. https://doi.org/10.1026/0012-1924/a000176

Seifried, E., Eckert, C., & Spinath, B. (2018). Optional learning opportunities: Who seizes them and what are the learning outcomes? *Teaching of Psychology, 45*(3), 246–250. https://doi.org/10.1177/0098628318779266

Seifried, E., Lenhard, W., & Spinath, B. (2015). Plagiarism detection: A comparison of teaching assistants and a software tool in identifying cheating in a psychology course. *Psychology Learning & Teaching, 14*(3), 236–249. https://doi.org/10.1177/1475725715617114

Seifried, E., Lenhard, W., & Spinath, B. (2017). Filtering essays by means of a software tool: Identifying poor essays. *Journal of Educational Computing Research, 55*(1), 26–45. https://doi.org/10.1177/0735633116652407

Spinath, B., & Seifried, E. (2012). Forschendes Lehren: Kontinuierliche Verbesserung einer Vorlesung [Forschendes Lehren: Continuous improvement of a lecture]. In M. Krämer, S. Dutke, & J. Barenberg (Eds.), *Psychologiedidaktik und Evaluation IX* [Psychology teaching and education IX] (pp. 171–180). Shaker.

Spinath, B., Seifried, E., & Eckert, C. (2014). Forschendes Lehren: Ein Ansatz zur kontinuierlichen Verbesserung von Hochschullehre [Forschendes Lehren: A concept to continuously improve teaching at universities]. *Journal Hochschuldidaktik, 25*(1+2), 14–16.

Spinath, B., Seifried, E., & Eckert, C. (2016). Forschendes Lehren: Ein Ansatz zur kontinuierlichen Verbesserung von Hochschullehre [Forschendes Lehren: A concept to continuously improve teaching at universities]. In M. Heiner, B. Baumert, S. Dany, T. Haertel, M. Quellmelz, & C. Terkowsky (Eds.), *Was ist gute Lehre? Perspektiven der Hochschuldidaktik* [What is good teaching? Perspectives on university pedagogy] (pp. 59–72). W. Bertelsmann.

Taylor, A. K., & Kowalski, P. (2014). Student misconceptions: Where do they come from and what can do? In V. A. Benassi, C. E. Overson, & C. M. Hakala (Eds.), *Applying science of learning in education: Infusing psychological science into the curriculum* (pp. 259–273). Society for the Teaching of Psychology.

Wigfield, A., & Eccles, J. S. (2000). Expectancy—Value theory of achievement motivation. *Contemporary Educational Psychology, 25*(1), 68–81. https://doi.org/10.1006/ceps.1999.1015

III

INTERNATIONAL APPROACHES

12

Assessing Learning Outcomes in Undergraduate Psychology Education

Lessons Learned From Five Countries

Jacquelyn Cranney, Julie A. Hulme, Julia Suleeman, Remo Job, and Dana S. Dunn

The value of higher education degree programs in general, and psychology undergraduate degree programs in particular, has recently been questioned; this is true not only in the United States (e.g., Halonen, 2011) but also in other Western countries (e.g., Trapp et al., 2011). In most countries, the undergraduate psychology degree program is popular. In some, because intake to accredited programs that lead to graduate professional training is restricted, most undergraduate students progress to that next stage of training (e.g., the Netherlands; van der Molen & Visser, 2008). For example, as indicated below, the vast majority (about 90%) of students in Italy go on to further study to pursue professional or research psychology.

However, it appears that in the majority of countries, fewer than 20% of psychology undergraduates progress to the limited places in graduate-level professional or research training psychology programs. The first question is why undergraduate psychology is so popular. Wilson (2009) asserted that students enrolling in introductory psychology are interested in finding out

We thank the reviewers for their constructive comments. Julia Suleeman thanks Dr. Octaviani Indrasari Ranakusuma (Dean of Faculty of Psychology, Universitas YARSI), Rika Eliana, M.Psi. (Vice Dean of Faculty of Psychology, Universitas Sumatera Utara), Dr. Esther Widhi (Head of Undergraduate Psychology Program, Faculty of Psychology, Universitas Bina Nusantara), Raymond Godwin, M.Si. (staff, Faculty of Psychology, Universitas Bina Nusantara), and Dr. Bagus Takwin, M. Hum. (Head, Social Psychology Study Program, Faculty of Psychology, Universitas Indonesia) for sharing valuable experiences in undertaking assessment for undergraduate psychology students.

https://doi.org/10.1037/0000183-013
Assessing Undergraduate Learning in Psychology: Strategies for Measuring and Improving Student Performance, S. A. Nolan, C. M. Hakala, and R. E. Landrum (Editors)
Copyright © 2021 by the American Psychological Association. All rights reserved.

more about themselves and about how to get along with others. Further, Bromnick and Horowitz (2013) asserted that psychology students want to "make a difference"—they don't particularly want status or wealth, but they want to make the world a better place. The second question to be addressed is what happens to the majority of psychology graduates who do not go on to further study in professional or research psychology. Researchers have found that Australian data indicate that many more final-year undergraduate students want to undertake professional training than there are training places available (Cranney et al., 2018). U.K. data indicate that only 15% of 2018 applicants to clinical psychology programs were successful in obtaining admission (see Clearing House for Postgraduate Courses in Clinical Psychology, 2018).

Whether final-year undergraduate students should or can progress to graduate-level professional training relates to (a) their ability, and (b) the demand and the number of training places available for professional and research psychologists. There do not appear to be informative data on the former; for the latter, there is some indication of shortages of professional psychologists and of training places (e.g., in Australia; Voudouris & Mrowinski, 2010). Ideally, from our biased perspective, there should be more training and employment opportunities for practicing professional psychologists. For example, we, the coauthors, all strongly agree that there should be full-time developmental and educational psychologists in every school (McGovern et al., 2010); however, in some countries, the trained psychologists are being replaced with personnel less qualified to deliver psychological services (e.g., teachers, Workplace Health and Wellbeing, Cornwall, 2019; undergraduate psychology major graduates, Health Education England, 2018). Two factors mitigate against increased training places: (a) cost (e.g., Australian psychology departments lose approximately $8,000/year per student in professional psychology graduate training—training is not directly funded and is usually subsidized by undergraduate student fees, Voudouris & Mrowinski, 2010; cf. clinical psychology training in the United Kingdom, which is fully funded by the National Health Service; Health Education England, 2020); and (b) the lack of appreciation by governments of the value of professional psychology, particularly those forms focusing on prevention (e.g., health, community, educational and developmental psychology).

How does this situation (i.e., most undergraduates not progressing to further professional training) relate to assessment and what is assessed? We propose that our profession must review the intended outcomes of undergraduate education, both at the introductory psychology and final-year major levels. What messages about psychological science and practice should every introductory and final-year psychology student receive? Moreover, we propose that graduates should appreciate that psychological science uniquely provides knowledge and evidence-based tools that can lead to more fulfilling academic, professional, and personal lives. That is, they should acquire a minimum level of psychological literacy—the capacity to intentionally use psychological science to pursue personal, professional, and societal goals (Cranney & Dunn, 2011).

The elements of psychological literacy at both levels (introductory level and minimum degree-program level expectations) relate to intended learning outcomes or graduate capabilities; these are relatively similar across nations (see the national sections later in this chapter).

Focusing on learning outcomes is consistent with backward design or constructive alignment, whereby the first step in curriculum design is determining the end goal (i.e., the learning outcomes), with further steps involving how to assess such outcomes and how to afford students opportunities to acquire such outcomes (Biggs, 1996; Wiggins & McTighe, 2005; see also Chapter 13, this volume). Backward design also emphasizes learning outcomes reflecting "enduring understandings" that continue to be useful in solving everyday life problems. For example, for most psychology major graduates, a thorough understanding of the difference between correlation and causation may be more useful in the long term than a capacity to precisely apply American Psychological Association (APA) Style.

Relatedly, assessment should be seen as an intervention (Bearman et al., 2016) that (a) provides students with knowledge, skills, and attitudes relevant to their future; and particularly (b) supports students' lifelong learning capacity. As many assessment scholars have indicated, standard assessment strategies of multiple-choice question exams and standard essays or lab reports often fall short of driving acquisition of higher level complex cognitive/emotional/behavioral capacities (e.g., the ability to apply knowledge and skills to real-life situations; the ability to engage in informed moral decision making; e.g., Sadler, 2016). This gap in assessment is likely driven by a number of factors, including (a) educator lack of knowledge of effective and efficient resources; (b) economically driven policies that do not allow adequate resourcing of effective learning, teaching, and assessment strategies; and (c) student expectations driven by prior experience of poor assessment practices.

In this chapter, we provide a brief overview of the assessment of undergraduate psychology learning outcomes in five nations, with a view to learning about similarities and differences. Importantly, this may lead to ideas about how we might work together across nations to resolve some of the issues that are raised and make the most of opportunities to optimize our undergraduate psychology programs for the benefit of students, psychology, and society.

ASSESSMENT IN AUSTRALIAN UNDERGRADUATE PSYCHOLOGY PROGRAMS

To become an endorsed practicing psychologist in one of nine recognized endorsement areas (i.e., clinical, clinical neuropsychology, community, counselling, educational and developmental, forensic, health, organizational, and sports), the standard education and training route is a 3-year undergraduate psychology major bachelor degree, an honors 4th year or equivalent, a 2-year master's in an endorsement area, and 2 years of endorsement supervision in the workplace. Other pathways to professional registration and endorsement are emerging, but it should be noted that approximately 16% of all university students in Australia take first-year psychology; fewer than 20% of psychology majors go on to the fourth honors year in psychology; and fewer than half of honors students go on to professional psychology training, including to research degrees in psychological science (Cranney et al., 2018). Limited research regarding the career aspirations and outcomes of undergraduate psychology majors indicate that

- at the University of New South Wales, Sydney (a highly rated research-intensive university), approximately two thirds of psychology major students reported that, in their first year, they intended to progress to graduate professional psychology training; however, by their (current) final year, this fraction had been reduced to approximately one half (Cranney et al., 2018).

- most students who do not go on to graduate study obtain positions in diverse service-oriented careers (Cranney et al., 2008).

- graduates of 3-year and 4-year psychology programs and current master's students report that their undergraduate degree prepared them well for a psychological research career (if that is what they wanted to do) but not for working in a global economy (Cranney et al., 2019).

Undergraduate psychology programs are accredited by the Australian Psychology Accreditation Council (APAC). In 2010, the revision of the standards included a major shift to the fuller specification of outcomes in the form of graduate attributes (knowledge, research skills, critical thinking skills, ethics and value, communication skills, and application), each with associated lower level learning outcomes (APAC, 2010). In 2019, a new set of undergraduate program competencies began to be evaluated during the accreditation cycle. These competencies included comprehending and applying psychological knowledge (across a range of topics), as well as the following:

- "Apply knowledge and skills of psychology in a manner that is reflexive, culturally appropriate and sensitive to the diversity of individuals";

- "Analyse and critique theory and research in the discipline of psychology and communicate these in written and oral formats";

- "Demonstrate an understanding of appropriate values and ethics in psychology"; "Demonstrate interpersonal skills and teamwork"; and

- "Demonstrate self-directed pursuit of scholarly inquiry in psychology." (APAC, 2019, p.11)

In addition, standards within the general domains are of interest:

- "Learning and teaching methods and environments are designed and used to enable students to achieve the program learning outcomes when assessed" (APAC, 2019, p. 9);

- "Cultural responsiveness, including with Aboriginal and Torres Strait Islander cultures is appropriately integrated within the program and clearly articulated as a required learning outcome" (APAC, 2019, p. 9);

- "Students are informed of the availability of personal and professional support services, and are equipped with skills to adequately maintain their own well-being" (APAC, 2019, p. 9).

One section of the standards entirely concerns assessment and includes (a) the requirements that all program learning outcomes (covering all required competencies) are assessed; (b) that there is a clear relationship between criterion-based assessment strategies and learning outcomes; (c) that multiple assessment tools, modes, and techniques are used; and (d) that moderation and other procedures ensure fair assessment and feedback. Accompanying the standards is an "Evidence Guide" that attempts to give some guidance (which is not part of the official standards); this document mentions formative feedback as being a desirable practice.

Some of the strengths of the 2019 standards include increased emphases on interpersonal communication and teamwork and on cultural responsivity. Some of the weaknesses include decreased emphases on research training and on application to personal, professional, and societal issues—the acquisition of psychological literacy. Indeed, the 2019 standards appear to be even more narrowly focused on graduate professional psychology competencies than were the 2010 standards; they appear to have ignored the literature on the advantages for the discipline and profession of psychology of taking account of the diverse career destinations and aspirations of undergraduate students. Against this narrow APAC perspective, undergraduate psychology educators continue to negotiate with department chairs to provide the resources to support meaningful learning and assessment activities (e.g., work-integrated learning experiences) that enhance the psychological literacy and employability of all psychology major students. Clearly, for the future of our students and our society, there is still much work to be done to optimize undergraduate leaning outcomes as driven by authentic assessment (see Chapter 13, this volume, for information about the Assessment Design Decisions Framework, an Australian effort to promote learning-oriented assessment).

ASSESSMENT FOR UNDERGRADUATE PSYCHOLOGY STUDENTS IN INDONESIA: WHAT IS NEEDED?

To understand the assessment for undergraduate psychology programs in Indonesia, we provide a brief history of the psychology program in Indonesia to provide context for understanding psychology and its development in the country. Following that context, we provide an argument that assessment should be aligned with the educational goals of the units, which in turn should reflect the program competencies expected from the graduates.

Brief History of Psychology Education and Training in Indonesia

Indonesian psychology training was founded in 1953, as part of the Faculty of Medicine at Universitas Indonesia (UI). UI is currently a state-run, high-level university with approximately 50,000 students. In 1960, psychology became an independent faculty of UI.[1] Initially, the psychology program focused on preparing clinical psychologists, with the length of study of 5½ to 6 years. From the beginning, the Faculty of Psychology supported two degree programs for psychology. Graduates from the first program were awarded *Sarjana Muda Psikologi* (a Bachelor of Arts [BA] in Psychology); those from the second program were awarded the psychologist degree, equal to a master's degree (even though it was not so labelled). Only those with the psychologist degree were allowed to practice as a psychologist in all clinical settings. All students in the preparation for the psychologist degree had to successfully complete internships in at least four areas: developmental psychology, industrial and organizational psychology, clinical psychology, and social or experimental psychology. Before the psychologist degree was awarded, students had to write at least two theses to reflect their understanding of how to apply psychological theory to certain phenomena and how to use research methods to analyze psychological data. Graduates were eligible to perform psychological practice after being registered with the Indonesian Psychology Association. Their competencies included (a) administering and interpreting psychological tests; (b) psycho-diagnostics; (c) counseling; and (d) therapy in clinical, child, industrial, and school psychology. It was intended that all students accepted at the Faculty of Psychology of UI would graduate with a psychologist degree. Only under special circumstances (mostly for not meeting the minimum requirements) were students not allowed to continue to the second degree program after they were awarded the BA in Psychology. Those with the psychologist degree were allowed to enroll in the doctoral program, if they wished. In this way, the educational system follows that in the Netherlands, which reflects the 300 years of Dutch colonial history of Indonesia.

Since 1992, the first 4 years of the psychology program has been called the undergraduate program (containing a required thesis); the remaining 2 years are called the professional program (Munandar, 2003). The students in professional psychology can choose to specialize in child psychology, clinical psychology, school psychology, or industrial and organizational psychology. In addition, master's programs in applied psychology and in psychology science are open for those who do not have the undergraduate psychology degree. Currently, the majority of graduates from the undergraduate psychology program choose to work rather than continue with further graduate study and, on average, they gain employment within 3 months of graduation (Career Development Center Universitas Indonesia, 2013). The types of jobs the sample of graduates obtain vary and are not necessarily related directly to

---

[1]Note that the term "Faculty" in Indonesia is roughly equivalent to the term "Department" in the United States.

psychology (e.g., computer programmers, banking officers who analyze data). The majority, however, still work in fields related to psychology (e.g., teaching, training, sales and marketing, research, human resources). More than 55% of the total sample of graduates also reported that they were ready to work and that the knowledge or skills they received through the psychology undergraduate program were appropriate for their job.

Assessment as Required by the National Board of Accreditation for Higher Education

There is no specific format of assessment required by the National Board of Accreditation for Higher Education (Peraturan BAN-PT No 2 Tahun 2017, 2017). For the accreditation procedure (which is repeated every 5 years), each study program has to provide examples of the assessment administered to the undergraduate students. Also, each study program has to assure that the assessments would guarantee the achievement of the appropriate educational goals. Nevertheless, a set of guidelines is provided by the Directorate of Higher Education regarding the competencies required for the graduates of the undergraduate psychology program (Peraturan Presiden nomor 8 Tahun 2012, 2012):

1. Able to apply the knowledge, skills, and technology provided by the undergraduate program to solve problems and able to adapt to the situation one faces;

2. Able to master theoretical concepts related to the discipline and its specific knowledge in certain areas and be able to formulate procedures for problem solving;

3. Able to make decisions based on analyses of information and data and be able to suggest a certain choice among the alternatives, either for oneself or for groups; and

4. Able to be responsible toward one's own job and toward the achievement of the organization's goals.

Because the Faculty of Psychology at UI was the first to offer psychology programs, and other faculties of psychology in Indonesia follow its curriculum, the UI assessment approach provides a glimpse of the overall assessment in psychology in Indonesia.

Assessment as Required at UI

UI does not explicitly outline the types of assessment required of students; rather, it states the general competencies expected as the educational achievement for the students at undergraduate, master's, and doctoral levels. For undergraduate psychology students, the following competencies are expected of graduates:

1. Able to analyze psychological symptoms in individuals, groups, organizations, and communities using the appropriate psychological theories;

2. Able to carry out psychological research on individuals, groups, organizations, and communities; and

3. Able to design an intervention for individuals, groups, organizations, and communities, using the principles of behavioral change.

UI is located in Jakarta, a city of 13 million people; thus, another competency required of alumni of the undergraduate psychology program is the understanding of urbanization and how it can cause certain problems for humans.

There are no specific assessment requirements, as long as each unit has at least two components of assessment throughout the semester. Therefore, it is up to the unit coordinators to design the appropriate assessment for their unit. Note that other faculties of psychology may have other emphases that reflect the uniqueness of their undergraduate programs. For example, the Faculty of Psychology at Universitas Gajah Mada emphasizes the development of Indonesian psychological theories as one goal of their programs (Walgito, 2008); the same faculty also has a center for Cultural and Indigenous Psychology.

How Assessment Is Typically Understood and Practiced

Five lecturers from four faculties of psychology (two from state and three from private universities) shared their experiences with assessments for undergraduate psychology students with one of this chapter's authors. Each has been teaching for at least 11 years in the same faculty. All have received training (delivered by their universities) on unit assessment as part of mandatory preparation to become lecturers. They all agreed that assessment is needed to evaluate whether the educational goals for the unit have been met by each student. To serve this purpose, at least two assessment tasks are given throughout the semester, usually consisting of a test in the middle of the semester and a final test. Some lecturers design their assessments by referring to what is provided by the unit textbooks, whereas others align their unit assessment to the educational goals specified by their respective study program.

The types of assessment also vary: quizzes, midterm tests, final examinations, as well as other assignments for individuals or groups, such as summaries and discussions of certain topics or key terms. Units that have comprehension as the goal have much easier assessment tasks compared with units that have application, analysis, or synthesis as the goal. Feedback and monitoring should be provided to ensure that student achievements are as intended. Group projects (e.g., short observation, a small-scale research project) are often used to reduce the number of assignments that lecturers have to grade; however, for some units, individual projects are preferred to encourage individual achievement of competencies for that unit. For example, in an Academic Writing unit, students are asked to write an introduction and literature review individually to ensure that they have the competency of clear writing. However, because the objective for the Experimental Psychology unit is that students should be able to use various tools in assessing constructs such as attention, perception, and memory, the assessment is a written report of experimental studies they run for younger students. Another problem that each lecturer faces is the enormous amount of time spent to prepare the unit and provide feedback for the assessments; these tasks have to be done by the lecturer alone—there is no tutorial system in Indonesia. Thus, it is not surprising that the favorite type of assessment is multiple-choice question exams. Unfortunately, there is no guarantee that the assessment is appropriate for that specific learning objective, because supervision of curriculum design and delivery never takes place.

Challenges for Psychology in Indonesia

Today, the number of undergraduate psychology programs in Indonesia exceeds 140. With a population close to 250 million, there is a huge need for psychology graduates and not only those with a bachelor's degree (Matindas, 2008). In addition, the practice of psychologists in Indonesia has moved from the clinical setting to nonclinical areas, such as school psychology and social psychology. Ideally, those with a psychology degree, either at the undergraduate or master's levels, can be involved in all areas of psychology, because Indonesia needs people who can apply psychology to solve problems, such as corruption or irresponsible driving (Sarwono, 2008). Most importantly, psychology is needed to educate people to oppose terrorism and to develop psychological responses to the country's frequent natural disasters (Sarwono, 2010).

In conclusion, assessment in undergraduate psychology programs in Indonesia is needed to ensure that graduates have the expected competencies; thus, assessment needs to be focused on the educational goals of each unit, reflecting the targeted competencies of the graduates.

PSYCHOLOGY EDUCATIONAL OUTCOMES AND ASSESSMENT IN ITALY: SLOW BUT TANGIBLE PROGRESS

To practice as a psychologist in Italy, a person needs to be licensed (or registered). As outlined by Job and colleagues (2009), licensure requires 5 years of university education plus an additional year of supervised practice—a system very much in line with the EuroPsy proposal. The EuroPsy project, founded by the European Union and by the European Federation of Psychologists' Associations, provides reference standards for the academic curricula in psychology; it is based on the 3-level framework (bachelor of arts, 3 years; master of arts, 2 years; supervised practice, 1 year). The intention is to provide for the professional competences of psychologists. The framework combines an "input" and an "output" model, the former based on the knowledge and understanding provided by the academic curricula and the latter based on competencies jointly provided by the university and the year of supervised practice, further refined through continuous professional development (e.g., Lunt et al., 2015).

Psychology students who decide to leave the program at the bachelor level (i.e., after 3 years) may apply for a license that allows them to work in activities variously named counseling, psychological support, and education. Few choose this option, both because most of them aspire to become full professional psychologists and because the job market is limited. As a consequence, there is a huge numerical disproportion between fully fledged psychologists and so-called junior psychologists (109,045 vs. 296 as of November 2018; see Consiglio Nazionale dell'Ordine degli Psicologi, 2020). In fact, most students with a bachelor's degree in psychology go on to one of the master's programs that usually cover one of the main professional areas (i.e., clinical, work/organizational, educational, forensic, or neuropsychology). This is a point of difference between Italy and the other countries discussed in this chapter.

The fact that at least some students do exit at the bachelor's level requires establishing outcomes at the undergraduate level that are effective both for enrolling in a relevant master's program as well as for working in counseling and education. Furthermore, it calls for assessment measures able to capture the relevant competencies in both areas.

The outcomes of undergraduate education are generally cast in terms of the Dublin descriptors, which have served as one of the foundations for the creation, in 2005, of the Framework for Qualifications of the European Higher Education Area (Ministry of Science, Technology and Innovation, 2014). They provide statements about typical expectations of achievements and abilities associated with each of the higher education cycles (i.e., bachelor, master, and doctorate). They are phrased in terms of competence levels and consist of the following five components: (a) knowledge and understanding, (b) applying knowledge and understanding, (c) making judgments, (d) communication, and (e) lifelong learning skills. Although the descriptors are a useful frame to characterize competencies in higher education, and they are general enough to subsume a net of interrelated competencies and abilities, they are not cast in terms of learning outcomes, and so most of them fail to specify both the intended subcompetencies (e.g., written communication) and the level at which the competency should be mastered (e.g., nativelike written communication of English as a foreign language). Thus, assessing outcomes in this framework may not be as straightforward as it could be.

Assessment of individuals' outcomes for single (or for a small set of) units within a degree program, as well as the assessment of the end-of-curriculum degree program outcomes, are routinely performed by teaching staff and by departments. Some form of assessment is also performed by universities in order to compare degree programs and departments. Finally, assessment is performed by both governmental agencies and private companies in order to evaluate cross-disciplinary and work-related competencies for new and recent graduates.

In Italy, assessment as a comprehensive, multilevel, and generative tool is receiving considerable attention due to the development of a national assessment procedure by the National Agency for the Evaluation of University and Research (ANVUR, 2018). The assessment focuses on the competencies of new graduates at the bachclor and master's levels, based on the assumption that it may contribute to the monitoring of the quality of the educational process by producing indicators usable for the accreditation and reaccreditation of departments and degree programs. The project (see Rumiati et al., 2018) is called TECO (Test of Competencies) and aims to assess both cross-disciplinary, enabling competencies (TECO-T) and disciplinary, content competencies (TECO-D). The cross-disciplinary competencies are literacy, numeracy (already available), civics, problem solving, and foreign language (English). TECO-D is under development by a working group on psychology. Assessment tapping different levels of competencies and/or different types of competencies is related to what assessment is used for, that is, the specific goals the assessment is supposed to support. Several issues follow from this.

First, outcomes of the assessment should be consistent with the level of competencies evaluated. It may be misleading to draw conclusions at one level considering assessment outcomes at a different level. Second, cross-disciplinary competencies, like those assessed by TECO-T, must be general enough to be detectable in all discipline areas (e.g., mathematics, biology, literature); however, this may leave out the assessment of competencies that, although not strictly disciplinary, may be particularly relevant for specific areas. For psychology, some of the competencies grouped under the umbrella of psychological literacy (Cranney & Dunn, 2011) may be extremely important to assess for undergraduate psychology students and yet pass undetected through TECO-T. Third, some degree of diversity across departments is positive, because it (a) may reflect a department's specialization in an area, hopefully increasing competencies in that area; and (b) allows students to have a fast entry to their area of interest. However, again, assessments may fail to detect such differentiation, which may hamper evaluation of students' competencies. To illustrate, our department values early acquisition of research abilities and motivates students to take an active part in lab meetings, research projects, and so on. If these competencies are not considered when assessing cross-disciplinary outcomes, students may feel a dissonance between what they value and the subject of their assessment.

Fourth, it makes sense to assess undergraduate students for some "work-related abilities" if students have been provided with relevant training opportunities during the curriculum (e.g., experience in the workplace, training with supervision). This is not always possible, as both the health sector and private enterprise prefer master's students over undergraduate students as trainees because of the paucity of positions and the expected higher degree of competencies of the former students. For these reasons, many Italian universities recur to the so-called indirect training: Professional psychologists in different areas of expertise are invited to give seminars and/or short modules on experiential and professional aspects of their work. Although both forms of training may provide information about the workplace of psychologists, only the former allows the acquisition of specific abilities, and the assessment of work-related abilities should thus be consistent with the specific form of training to which students have been exposed.

The fact that assessment is a multifaceted and multilevel enterprise poses problems of consistency and congruency, but it also allows shaping the assessment to the desired goal. Thus, it may be assumed that training in the areas of psychological literacy or in more specific aspects, such as research abilities, results in the acquisition of related competencies that may be part of the outcomes tested at different levels, from specific to general. In this case, the assessment would be viable and fair. However, some relevant and important outcomes may not be detected. A possible solution is to identify assessment tools that vary based on level (e.g., general) and area of knowledge (e.g., behavioral sciences) in such a way as to maximize the congruency between the competencies that have been acquired and the competencies that are tested.

ASSESSMENT IN UNDERGRADUATE PSYCHOLOGY PROGRAMS IN THE UNITED KINGDOM: EVOLUTION, NOT REVOLUTION

Psychology is a popular choice for undergraduate study in the United Kingdom, with approximately 12,000 students graduating with bachelor's degrees every year. However, of the large numbers of psychology graduates, only around 15% progress to further training and careers in professional psychology (i.e., graduate training leading to registration), with the remaining 85% pursuing careers in diverse settings, including health and social care, government, education, business and marketing, and the criminal justice system. Graduate employability and "value for money" are matters of deep concern to the U.K. government, and to students, in the context of student fees (currently £9250 per year for a 3-year degree in England), increasing student debt, and relatively high participation rates in higher education (approximately 48% of 18–21-year-olds; National Statistics, United Kingdom, 2019).

Psychology departments have come under pressure, therefore, to articulate the employability benefits of a psychology degree. The importance of this has been exacerbated given the relatively low proportion of students pursuing careers in psychological professions, and the fact that students take approximately 5 years from graduation to enter their chosen career (Morrison Coulthard, 2017). The pressure for "value" has led to a shift in focus of the undergraduate curriculum, from traditional, science-based, and theoretical to an emphasis on psychological literacy, as well as employability. This process started with a growing awareness of psychological literacy, first in the United States and then in the United Kingdom (Halpern, 2010; Trapp et al., 2011), and has gradually become accepted by educators and students. Hulme and Kitching (2015) conducted focus groups with academics across all four nations of the United Kingdom; they identified trends in psychology higher education and reported that departments were increasingly recognizing the value of applied psychological knowledge and research, as well as thinking about ways in which this could be reflected within the curriculum. This was perceived as an opportunity and a challenge. For example, one participant stated: "Engagement with communities, organisations and business has to be a way forward. How Psychology does that is an interesting one . . . in mainstream psychology, how do we develop what we are terming civic engagement?" (Hulme & Kitching, p. 15). However, large class sizes were seen as a barrier, and some providers were struggling to adjust teaching and assessment methods to incorporate the focus on application: "How you develop modules that can engage three hundred into the communities is more of a bigger challenge" (Hulme & Kitching, p. 15).

Along with the "bottom-up" drive to integrate psychological literacy into the curriculum, the bodies that govern psychology education in the United Kingdom have started to apply "top-down" pressure. In the United Kingdom, the primary curriculum driver is the Quality Assurance Agency (QAA) Subject Benchmark Statement, which defines the core content, skills, and attributes associated with the successful study of any subject in higher education. The most recent QAA Subject Benchmark Statement for Psychology (Quality Assurance Agency, 2019) introduced a new set of guiding principles, including that studying psychology would "lead to an understanding of real life applications of theory to the full range of experience and behaviour and the application of psychological understanding to real world questions" (p. 4). This statement has been incorporated into the accreditation standards for undergraduate psychology of the British Psychological Society (BPS, 2019). In the United Kingdom, students must achieve an accredited undergraduate degree in order to be able to pursue graduate training (to master's or doctoral level, depending on the specialism) to become a professional psychologist registered with the U.K. Health and Care Professions Council (HCPC); thus, the vast majority of U.K. bachelor's degrees are accredited. The psychology curriculum is being pushed toward a more applied focus, motivated by student and academic interests, and reinforced by regulatory bodies. This is also the case in the United States and in Italy, where congruent changes in assessment strategies have not always taken place.

As noted earlier (Biggs, 1996), effective learning requires constructive alignment of learning outcomes, learning activities, and assessments through backward design. A challenge for U.K. psychology departments then has been to realign the curriculum to incorporate psychological literacy into all of these aspects. Since the publication of Trapp and colleagues' (2011) report, the momentum to develop psychological literacy provision has been growing and, alongside application incorporated into learning outcomes and some classroom activities, some programs have begun to move away from traditional modes of assessment (i.e., essays, lab reports, and exams) and to introduce more applied and problem-based assessments, as discussed below. To some extent, though, uptake has been patchy, with pockets of strong practice in some institutions, whilst others still primarily assess achievement through traditional methods.

In part, where practice has changed, there has been recognition of the longer term benefits of learning that can be achieved through coursework assignment assessment, as opposed to examination assessment (e.g., Gibbs & Simpson, 2005), given the transferable nature of the former kind of learning. In psychology departments with a growing focus on employability and psychological literacy, programs are using more coursework assignments, fewer exams, and more modes of continuous and formative assessment. As Gibbs and Simpson (2005) argued,

> Much assessment simply fails to engage students with appropriate types of learning. Submitting a lab report of a teacher-designed lab is unlikely to help students to learn how to design experiments. Probably the only way to learn how to solve problems is to solve lots of problems. Probably the only way to gain facility with the discourse of a discipline is to undertake plenty of practice in using that discourse, for example through writing. Assignments are the main way in which such practice is generated. (p. 12)

In the United Kingdom, assessment is recognized in driving learning as a tool to engage students, stimulate their curiosity, and provoke them into reflection, self-assessment, and self-improvement (Bloxham, 2014). This recognition has moved psychology educators to embed problem-solving skills into assessments. Similarly, there has been a strong focus on enhancing feedback as a tool to promote learning (Winstone et al., 2017).

Early innovations were largely based upon Norton's (2004) Psychology Applied Learning Scenarios and similar approaches. Vignettes were used to present a short case study, in which students were asked to define a problem, offer an appropriate solution, and explain their ideas using psychological theory. For example, students were presented with clinical cases for analysis and asked to recommend treatment or are tasked with observing and finding an approach to support a lecturer with psychological evidence to improve their teaching.

In addition to incorporating applied learning tasks, over time, there has been a shift towards increasing use of authentic assessment (Gulikers et al., 2004), with employers collaborating in setting assessments that reflect real-world problems that graduate employees might be expected to solve in the workplace. An example of this is the "Making a Difference in Psychology" module at Keele University (Kent & Skipper, 2015), in which employers set problem-based assessments (e.g., supporting children in care to enter higher education). Students design an intervention and method of evaluation and write a "research-informed rationale" to explain the psychology underpinning their proposals. Some of the students' submissions have influenced employer practices—they have had "real-world" impact.

Gradually, this sort of approach is becoming more popular within psychology in the United Kingdom, with practical examples presented in a compendium

(Taylor & Hulme, 2015). These cases demonstrate a wide variety of assessment practices, including reflections on placement activities, personal employability, blogging to make psychology accessible to the public, and critically evaluating news stories with reference to original research. Currently, it seems that applied and authentic assessment practices are largely confined to specific modules, rather than cutting across at degree program level (Taylor & Hulme, 2018). However, the growth in applied assessment practices looks set to continue (despite challenges with class sizes) through a process of gradual evolution rather than rapid revolution.

ASSESSMENT IN PSYCHOLOGY DEPARTMENTS IN THE UNITED STATES: A SNAPSHOT OF MORE PROMISE THAN PROGRESS

The assessment of teaching and learning in psychology within higher education in the United States remains an important goal of psychology educators. At present, however, assessment is but one flash point among many that both require and deserve attention from faculty and administrators—others include whether psychology is a good choice for undergraduates and how psychology curricula can better ease students into the workforce. Still, most institutions feel pressure to do some assessment evaluation activities across academic programs in order to satisfy one of the six regional accrediting bodies across the United States (my college, for example, is accredited by the Middle States Commission on Higher Education; https://www.msche.org/), whose role it is to ensure that colleges and universities are delivering on their promise to educate students in ways that will prepare them either to enter the workforce immediately after graduation or to pursue graduate education. If nothing else, such accreditation pressure ensures that psychology departments and programs pursue some assessment activities in order to demonstrate that students are learning within the major and that teaching practices are effective.

One overarching challenge for U.S. colleges and universities is lack of agreement where standardized institutional assessments are concerned. At present, relatively few standardized global assessments are popular—other than, perhaps, the AAC&U Value Rubrics (2019; see Chapter 15, this volume). Simply put, many institutions want their own unique assessment measure(s) that capture the pedagogical goals of their respective mission statements. There is, then, no shared vision for discipline-level assessments, which complicates the normative goals of high-quality assessment practices.

Paths of Assessment Practice in Psychology

Some psychology departments craft their own internal, local assessments tools that are often designed to demonstrate learning linked to particular strengths or academic interests within a program. Such tools can be time consuming to create and validate, but they have the advantage of allowing these departments to focus on and often tout what they do best (e.g., Brito et al., 2004). Other programs adopt an assessment of general learning in psychology tool that can be administered towards the end of students' 4-year degrees in psychology. These assessment tools are available for purchase from purveyors like the Educational Testing Service (ETS; 2020). ETS produces the *Major Field Test for Psychology*, a measure that contains 140 multiple-choice questions reflecting unit content that psychology majors would be expected to acquire over the course of their education (e.g., understanding aspects of experiments, interpreting graphs showing psychological data). The summary data from the test can be used to help a department identify areas where students are clearly learning material (e.g., lifespan development), as well as those where student performance is lacking (e.g., neuroscience). Unit content related to the latter then can be revised, and an evaluation of whether improvement has occurred can be undertaken when future cohorts complete the *Major Field Test for Psychology*.

Between the poles of locally generated and standardized assessments lies a considerable number of resources made available by the APA, chiefly through its Education Directorate. Chief among these resources is the *APA Guidelines for the Undergraduate Psychology Major: Version 2.0* (*Guidelines 2.0*; APA, 2013). The *Guidelines 2.0* contain a framework for teaching and learning linked to four skills-based goals and one content-based goal. Goal 1 (Knowledge Base in Psychology) is content based, as it focuses on outlining the fundamental disciplinary material that psychology majors should learn, understand, and use following their education. Goal 2 (Scientific Inquiry and Critical Thinking) explicates the inferential and methodological skills psychology majors should acquire during their foundational education. Goal 3 (Ethical and Social Responsibility) considers ethical and social skills that students should learn and apply in professional as well as personal situations. Goal 4 (Communication) explores those skills that allow students to demonstrate their oral, written, and interpersonal abilities linked to psychology (e.g., explaining complex research results in lay terms). Finally, Goal 5 (Professional Development) specifically identifies skills linked to teamwork, project management, focused self-reflection, and general career preparation.

Each of the five *Guidelines 2.0* goals contains a set of explicit student learning outcomes that can be tied to measurable behaviors. When a psychology department or program uses the *Guidelines 2.0*, one or two learning outcomes tied to a given goal can be assessed within a particular unit/module. For example, within a capstone seminar (possibly the last required unit in a major curriculum), students could be expected to demonstrate scientific inquiry and critical thinking skills by designing an empirical study tied to an original hypothesis, collecting relevant data, and then interpreting the psychological import of the results and sharing them in oral or written form (which could also be linked to communication skills tied to Goal 4, and so on).

By assessing only a subset of learning outcomes tied to one or two goals in a given unit or units, psychology teachers can focus on demonstrating that their majors are (or are not) acquiring content- or skills-based knowledge deemed to be essential to psychology and its future utility in their lives (i.e., for the workforce or further education). If the assessment data indicate sufficient student learning is taking place among, for example, 80% or 90% of students in a given unit, then no modifications in teaching (or what materials are used) are needed. If, however, the assessment results point to lower knowledge of skills acquisition among the students (e.g., only 60% meet the learning criteria), then the results can be used for major or minor revisions to a given unit, its content, and so on. Such assessment-based interventions ensure that units evolve to meet student needs across time, while also showing that intended learning outcomes are actually being acquired or even exceeded.

Remaining Challenges for Assessment in Psychology in the United States

The main challenge for psychology departments and programs (in addition to the sense that too many demands are being put on faculty beyond those linked to teaching, scholarship, and institutional service) remains actually *using* the data from assessment to "close the loop"—to refine, revise, and improve how teaching occurs in face-to-face, hybrid, or online modes. Too many program directors end up collecting reams of assessment data in a routine manner, but then never use the data to implement changes in their curriculum. Other programs become overly enthused by assessment, do too much of it, and then become exhausted, even "burned out" by the experience—and then react by doing too little assessment evaluation. For effective assessment to achieve a firmer toehold in the United States, the practice of conducting and evaluating authentic assessment must become a routine part of faculty life and be done in moderation, so that modest but effective changes can inform the process of teaching and learning in the psychology classroom. Further discussion of assessment prospects and practices linked primarily to efforts in the United States can be found in Dunn et al. (2004, 2011, 2013).

CONCLUSION AND RECOMMENDATIONS

Interestingly, there appear to be more similarities than differences among the different nations in terms of issues regarding assessment. These points of commonality include:

- some commonality in intended generic and psychology-specific learning outcomes, particularly around a growing emphasis on psychological literacy;

- a reasonably common situation (with exceptions, such as Italy) whereby there are (a) approximately five times as many psychology major graduates as graduate places, and (b) highly diverse career destinations of the majority of graduates;

- a tension in undergraduate programs between providing the basis for a career in professional or research psychology versus a more liberal arts and sciences education;

- national/regional transdisciplinary and disciplinary/professional accreditation body demands (in terms of intended outcomes/competencies and the assessment of these) and the tensions between the transdisciplinary and disciplinary;

- particular research or professional strengths of the individual department, which may not be so easily "showcased" by standardized learning outcome assessment;

- lack of personalization of learning outcomes and their assessment in terms of the individual student's interests; for example, the student may be learning more than what is assessed, and so they may feel that their learning is undervalued;

- the increasing national emphasis on ensuring the value of higher education learning outcomes/competencies in terms of preparation for employment or for graduate study;

- lack of training of faculty in authentic assessment (i.e., a move away from multiple-choice final exams and toward development and assessment of transferable, evidence-based problem-solving skills for application in professional and societal domains);

- lack of resourcing of effective, evaluated authentic assessment at a unit and program level that will both support student motivation to learn and better prepare them for employment and graduate study; and

- the need for innovative solutions to feasible authentic assessment (e.g., technologically supported calibrated self- and peer-assessment).

In terms of differences, there are not many, and these relate more to recommendations for solutions regarding the issues previously raised. These include

- increased emphasis on research training and, in particular, critical thinking skills (the United Kingdom requires an independent research project in its 3-year program, whereas in the U.S. 4-year program, it is not necessarily required)—the minimal aim should be to produce graduates with an appreciation of what is required to undertake rigorous basic and applied research so, at the very least, they are accomplished critics of claims regarding human behavior;

- increased emphasis on assessment of whole-of-program learning outcomes (as can happen in the United States) over and above assessment of unit-level outcomes (the primary emphasis in the United Kingdom and Italy); such assessment should also increase students' awareness of the value of their undergraduate education (this could be measured!);

- increased emphasis on psychological literacy as the international "umbrella" graduate outcome that emphasizes application, including evidence-based strategies for career development learning (Cranney & Morris, 2020);

- explicit delineation of career development learning (APA, 2013); this provides impetus for departments to develop and assess this intended outcome/goal;

- increased emphasis on the development and assessment of undergraduate student capability to address local/national behavioral issues, as is the case in Indonesia (a benefit to the graduate in terms of employability, to the discipline in terms of reputation and, of course, to society in terms of potential solutions to the behavioral issues); and

- increased emphasis on authentic assessment of psychological literacy (as is the case in the United Kingdom, as evidenced by the provision of accessible examples of such; e.g., Taylor & Hulme, 2015, 2018).

In addition, there are recommendations arising from the commonalities, such as

- increased emphasis on personalized assessment; this may vary as a function of entry criteria for programs (e.g., in some Italian undergraduate research-centric programs, the entry is highly selective with few places, and so one might expect higher achievement of research skills; cf. more "liberal-entry" and generalized programs in other countries);

- increased emphasis on both common learning outcomes and some commonality in methods of assessment; note that, although (a) the Bologna-aligned EuroPsy process specified common learning outcomes/competencies and made suggestions for common assessments (Lunt et al., 2011) that have influenced institutional curricula and professional mobility (McElvaney, 2018), and (b) international organizations have specified professional psychology competencies (e.g., International Association of Applied Psychology and International Union of Psychological Science, 2016), national-level licensure/certification for professional psychologists is where the power and resources for assessment and evaluation is based; and

- increased need for training of faculty in authentic assessment and, in particular, in the process of backward design and its evaluation.

Given the often conflicting assessment aims of institutional/regional bodies, or the too-narrow focus of professional psychology bodies, the implementation of these idea may best be achieved by psychology educators working collaboratively through national (e.g., BPS: Undergraduate Education Committee, and Partnership and Accreditation Committee) or international (e.g., European Society for Psychology Learning and Teaching; International Council of Psychology Education) disciplinary/professional bodies to create feasible common and potentially internationally aligned forms of assessment through accreditation or other quality assurance schemes. Moreover, such bodies could promote relevant faculty development through supporting/instigating psychology education conferences, grants, and awards, whereby our evidence-based practice is shared, with the aim of greater student employability and global citizenship, that is, a more applied focus that can benefit society generally.

REFERENCES

American Psychological Association. (2013). *APA guidelines for the undergraduate psychology major: Version 2.0.* https://www.apa.org/ed/precollege/about/psymajor-guidelines.pdf

ANVUR, National Agency of Evaluation of the University System and Research. (2018). *TECO-D/Psychology working group.* https://www.anvur.it/gruppo-di-lavoro-ric/gruppo-di-lavoro-teco-d-psicologia/

Association of American Colleges and Universities. (2019). *VALUE rubrics.* https://www.aacu.org/value-rubrics

Australian Psychology Accreditation Council. (2010). *Rules for accreditation and accreditation standards for psychology courses* (Version 10). https://www.psychologycouncil.org.au/standards_2010

Australian Psychology Accreditation Council. (2019). *Accreditation standards for psychology programs.* https://www.psychologycouncil.org.au/sites/default/files/public/Standards_20180912_Published_Final_v1.2.pdf

Bearman, M., Dawson, P., Boud, D., Bennett, S., Hall, M., & Molloy, E. (2016). Support for assessment practice: Developing the Assessment Design Decisions Framework. *Teaching in Higher Education, 21*(5), 545–556. https://doi.org/10.1080/13562517.2016.1160217

Biggs, J. (1996). Constructive alignment in university teaching. *HERDSA Review of Higher Education, 1,* 5–22. https://tru.ca/__shared/assets/herdsa33493.pdf

Bloxham, S. (2014). Assessing assessment: New developments in assessment design, feedback practices and marking in higher education. In H. Fry, S. Ketteridge, & S. Marshall (Eds.), *A handbook for teaching and learning in higher education: Enhancing academic practice* (4th ed., pp. 107–122). Taylor & Francis. https://www.crcpress.com/A-Handbook-for-Teaching-and-Learning-in-Higher-Education-Enhancing-Academic/Marshall/p/book/9780367200824

British Psychological Society. (2019). *Standards for the accreditation of undergraduate, conversion and integrated Masters programmes in psychology.* https://www.bps.org.uk/sites/www.bps.org.uk/files/Accreditation/Undergraduate%20Accreditation%20Handbook%202019.pdf

Brito, C. F., Sharma, A., & Bernas, R. S. (2004). Assessing student learning using a local comprehensive exam: Insights from Eastern Illinois University. In D. S. Dunn, C. M. Mehrotra, & J. S. Halonen (Eds.), *Measuring up: Educational assessment challenges and practices for psychology* (pp. 209–224). American Psychological Association. https://doi.org/10.1037/10807-011

Bromnick, R., & Horowitz, A. (2013). *Reframing employability: Exploring career-related values in psychology undergraduates* [Paper presentation]. Higher Education Academy: STEM 2013 Annual Meeting, Birmingham, England. https://www.heacademy.ac.uk/system/files/resources/reframing_employability_exploring_career-related_values_in_psychology_undergraduates.pdf

Career Development Center Universitas Indonesia. (2013). *HASIL Tracer study UI 2010.* http://cdc.ui.ac.id/index.php?option=com_content&task=view&id=777&Itemid=121

Clearing House for Postgraduate Courses in Clinical Psychology. (2018). *Application: Numbers.* http://www.leeds.ac.uk/chpccp/numbers.html

Consiglio Nazonale dell'Ordine degli Psicologi. (2020). https://www.psy.it

Cranney, J., Botwood, L., & Mellish, L. (2019). *Student, graduate and employer perspectives on psychology undergraduate education in Australia: A pilot study* [Unpublished manuscript]. The University of New South Wales.

Cranney, J., & Dunn, D. S. (Eds.). (2011). *The psychologically literate citizen: Foundations and global perspectives*. Oxford University Press. https://doi.org/10.1093/acprof:oso/9780199794942.001.0001

Cranney, J., & Morris, S. (2020). Psychological literacy in undergraduate psychology education and beyond [Manuscript submitted for publication]. In P. Graf & D. Dozois (Eds.), *Handbook of applied psychology*. Wiley.

Cranney, J., Morris, S., Levy, N., & Mellish, L. (2018, October). *Career development learning in a capstone course* [Paper presentation]. UNSW Sydney, Learning and Teaching Forum, Sydney, New South Wales, Australia.

Cranney, J., Provost, S., Katsikitis, M., Martin, F., White, F., & Cohen, L. (2008). *Designing a diverse, future-oriented vision for undergraduate psychology in Australia*. http://www.olt.gov.au/resource-future-psychology-unsw-2008

Dunn, D. S., Baker, S. C., Mehrotra, C. M., Landrum, R. E., & McCarthy, M. A. (Eds.). (2013). *Assessing teaching and learning in psychology: Current and future perspectives*. Wadsworth, Cengage Learning.

Dunn, D. S., McCarthy, M. A., Baker, S. C., & Halonen, J. S. (2011). *Using quality benchmarks for assessing and developing undergraduate programs*. Jossey-Bass.

Dunn, D. S., Mehrotra, C. M., & Halonen, J. S. (Eds.). (2004). *Measuring up: Educational assessment challenges and practices for psychology*. American Psychological Association. https://doi.org/10.1037/10807-000

Educational Testing Service. (2020). *ETS major field test for psychology*. https://www.ets.org/mft/about/content/psychology

Gibbs, G., & Simpson, C. (2005). Conditions under which assessment supports students' learning. *Learning and Teaching in Higher Education, 1*, 3–31.

Gulikers, J. T. M., Bastiaens, T. J., & Kirschner, P. A. (2004). A five-dimensional framework for authentic assessment. *Educational Technology Research and Development, 52*, 67–86. https://doi.org/10.1007/BF02504676

Halonen, J. S. (2011). *Are there too many psychology majors? White paper for the State University System of Florida Board of Governors*. cogdop.org/page_attachments/0000/0199/FLA_White_Paper_for_cogop_posting.pdf

Halpern, D. F. (Ed.). (2010). *Undergraduate education in psychology: A blueprint for the future of the discipline*. American Psychological Association. https://doi.org/10.1037/12063-000

Health Education England. (2018). *Mental health*. https://www.hee.nhs.uk/our-work/mental-health

Health Education England. (2020). *Clinical psychologist education funding review*. https://www.hee.nhs.uk/news-blogs-events/news/clinical-psychologist-education-funding-review

Hulme, J. A., & Kitching, H. J. (2015). *Learning and teaching issues in the discipline: Psychology*. British Psychological Society.

International Association of Applied Psychology and International Union of Psychological Science. (2016). *International declaration of core competences in professional psychology*. http://www.iupsys.net/dotAsset/1fd6486e-b3d5-4185-97d0-71f512c42c8f.pdf

Job, R., Tonzar, C., & Lotto, L. (2009). Italian University curricula in psychology: An appraisal of the EUROPSY project. In S. McCarthy, V. Karandashev, M. Stevens, A. Thatcher, J. Jaafar, K. Moore, A. Trapp, & C. Brewer (Eds.), *Teaching psychology around the world* (Vol. 2, pp. 308–317). Cambridge Scholar.

Kent, A., & Skipper, Y. (2015). Making a difference with psychology: Reporting on a module to develop psychological literacy in final year undergraduate students. *Psychology Teaching Review, 21*(2), 35–47. http://eprints.keele.ac.uk/1882/

Lunt, I., Job, R., Lecuyer, R., Peiro, J. M., Gorbena, S., & EuroPsy Steering Group for Psychology. (2011). *Tuning-EuroPsy: Reference points for the design and delivery of degree programmes in psychology*. University de Deusto. http://www.deusto-publicaciones.es/deusto/pdfs/tuning/tuning27.pdf

Lunt, I., Peiró, J. M., Poortinga, Y., & Roe, R. A. (2015). *EuroPsy: Standards and quality in education for psychologists*. Hogrefe.

Matindas, D. S. (2008). Indonesia butuh psikolog, bukan sekedar sarjana psikologi [Indonesia needs psychologists, not only Bachelor of Arts in psychology]. In W. Dahlan, B. Harbunangin, J. A. A. Rumeser, & L. S. Sriamin (Eds.), *Dialog Psikologi Indonesia: Doeloe, kini dan esok* (pp. 79–91). HIMPSI Jaya.

McElvaney, R. (2018). *History of the competency movement in Europe*. https://europsy.eu/_webdata/asppb_history_competency_europe_efpa_oct18.pdf

McGovern, T. V., Corey, L. A., Cranney, J., Dixon, W. E., Jr., Holmes, J. D., Kuebli, J. E., Ritchey, K. A., Smith, R. A., & Walker, S. J. (2010). Psychologically literate citizens. In D. F. Halpern (Ed.), *Undergraduate education in psychology: Blueprint for the future of the discipline* (pp. 9–27). American Psychological Association. https://doi.org/10.1037/12063-001

Middle States Commission on Higher Education. (2020). https://www.msche.org/

Ministry of Science, Technology, and Innovation. (2014). *A framework for qualifications of the European higher education area*. http://ecahe.eu/w/index.php/Framework_for_Qualifications_of_the_European_Higher_Education_Area

Morrison Coulthard, L. (2017). *BPS careers destinations (phase 3) survey, 2016 Report*. The British Psychological Society. https://www.bps.org.uk/sites/bps.org.uk/files/News/News%20-%20Files/Careers%20destination%20survey.pdf

Munandar, A. S. (2003). Proses pengembangan pendidikan psikologi di Indonesia [Process of the development of psychology education in Indonesia]. In M. P. Satiadarma (Ed.), *Perjalanan Emas Pendidikan Psikologi UI* (pp. 70–77). Fakultas Psikologi Universitas Indonesia.

National Statistics, United Kingdom. (2019). *Participation rates in higher education*. https://www.gov.uk/government/statistics/participation-rates-in-higher-education-2006-to-2018

Norton, L. (2004). *Psychology applied learning scenarios*. Higher Education Academy. https://www.heacademy.ac.uk/system/files/psychology-applied-learning-scenarios.pdfPeraturan BAN-PT No 2

Peraturan Presiden nomor 8 Tahun 2012. (2012). *Peraturan Presiden nomor 8 Tahun 2012 tentang Kerangka Kualifikasi Nasional Indonesia*. http://sipuu.setkab.go.id/PUUdoc/17403/Perpres0082012.pdf

Quality Assurance Agency [QAA]. (2019). *Subject benchmark statement for psychology*. https://www.qaa.ac.uk/docs/qaa/subject-benchmark-statements/subject-benchmark-statement-psychology.pdf?sfvrsn=6935c881_13

Rumiati, R. I., Ciolfi, A., Di Benedetto, A., Sabella, M., Infurna, M. R., Ancaiani, A., & Checchia, D. (2018). Key-competences in higher education as a tool for democracy. *Form@re—Open Journal Per La Formazione in Rete, 18*(3), 7–18. https://doi.org/10.13128/formare-24684

Sadler, D. R. (2016). Three in-course assessment reforms to improve higher education learning outcomes. *Assessment & Evaluation in Higher Education, 41*(7), 1081–1099. https://doi.org/10.1080/02602938.2015.1064858

Sarwono, S. W. (2008). Psikologi Indonesia dalam perspektif internasional [Indonesian psychology in international perspective]. In S. W. Sarwono, E. Markum, R. W. Matindas, W. Dahlan, W. W. D. Mansoer, J. A. A. Rumeser, . . . (Eds.), *Dialog Psikologi Indonesia: Doeloe, kini dan esok* (pp. 165–183). HIMPSI Jaya.

Sarwono, S. W. (2010, July 8–11). *Towards an Asian psychology: Learning from Indonesian experience* [Keynote address]. International Conference on Psychology Education, Sydney, Australia.

Tahun 2017. (2017). *Peraturan BAN-PT No 2 tahun 2017 tentang SAN-Dikti*.

Taylor, J., & Hulme, J. A. (2015). *Psychological literacy: A compendium of practice.* http://eprints.keele.ac.uk/1005/1/psychological%20literacy%20compendium%20final2.pdf

Taylor, J., & Hulme, J. A. (2018). An overview of psychological literacy in practice from the United Kingdom. In G. J. Rich, A. Padilla-López, L. K. de Souza, L. Zinkiewicz, J. Taylor, & J. L. S. B. Jaafar (Eds.), *Teaching psychology around the world* (Vol. 4, pp. 362–379). Cambridge Scholars.

Trapp, A., Banister, P., Ellis, J., Latto, R., Miell, D., & Upton, D. (2011). *The future of undergraduate psychology in the United Kingdom.* U.K. Higher Education Academy Psychology Network. https://www.advance-he.ac.uk/knowledge-hub/future-undergraduate-psychology-united-kingdom

van der Molen, H. T., & Visser, K. H. (2008). Accountability of psychology in the Netherlands. In J. E. Hall & E. M. Altmaier (Eds.), *Global promise: Quality assurance and accountability in professional psychology* (pp. 148–163). Oxford University Press. https://doi.org/10.1093/acprof:oso/9780195306088.003.0007

Voudouris, N. J., & Mrowinski, V. (2010). Alarming drop in availability of postgraduate psychology training. *InPsych, 32*, 20–23.

Walgito, B. (2008). Kebanyakan teori masih dari Barat. [Most theories are from the West] In S. W. Sarwono, E. Markum, R. W. Matindas, W. Dahlan, W. W. D. Mansoer, J. A. A. Rumeser, . . . (Eds.), *Dialog Psikologi Indonesia: Doeloe, kini dan esok* (pp. 3–11). HIMPSI Jaya.

Wiggins, G., & McTighe, J. (2005). *Understanding by design* (2nd ed.). Association for Supervision and Curriculum Development. http://isbninspire.com/pdf123/offer.php?id=1416600353

Wilson, T. D. (2009). Know Thyself. *Perspectives on Psychological Science, 4*(4), 384–389. https://doi.org/10.1111/j.1745-6924.2009.01143.x

Winstone, N. E., Nash, R. A., Parker, M., & Rowntree, J. (2017). Supporting learners' agentic engagement with feedback: A systematic review and a taxonomy of recipience processes. *Educational Psychologist, 52*(1), 17–37. https://doi.org/10.1080/00461520.2016.1207538

Workplace Health and Wellbeing, Cornwall. (2019). *How do I become a health and wellbeing champion?* https://www.whwcornwall.co.uk/health-champions/what-is-a-health—wellbeing-champion/

13

Applying the Assessment Design Decisions Framework Internationally

Jacquelyn Cranney, Dana S. Dunn, and Suzanne C. Baker

As the chapters in this volume make abundantly clear, undergraduate psychology assessment efforts are multifaceted and highly diverse. Growth and progress have resulted in a variety of approaches that instructors can tailor to specific learning environments and program goals. In this chapter, we take the view that although our own assessment practices may be adequate and often innovative, and even highly effective, it is useful to learn from others to gain fresh perspectives and ideas.

We define *assessment* as the "graded and non-graded tasks, undertaken by an enrolled student as part of their formal study, where the learner's performance is judged by others (teachers or peers)" (Bearman et al., 2016, p. 547). From a psychology education perspective, assessment includes the reliable and valid measurement of intended learning outcomes, including the appropriate application of psychological knowledge, skills, and attitudes by university-level students.

To help structure our "looking outside the box," we use a framework created by a multi-institutional Australian project on learning-oriented assessment. This approach, the Assessment Design Decision Framework (ADDF), takes an educator "work-as-done" (vs. "work-as-imagined") perspective (Bearman et al., 2016, p. 546). That is, in contrast to education theory or institutional policy, the ADDF is based on research that focuses on the reality of the educator's decision making in local educational contexts.

https://doi.org/10.1037/0000183-014
Assessing Undergraduate Learning in Psychology: Strategies for Measuring and Improving Student Performance, S. A. Nolan, C. M. Hakala, and R. E. Landrum (Editors)

More specifically, Bearman and colleagues (2016) identified three levels of assessment decision making: (a) policy level (e.g., institutional policy prescribing that the maximum number of assessments for any unit should be three)—these decisions are often made by leaders or managers who are no longer responsible for unit/module design or delivery; (b) unit-level design decisions made by a unit convener or an instructional team (e.g., determining that there should be weekly formative quizzes, each worth a small percentage of the final grade, and that all 12 quizzes are described as one form of assessment for the purposes of meeting institutional policy requirements); and (c) decisions about student assessment performance, usually by casual or sessional tutors (e.g., marking an essay by making evaluative judgements against a rubric).

To illustrate the difference between "work as imagined" (e.g., as determined by policy and/or educational theory) and "work as done" (i.e., how educators actually make assessment design and delivery decisions), here is an example from one coauthor's experience. Driven by educational theory and research, Cranney and Morris (2018) saw the need to create a capstone unit for senior undergraduate psychology students that (a) allowed students to integrate and apply knowledge from diverse areas of psychology, and (b) supported students in their career development learning. During the design phase of this unit, it was clear that the research (work as imagined) pointed toward work-integrated learning (WIL) as being a learning, teaching, and assessment (LTA) strategy that would meet these two needs (especially the latter). The unit designers rejected that approach on the basis that their local School of Psychology culture would be unlikely to ever support the necessary staff resources to run WIL, which usually involves intensive interaction with industry partners. Thus, a less authentic LTA strategy, involving in-house career development learning and reflection, was chosen (work as done). More recently, draft institutional policy has signaled that WIL is to be a significant part of every degree program (work as imagined). In attempting to at least partly meet the intent of this policy decision, we have recently integrated an "informational interview" requirement (work as done) in the career development learning component. The informational interview requires that students locate a person in a career position that they aspire to, interview that person, and then write a guided reflection on the experience. This compromise LTA strategy allows a slightly more authentic assessment than the previous LTA strategy and has not significantly impacted on the limited resources available. In summary, resource constraints at the assessment delivery level means that "work as imagined" is not possible, so a compromise results in "work as done."

In this chapter, we provide ideas, examples, and critiques from several international sources, with the aim of stimulating innovative and effective assessment decision making and practice at the front line of assessment. It should be noted that, in considering student acquisition of learning outcomes, a number of input factors, such as learning environment and student effort, are acknowledged and discussed where appropriate. We first introduce the

ADDF, then we highlight international assessment practices where relevant, and finally we provide some conclusions and recommendations that are linked to the adoption of some selected assessment practices.

OVERVIEW OF THE ADDF

Bearman and colleagues (2016) argued that although in theory it is desirable to focus on learners and their experience of assessment, in reality it is the educator who usually makes decisions about assessments. These decisions are often difficult, given the multiple constraints on educator practice, including institutional policy and increasing demands on educators' time (Walvoord, 2004). The ADDF aims to keep the focus on both the learner's experience and the educator's reality. In the following sections, we briefly consider the categories of the ADDF and provide ideas, examples, and critiques, including international perspectives, and how these can be applied to undergraduate psychology education.

The ADDF is composed of six categories of factors that influence and structure assessment-related decisions. Briefly, these categories include (a) purposes of assessment (e.g., promoting student learning; providing grades as a measure of learning; developing graduates' capacity to make evaluative judgments); (b) learner outcomes (e.g., of unit or program, of professional competency requirements); (c) contexts of assessment (e.g., student characteristics, institutional policies, program characteristics, mode of instruction); (d) tasks (e.g., student assignments that develop and demonstrate learning) and their characteristics; (e) feedback (purposes, opportunities, characteristics); and (f) interactions (e.g., the relationships between the assessment task and student or instructor attitudes). We refer readers to Bearman and colleagues (2016) for a complete description of the framework.

PURPOSES OF ASSESSMENT

Why assess teaching and learning? In the first place, and arguably most importantly, assessment can support student learning. By "support," most educators mean that there is some evidence that particular pedagogical practices have actually led to the retention of key discipline-based information and related skills by students. Such assessment support provides a source of confidence for students, families (who are often paying for their education), degree-granting institutions (who seek to meet their advertised objectives), boards of trustees or regents (who are obligated to ensure an institution is credibly educating its students), and accrediting bodies for higher education. More than that, routine assessment is a means for ensuring that materials and methods for teaching units in undergraduate psychology curricula are being updated on the basis of student performance. In other words, what is working well is retained, and practices or content that are problematic are revised in the next iteration of a unit.

Such ongoing assessment is related to a second concern, the assignment of grades, which represents a summative assessment of student learning. Generally speaking, the grades students earn serve to certify their learning within the discipline (i.e., generally, higher grades correspond to greater learning). Grades and, eventually, an accompanying degree (or multiple degrees) inform potential employers and graduate schools that students have demonstrated discernable levels of learning and acquired particular expertise within their chosen field. Of course, many employers and postgraduate programs are more interested in students' continued ability to learn than they are in grades per se (at least until the latter fall to some point on the grading continuum where the link to knowledge and skill acquisition may be in doubt).

The problem with exclusive reliance on unit grades as summative assessments is that they are often biased toward retention of unit content (i.e., facts, declarative knowledge) and rarely focus on more authentic assessments that involve complex cognitive functioning (e.g., the application of knowledge and skills to solving complex problems). As is appropriate to higher education, many educators prefer to use authentic activities, but it is often the case that such activities can only be feasibly used in formative assessments. Such activities require students to use the knowledge they have gained in realistic tasks that reflect the application of ideas (e.g., using a particular psychological theory to explain the nature of some novel behavior, using research and writing skills to craft a persuasive speech aimed at reducing problem behaviors).

This notion of application is important because it is linked to a third purpose of assessment noted in the ADDF: equipping learners for future judgments. One of the real challenges for assessment is showing that psychological knowledge and skills gained in one domain can be successfully transferred to other domains. Can students use their knowledge to identify and interpret related behaviors in distinctly different situations, at different times, and in other places? High-quality assessments enable students the opportunity to display deep learning, where concepts can be readily applied to new situations in order to offer psychological insights. Would-be employers and graduate programs also value this third arena of evidence, where classroom learning is shown to be applicable to real world challenges.

Psychology educators in the United States have long called for greater reliance on authentic assessments rather than more summative assessments aimed at tracking low-level knowledge. However, the former are more challenging to create from scratch, whereas the latter are often available as standardized tests that can readily be used to survey students and then be quickly scored and analyzed. Both approaches to assessment have their merits, of course, but giving students the opportunity to behaviorally demonstrate what they have learned may better represent learning outcomes than do "paper and pencil" measures.

Still, there is much to assess—performance within the major in particular units, learning in the all-important introductory unit (the only exposure to psychology for the vast majority of college and university students), and capstone unit experiences where psychology majors ideally tie together learned material from their previous unit work into some elaborate final project (e.g., literature review paper, experiment, oral presentation or poster session presentation, service learning project). Ideally (work as imagined), psychology educators should expend efforts deciding when and where more authentic assessments are most appropriate and where low-level summative measures best fit the need. Given the reality that some universities have final-year undergraduate classes of over 600 psychology major students, however, the challenge is to find scalable solutions to conducting more authentic assessments. Recent work in medical education, whereby artificial intelligence enables objective video-based measures of medical students' communication capacity with simulated patients (Liu et al., 2019), allows us to believe that technological solutions may help to provide some solutions in the medium to long term. In the meantime, although it is a challenge, educators should continue to develop reasonable assessments that approach the desired outcomes.

Although educators can follow the five educational goals laid out in the helpful and popular *American Psychological Association Guidelines for the Undergraduate Psychology Major 2.0* (APA, 2013) or the APA's nascent Introductory Psychology Initiative, they are free to adopt alternative perspectives, such as that of psychological literacy (i.e., the capacity to intentionally apply psychological principles to achieve personal, professional, and societal goals; Cranney & Dunn, 2011a). Teachers can assess psychological literacy by examining how students apply psychological knowledge and skills to their daily lives—to how they function in the workplace, in their personal lives, and in their wider social context (Hulme & Cranney, in press). Cranney et al. (2011) gave many examples of how this can be readily achieved within the undergraduate psychology curriculum. For example, after studying learning theories, students could perform a content analysis of print, televised, and online media advertisements in order to identify the particular learning principles being applied in each media outlet. Taylor and Hulme (2018) compiled an *International Edition of the Psychological Literacy Compendium*, which gives examples of learning, teaching, and assessment strategies from several nations (see the Tasks, Feedback Processes, and Interactions section of this chapter); moreover, the https://www.psychliteracy.com/resources webpage is currently being populated with examples of diverse international practice.

LEARNER OUTCOMES

The ADDF asks the question "How does assessment align with, and promote, desired learner outcomes, including: (1) unit/module learning outcomes; (2) overall program learning outcomes; (3) professional requirements; and (4) learners' general professional or intellectual development" (Bearman et al., 2016, p. 552)? The first reference point for any educator should be: What should the student learn in this unit—what are the intended learner/learning outcomes? However, as Bearman and colleagues (2016) pointed out, there "are little data that reveal the reasons for educators' assessment choices" (p. 546), which suggests that the educators themselves may not be clear regarding what they want the student to learn and why. Indeed, learner outcomes should first be specified for the entire program, and the unit-by-unit support of the gradual development of those outcomes should be mapped across the program, both to ensure a scaffolded learning experience and to demonstrate to accreditation bodies where the intended learning outcomes or competencies are being assessed and how (e.g., Australian Psychology Accreditation Council, 2019, Domains 3 and 5).

Thus, in considering assessment, psychology educators need to first identify intended outcomes for undergraduate psychology. In the United Kingdom, psychological literacy has been specified by the accreditation body as a general learning outcome, and Hulme and Cranney (in press) provided LTA examples at both the unit and program level. This approach meets all of the ADDF learner outcome alignment facets (Bearman et al., 2016), although, in reality, the United Kingdom work has only recently begun.

The U.S. *Guidelines for the Undergraduate Psychology Major 2.0* (*Guidelines 2.0*; APA, 2013) specify the following five program learning goals, of which the first refers to content and the other four are skills-oriented: (a) knowledge base, (b) scientific inquiry and critical thinking, (c) ethical and social responsibility in a diverse world, (d) communication, and (e) professional development. Each goal has a set of explicit student learning outcomes that can be tied to measurable behaviors, and the *Guidelines 2.0* provide example contexts where foundational learning (what students new to the major can reasonably be expected to know and demonstrate) and baccalaureate indicators (what senior majors can be expected to know and demonstrate) can be assessed. Further, successful learning linked to each goal can be described by appropriate action verbs (e.g., students who have acquired professional development skills can be characterized as "collaborative" and "efficient").

Are there other tools available that can be used to validly and reliably assess these learning goals? *The Assessment CyberGuide for Learning Goals and Outcomes* (*CyberGuide*; APA Education Directorate, 2009) is a resource designed to support the *Guidelines* and their implementation. Materials shared within the *CyberGuide* aim to help departments and faculty members create and implement appropriate assessment plans that will provide fruitful results. Other assessment resources include *Using Quality Benchmarks for Assessing and Developing Undergraduate Programs* (Dunn et al., 2011), *Assessing Teaching and Learning in Psychology: Current and Future Perspectives* (Dunn et al., 2013), and *Measuring Up: Educational Assessment Challenges and Practices for Psychology* (Dunn et al., 2004).

In terms of the development and assessment of the *Guidelines 2.0* learning goals, perhaps the most notable shortcomings are in the everyday application of knowledge (see Subgoals 1.2, 1.3; for more details, the reader can refer to the original document linked in the reference list), incorporating sociocultural factors in scientific inquiry (i.e., Subgoal 2.5), demonstrating positive interpersonal skills (i.e., Subgoals 3.2, 4.3, 5.4), adopting values that build communities at local, national, and global levels (i.e., Subgoal 3.3), and demonstrating self-management (i.e., Subgoal 5.2) and career literacy (i.e., Subgoals 5.1, 5.5) (see the ADDF reference to general professional development as a learning outcome; Bearman et al., 2016). To be sure, these learning outcomes are challenging to assess, a situation that may reflect a lack of positive motivation on the part of psychology educators or perhaps a lack of negative motivation (i.e., punitive incentives) associated with regulatory or accrediting bodies. Certainly, it will take time, funds, and creativity to develop and reliably/validly assess many of the learning outcomes tied to the five goals.

As an example of the challenges involved, let's take "demonstrating positive interpersonal skills," a quality relevant to three APA subgoals. There are three aspects to consider here. First, what is the psychological science linked to effective interpersonal skills? Does it entail, for example, forming and then maintaining/improving positive interpersonal relationships? If so, these aspects are clearly a part of Goal 1 (knowledge base). Secondly, psychology educators need to construct learning environments where evidence-based skills can be acquired across several units, allowing for the scaffolding of increasingly complex skills. Thirdly, there is the requirement for assessing both the knowledge related to and the evidence-based skills tied to positive interpersonal skills.

Fortunately, there are well-established good practices for developing (e.g., Dunlosky et al., 2013) and assessing (e.g., Boud, 2010) psychology's knowledge base. Thus, if educators are motivated to learn about and implement these practices (e.g., by providing opportunities for developing mastery of the discipline's declarative knowledge through online interactive multiple-choice testing), then it is the student's responsibility to study effectively to succeed within the parameters of such assessments. However, in terms of actual *skill* development and assessment, there may be several barriers, including guidance for educators as to how to most effectively provide students with opportunities to develop these skills (but see Morris et al., 2018, for some introductory techniques) and a lack of time and space in the curriculum. For example, if the educator is to assess specific "in vivo" interpersonal skills for each student, how will this be accomplished? As a comparison, the highly resource-intensive Objective Structured Clinical Examination (OSCE; e.g., Norris et al., 2017; Ross et al., 1988) involves realistic scenarios for the assessment of clinical skills in a small number of clinical psychology graduate students. How can such a high-validity assessment approach be created and feasibly implemented for the hundreds of students often enrolled in an undergraduate class? Similar issues have been raised with the recently revised undergraduate competency of interpersonal and teamwork skills that must be assessed as part of program accreditation (Australian Psychology Accreditation Council, 2019). Valid and reliable assessment of complex skill-based learner outcomes (work as imagined) may fail when faced with the realities of poor resource allocation and workplace culture (work as done).

One answer may be in what the Association of American Colleges & Universities (AAC&U) has provided by way of rubrics for key graduate capabilities, including demonstrating teamwork (AAC&U, 2019; see also Polly et al., 2018, for an example within Australian medical sciences education). The use of these rubrics could be integrated into units where team or group work is integral to the related learning, teaching, and assessment strategies. It also may be possible that the actual assessment could be undertaken by peers, with the occasional or capstone authentication of such skills by teachers, perhaps facilitated by technology (e.g., teamwork performance being assessed through computerized recognition of evidence-based constructive communication behavior; see Liu et al., 2019).

Finally, there is the development and assessment of the values underlying the "positive" in "positive interpersonal interactions," which is obviously connected to aspects of Goal 3. Like skills, values are most validly assessed through behaviors. Within the degree program, there could be scaffolding of the development of these values-in-action—starting with classroom simulations, and culminating in capstone experiences. Such scaffolded LTA activities should lead to the development and assessment of professional skills for all psychology graduates, thus addressing the general professional facet of the ADDF learner outcome assessment alignment requirement (see Bearman et al., 2016).

Clearly, a whole-program approach is necessary to adequately scaffold learning experiences, and innovative approaches to *feasible*, valid, and reliable assessment of these interpersonal skills are required. There appear to be few innovative examples that efficiently assess the capacity for positive interpersonal relationships in psychology undergraduate education, although one example that could be scaled up is presented by Hammar Chiriac et al. (2018). This gap gives a clear focus for future work that could benefit many psychology programs.

In terms of international perspectives on learning outcomes and their assessment, Cranney et al. (2020) conclude that there is considerable overlap in the intended learning outcomes of undergraduate programs internationally. This was also recognized by McGovern and colleagues (2010) in their initial conceptualization of psychological literacy as the congruence of international lists of learning outcomes. Other countries have perhaps realized earlier than the United States the importance of assessing the *application* of knowledge, skills, and attitudes, as can be seen in their accreditation standards and program aims (e.g., Indonesia: Sarwono, 2011; United Kingdom: Quality Assurance Agency, 2016). However, U.S. psychology educators should take pride in their current *Guidelines 2.0*, which emphasizes both broader societal issues (Goal 3) and evidence-based career-related skills (Goal 5). The former goal is perhaps the focus of excitement for many beginning college and university students; the latter goal is perhaps the realistic focus of mature-aged students and parents of younger students. Regardless, we must, through our assessment practices, support student acquisition of these intended learning outcomes through the programmatic approach of the ADDF (Bearman et al., 2016).

It is to our great advantage to share innovative practices, given the common constraint of resources, and the many contextual considerations, which we highlight in the next section.

CONTEXTS OF ASSESSMENT

There are many "contexts" that influence assessment. One of the most challenging noted by the ADDF, and the one that we focus on here, is "Departmental, disciplinary and personal norms, expectations and ideas" (Bearman et al., 2016). The *Guidelines 2.0* is a student-centered document (work-as-imagined), but it is the department or program and its faculty who design and deliver the curriculum and who determine opportunities for student learning, including assessment activities (work-as-done). How committed are the department chair, undergraduate degree program director, and associated instructors to the idea that maximizing opportunities for student acquisition of the program learning outcomes is paramount? Balancing this agenda with other demands on their time can be challenging, and it is still the case that many faculty members adopt a Social Darwinian approach to their teaching (i.e., survival of the fittest—perhaps more prevalent in countries where higher education is free to the student) or see teaching as a major imposition on their research time. In terms of psychology, not enough department chairs realize that providing an education that is valued by graduates could have major positive impacts on the reputation of the science and profession of psychology (Crowe, 2012), particularly when 3.5% of U.S. majors are psychology majors (National Center for Education Statistics, 2015–2016). A key point here is that psychology graduates pursue highly diverse careers (e.g., Dunn & Halonen, 2017) and so have the potential to have broad societal impact. Thus, making explicit the value of psychological science to personal, professional, and societal goals through authentic learning, teaching, and assessment strategies should be a key goal for every department chair.

TASKS, FEEDBACK PROCESSES, AND INTERACTIONS

We briefly address selected aspects of the last three ADDF categories in this section by giving some "task" examples from the literature and by commenting on aspects of feedback and interactions, including the educator–assessor's rationale for the assessment task and reflection on the feasibility of the assessment task (design and delivery). Note that Bearman and colleagues (2016) provided a framework within which many U.S. educators already practice; nevertheless, we have chosen some tasks from other countries to illustrate these aspects of the ADDF.

Firstly, Bearman and colleagues (2016) stated that "assessment always acts as an intervention into student learning . . . feedback processes are critical to effective learning through assessment . . . iterative opportunities for learners to incorporate feedback is a key component of the learning process" (p. 547). One example of feedback processes in practice is Broadbent et al.'s (2018) study in a large Australian undergraduate health psychology class, which involved three written assessments (same structure, different topics) during the session. The introduction of highly moderated and timely audio feedback for each of these assessments led to both a significant improvement in student evaluations of the unit and a progressive increase in student grades.

Second, and relatedly, Bearman and colleagues (2016) claimed that "assessment practices should develop learners' own capacities to evaluate their own work to prepare them for future challenges beyond the support of teachers and courses" (p. 547). For example, in a study conducted in Taiwan, Sung et al. (2003) instructed undergraduate students to use web-based self- and peer-assessment procedures to integrate the writing and evaluation of proposals for psychology experiments. Students submitted their draft proposal through a web portal and self-assessed their proposal along a number of dimensions. Students were assigned to small groups and then individually peer-rated the proposals of their other group members. They then discussed their self- and peer-ratings and then self- and peer-rated a second time. This was followed by a group defense of their revisions to the whole class, after which they received whole-class general feedback from the instructor on student comparative performance. Finally, students revised and resubmitted their proposals. Instructors rated both the draft and final proposals using the same criteria, and, as hypothesized, the ratings on the final proposals were higher than those of the draft. The interrater reliability of the group members' ratings also increased after their discussion. The authors concluded that the self- and peer-assessment and group discussion procedure could "help students to elaborate their experiment design knowledge" (p. 333), as indicated by the increased final proposal grade. Note that there was no comparison group that did not undertake this procedure. In terms of Bearman and colleagues' assertions above, these results imply that students can learn that peer-assessment and peer-discussion could improve knowledge, self-knowledge, and self-assessment, and that this process could be generalized to other contexts (e.g., the work-place). Note also that this kind of practice provides feedback on the student's first draft, in line with Bearman and colleagues' first assertion.

In another study conducted in Taiwan, Chen (2010) made the argument that mobile self- and peer-assessment systems, using explicit assessment criteria, provided considerable flexibility and, in particular, allowed multiple opportunities for reflection on feedback; it thus also allowed students to work toward improved assessment outcomes. Essentially, Chen argued that the "benefit of self- and peer-assessment [is that] students engage in learning by internalizing academic standards and by making judgments about their own and peer performance in relation to these standards" (p. 230). Students in this study improved performance across the peer-feedback rounds, although there was still a significant mismatch between final student and instructor rankings, which suggests that the degree of internalization was not adequate. Chen stated that this informs further work, which is in line with the "interactions" ADDF category. Note that in this study there was not a comparison group.

In an example from Belgium and the Netherlands, Dochy et al. (1999) made the point that there is a growing demand for lifelong learning and for practitioners who are able to reflect continuously and critically upon their own professional behavior and learning processes. On the basis of their review of studies on self-, peer-, and coassessment, they concluded that the use of a combination of these assessment forms "encourages students to become more responsible and reflective" (p. 331), thus building their capacity for adaptive professional behavior. The authors gave guidelines for educators, but the main messages from this review are that assessment should support learning and should prepare students for professional life.

In a study conducted in Canada, Jhangiani (2016) asked psychology students in a brief assessable "practice" exam to double-blindly peer-assess two students' responses and to discuss their assessment with a fellow student who had undertaken that same peer assessment. Half the students undertook this peer assessment exercise before the subsequent ("real") exam and half afterwards. The former students did better than the latter, even when class attendance and previous academic performance were taken into account. This experimental study supports the benefits of peer-assessment and feedback (Bearman et al., 2016), as well as spaced learning and repeated testing (Dunlosky et al., 2013).

These findings are generally congruent with an early study by Falchikov (1986) in the United Kingdom that required students to collaboratively construct the marking rubric for their psychology essays and then mark their own essays. The system produced primarily positive results and led to the author's conclusion that

> students found that the schemes of both self and peer assessment made them think more, learn more, and become more critical and structured. . . . Furthermore, they found the scheme challenging, helpful and beneficial, in spite of being hard and time-consuming." (p. 161)

In a similar study conducted in Hong Kong, Mok et al. (2006) came to similar conclusions based on increases in metacognitive functioning—students became more aware of their own learning processes.

Coulson et al. (2007) in a U.K. study argued that self-reflection is the basis for critical thinking, and they presented a two-dimensional matrix for conceptualizing reflection tasks. Note that although students are often required to self-reflect, they are not given guidance in how to do so—this paper provided such guidance. Coulson and colleagues integrated reflective exercises, including self-assessment, into a psychology unit and found that these students performed better on (identical) assessments compared to students from the previous cohort who did not have reflection exercises. These researchers illustrated the value of self-reflection (which included self-assessment). As indicated above, this contributed to the students' capacity to be reflective professional practitioners, which is particularly relevant to Goal 5 (career development learning) of the *Guidelines 2.0* (APA, 2013).

In summary, although in this section we have focused primarily on assessment tasks that require self-, peer-, and coassessment, these illustrate not only the value of various forms of feedback but also the importance of the educator–assessor in taking a scientist–educator approach (Bernstein, 2011) to both their choice and evaluation of their assessment tasks (this relates to Bearman et al.'s, 2016, notion of "interaction"). As Bearman et al. (2016) emphasized, however, the feasibility of that assessment task for not only the student but also the educator needs to be a central aspect of the decision process.

ADOPTING AND ADAPTING INTERNATIONAL ASSESSMENT PRACTICES IN PSYCHOLOGY PROGRAMS: MODEST PROPOSALS AND RECOMMENDATIONS

It is often acknowledged that changing assessment practices is difficult from a top-down institutional and national guidelines approach (Bearman et al., 2016; Sadler, 2016). For example, some educational institutions have been slow to adopt routine assessment practices unless encouraged—or compelled—to do so by regional accrediting bodies (e.g., AAC&U, Middle States Commission on Higher Education, Southern Association of Colleges and Schools).

The ADDF introduced here acknowledges that educators at the front lines often resist imposed changes (whether evidence-based or not) to their assessment practices (see Bearman et al., 2016). Educational contexts are highly complex, and there are many stakeholders with different motivations, ranging from the student who wants to learn or who just wants the degree to accreditation/quality assurance bodies and the higher education institutions that must show compliance with those standards. Bearman and colleagues (2016) concluded with five propositions to guide effective assessment approaches, which again illustrate the complexities of assessment decision-making: (a) benefit the learner but support the educator; (b) design is individual but also distributed; (c) holistic design processes blend with strategic decisions; (d) think conceptually, relationally, and pragmatically; and (e) think locally but also outside the proverbial box.

We believe that psychology educators can feasibly consider taking steps to best serve their programs and students, as well as to solidify their assessment practices. To begin, we recommend that departments focus on promoting and assessing psychological literacy as a primary motivator for both psychology educators and their students (Cranney & Dunn, 2011b; Hulme & Cranney, in press). This is "thinking beyond the square" as recommended by Bearman and colleagues (2016, p. 554), in that doing so will emphasize the importance of demonstrating how practical and applicable skills acquired in the psychology major can inform students' future careers, postgraduate educational plans (if any), and personal lives. In other words, educators could champion and document those aspects of psychological science that enhance daily living—

a choice that does not preclude also tracking the more traditional metrics linked to the psychology curriculum (e.g., knowledge of unit content). From this perspective, for example, showing how students learn to (a) exercise self-management skills and relatedly, and (b) promote well-being of the self and others is an important goal that could be assessed (Morris et al., 2018). Given the increasing concerns in our international communities about promoting health and well-being and about preventing severe psychological distress, this would seem a worthwhile goal from an international perspective and one worth sharing strategies for development and assessment.

We also urge department chairs and program directors to concentrate on filling in the gaps in the development and assessment of learning goals in psychology. All too often energy is directed at data collection rather than the subsequent use of assessment results to revise and refine what happens in the classroom or in online teaching. This aspect of assessment is often referred to as "closing the loop," and it can very often be the important task that is overlooked or forgotten in the rush to measure student performance. Department chairs must also be cognizant of what assessment practices can feasibly be undertaken by their faculty members.

In conclusion, we hope that our discussion of assessment using the ADDF to throw a light on international practice will inform department chairs and university and college education leaders, so that they are better able to support those at the front lines of assessment.

REFERENCES

American Association of Colleges & Universities. (2019). *VALUE rubrics*. https://www.aacu.org/value-rubrics

American Psychological Association. (2013). *Guidelines for the undergraduate psychology major: Version 2.0.* https://www.apa.org/ed/precollege/about/psymajor-guidelines.pdf

American Psychological Association Education Directorate. (2009). *The assessment cyberguide for learning goals and outcomes* (2nd ed.). https://www.apa.org/ed/governance/bea/assessment-cyberguide-v2.pdf

Australian Psychology Accreditation Council. (2019). *Accreditation standards for psychology programs*. https://www.psychologycouncil.org.au/standards_review

Bearman, M., Dawson, P., Boud, D., Bennett, S., Hall, M., & Molloy, E. (2016). Support for assessment practice: Developing the Assessment Design Decisions Framework. *Teaching in Higher Education: Critical Perspectives*, *21*(5), 545–556. https://doi.org/10.1080/13562517.2016.1160217

Bernstein, D. (2011). A scientist–educator perspective on psychological literacy. In J. Cranney & D. S. Dunn (Eds.), *The psychologically literate citizen: Foundations and global perspectives* (pp. 281–295). Oxford University Press.

Boud, D. (2010). *Assessment 2020: Seven propositions for assessment reform in higher education*. Australian Learning and Teaching Council. https://www.uts.edu.au/sites/default/files/Assessment-2020_propositions_final.pdf

Broadbent, J., Panadero, E., & Boud, D. (2018). Implementing summative assessment with a formative flavour: A case study in a large class. *Assessment & Evaluation in Higher Education*, *43*(2), 307–322. https://doi.org/10.1080/02602938.2017.1343455

Chen, C.-H. (2010). The implementation and evaluation of a mobile self- and peer-assessment system. *Computers & Education*, *55*(1), 229–236. https://doi.org/10.1016/j.compedu.2010.01.008

Coulson, M., Torrance, S., & Nunn, S. (2007). Fostering reflective thinking with the Learning Achievement Self-Evaluation Record (LASER). *Psychology Learning & Teaching, 6*(1), 12–19. https://doi.org/10.2304/plat.2007.6.1.12

Cranney, J., & Dunn, D. S. (2011a). Psychological literacy and the psychologically literate citizen: New frontiers for a global discipline. In J. Cranney & D. S. Dunn (Eds.), *The psychologically literate citizen: Foundations and global perspectives* (pp. 3–12). Oxford University Press. https://doi.org/10.1093/acprof:oso/9780199794942.003.0014

Cranney, J., & Dunn, D. S. (Eds.). (2011b). *The psychologically literate citizen: Foundations and global perspectives.* Oxford University Press. https://doi.org/10.1093/acprof:oso/9780199794942.001.0001

Cranney, J., Hulme, J., Suleeman, J., Job, R., & Dunn, D. (2020). *Undergraduate psychology education and assessment: International perspectives* [Manuscript submitted for publication].

Cranney, J., & Morris, S. (2018). Undergraduate capstone experiences and psychological literacy. In G. J. Rich, A. Padilla-López, L. K. de Souza, L. Zinkiewicz, J. Taylor, & J. L. S. B. Jaafar. (Eds.), *Teaching psychology around the world* (Vol. 4, pp. 306–328). Cambridge Scholars Press.

Cranney, J., Morris, S., Martin, F. H., Provost, S., Zinkiewicz, L., Reece, J., Milne-Home, J., Burton, L. J., White, F. A., Homewood, J., Earl, J. K., & McCarthy, S. (2011). Psychological literacy and applied psychology in undergraduate education. In J. Cranney & D. S. Dunn (Eds.), *The psychologically literate citizen: Foundations and global perspectives* (pp. 146–164). Oxford University Press. https://doi.org/10.1093/acprof:oso/9780199794942.003.0041

Crowe, S. (Ed.). (2012). *Psychology 2020: The 2011–2012 presidential initiative on the future of psychological science in Australia.* Australian Psychological Society. https://www.psychology.org.au/publications/inpsych/2012/october/crowe

Dochy, F., Segers, M., & Sluijsmans, D. (1999). The use of self-, peer and co-assessment in higher education: A review. *Studies in Higher Education, 24*(3), 331–350. https://doi.org/10.1080/03075079912331379935

Dunlosky, J., Rawson, K. A., Marsh, E. J., Nathan, M. J., & Willingham, D. T. (2013). Improving students' learning with effective learning techniques: Promising directions from cognitive and educational psychology. *Psychological Science in the Public Interest, 14*(1), 4–58. https://doi.org/10.1177/1529100612453266

Dunn, D. S., Baker, S. C., Mehrotra, C. M., Landrum, R. E., & McCarthy, M. A. (Eds.). (2013). *Assessing teaching and learning in psychology: Current and future perspectives.* Wadsworth, Cengage Learning.

Dunn, D. S., & Halonen, J. S. (2017). *The psychology major's companion: Everything you need to know to get where you want to go.* Worth.

Dunn, D. S., McCarthy, M. A., Baker, S. C., & Halonen, J. S. (2011). *Using quality benchmarks for assessing and developing undergraduate programs.* Jossey-Bass.

Dunn, D. S., Mehrotra, C. M., & Halonen, J. S. (Eds.). (2004). *Measuring up: Educational assessment challenges and practices for psychology.* American Psychological Association. https://doi.org/10.1037/10807-000

Falchikov, N. (1986). Product comparisons and process benefits of collaborative peer group and self assessments. *Assessment & Evaluation in Higher Education, 11*(2), 146–166. https://doi.org/10.1080/0260293860110206

Hammar Chiriac, E., Rosander, M., & Wiggins, S. (2018). Enhancing psychological literacy through a group selection exercise. In J. Taylor & J. Hulme (Eds.), *International edition of the psychological literacy compendium* (pp. 10–12). http://eprints.bournemouth.ac.uk/30425/1/International%20edition%20Psychological%20Literacy%20Compendium%20Final.pdf

Hulme, J., & Cranney, J. (in press). Psychological literacy and learning for life. In J. Zumbach, D. Bernstein, S. Narciss, & G. Marsico (Eds.), *International handbook of psychology learning and teaching.* Springer International.

Jhangiani, R. S. (2016). The impact of participating in a peer assessment activity on subsequent academic performance. *Teaching of Psychology, 43*(3), 180–186. https://doi.org/10.1177/0098628316649312

Liu, C., Lim, R., Taylor, S., & Calvo, R. A. (2019). Students' behavioural engagement in reviewing their tele-consultation feedback within an online clinical communication skills platform. *Computers in Human Behavior, 94*, 35–44. https://doi.org/10.1016/j.chb.2019.01.002

McGovern, T. V., Corey, L. A., Cranney, J., Dixon, W. E., Jr., Holmes, J. D., Kuebli, J. E., Ritchey, K. A., Smith, R. A., & Walker, S. (2010). Psychologically literate citizens. In D. F. Halpern (Ed.), *Undergraduate education in psychology: A blueprint for the future of the discipline* (pp. 9–27). American Psychological Association. https://doi.org/10.1037/12063-001

Mok, M. M. C., Lung, C. L., Cheng, D. P. W., Cheung, R. H. P., & Ng, M. L. (2006). Self-assessment in higher education: Experience in using a metacognitive approach in five case studies. *Assessment & Evaluation in Higher Education, 31*(4), 415–433. https://doi.org/10.1080/02602930600679100

Morris, S., Cranney, J., Baldwin, P., Mellish, L., & Krochmalik, A. (2018). *The rubber brain: A toolkit for optimising your study, work, and life.* Australian Academic Press Group.

National Center for Education Statistics, Institute of Education Services. (2015–2016). *Enrollment in postsecondary education, by level of enrollment, level of institution, student age, and major field of study: 2015–16.* https://nces.ed.gov/programs/digest/d17/tables/dt17_311.60.asp?current=yes

Norris, K., Matthewson, M. L., Van Niekirk, L., Bruno, R. B., & Scott, J. L. (2017, September 15–17). *Objective Structured Clinical Evaluations (OSCEs) in postgraduate psychology training programs: The future of competency-based assessment?* [Paper presentation]. AusPLaT-Australian Psychology Learning and Teaching Conference, Ipswich, Queensland, Australia. http://ecite.utas.edu.au/118000

Polly, P., Yang, J. L., Jones, N., Thai, T., Luo, A., Herbert, C., Lewis, T., Vickery, R., Richardson, A., & Schibeci, S. (2018). The teacher–student journey: Program-wide teamwork skills development and evaluation in the medical sciences. *The International Journal of Assessment and Evaluation, 24*(4), 1–24. https://doi.org/10.18848/2327-7920/CGP/v24i04/1-24

Quality Assurance Agency for Higher Education (QAA). (2016). *Subject benchmark statement: Psychology. October 2016.* https://dera.ioe.ac.uk//27668

Ross, M., Carroll, G., Knight, J., Chamberlain, M., Fothergill-Bourbonnais, F., & Linton, J. (1988). Using the OSCE to measure clinical skills performance in nursing. *Journal of Advanced Nursing, 13*(1), 45–56. https://doi.org/10.1111/j.1365-2648.1988.tb01390.x

Sadler, R. D. (2016). Three in-course assessment reforms to improve higher education learning outcomes. *Assessment & Evaluation in Higher Education, 41*(7), 1081–1099. https://doi.org/10.1080/02602938.2015.1064858

Sarwono, S. W. (2011). An Indonesian perspective on psychological literacy. In J. Cranney & D. S. Dunn (Eds.), *The psychologically literate citizen: Foundations and global perspectives* (pp. 178–190). Oxford University Press. https://doi.org/10.1093/acprof:oso/9780199794942.003.0046

Sung, Y.-T., Lin, C.-S., Lee, C.-L., & Chang, K.-E. (2003). Evaluating proposals for experiments: An application of web-based self-assessment and peer-assessment. *Teaching of Psychology, 30*(4), 331–334. https://doi.org/10.1207/S15328023TOP3004_06

Taylor, J., & Hulme, J. (Eds.). (2018). *International edition of the psychological literacy compendium.* https://static1.squarespace.com/static/57058d3cf850825efa99f692/t/5a9882230d929772c8d6cc12/1519944233794/International+edition+Psychological+Literacy+Compendium+Final.pdf

Walvoord, B. E. (2004). *Assessment clear and simple: A practical guide for institutions, departments, and general education.* Jossey-Bass.

14

Measuring the Generic Skills of Higher Education Students and Graduates

Implementation of the CLA+ International

Doris Zahner, Dirk Van Damme, Roger Benjamin, and Jonathan Lehrfeld

In many parts of the world, higher education systems are going through a process of transformation. Technological changes and associated developments in the economy and labor markets have pushed the demand for high-skilled workers and professionals to unprecedented levels. Higher education has become the most important route for the human capital development of a country. Higher education is the part of the learning trajectory where young people acquire the higher levels of generic and specific skills that are needed in the knowledge economy. At the individual level, a higher education qualification still offers the prospect of significant benefits in employability and earnings, despite the fact that, in most countries, the enrollment and graduation rates have increased massively. The higher education system also plays an important role in developing the social and emotional skills needed to become effective citizens able to participate in the social and political processes of developed economies. Higher education attainment rates also correlate strongly with indicators of social capital and social cohesion, such as interpersonal trust and volunteering. But how do we know that higher education systems and individual institutions effectively fulfill this role of developing the skills that matter?

The Organisation for Economic Cooperation and Development (OECD), whose mission is to promote policies that will improve the economic and social well-being of people around the world, has an assessment of foundation skills called the Survey of Adult Skills (more formally called the Program for

https://doi.org/10.1037/0000183-015
Assessing Undergraduate Learning in Psychology: Strategies for Measuring and Improving Student Performance, S. A. Nolan, C. M. Hakala, and R. E. Landrum (Editors)

the International Assessment of Adult Competencies [PIAAC]). The PIAAC measures skills such as literacy, numeracy, and problem solving in digital environments. Results from PIAAC studies have demonstrated that higher education qualifications, the most commonly used measure of human capital, are a poor indicator of the actual skills level of the population (OECD, 2016). There is also growing evidence that qualifications do not match skills (McGowan & Andrews, 2015).

In contrast, the OECD has an international large-scale assessment of 15-year-old students' academic performance in mathematics, science, and reading (in their native languages) in secondary school systems. This assessment, the Programme for International Student Assessment (PISA), has been administered to students in participating countries since the year 2000 and currently has over 75 participating countries. Whereas PISA has become the global benchmark of learning outcomes of 15-year-old students, and hence of the quality of school systems, there is no valid and reliable measure of learning outcomes of higher education students and graduates.

This puts a severe strain on the credibility of higher education systems and institutions to effectively develop the skills that matter for today's and tomorrow's knowledge economy and society. Massification (unprecedented growth) and grade inflation further underscore doubts regarding the value of degrees and qualifications. There are signs that global employers have begun to distrust university qualifications and have developed their own assessment tools and procedures to test students for the skills that they think are important. Also, governments worry that both the overall cost and the per-student cost is rising, confronting universities with concerns about efficiency and "value-for-money." Additionally, there is an increasing shift of the balance in the funding mix of higher education from public to private sources, thereby increasing the cost for students and families. Students end up paying more for the degree they hope to earn—then they also become stakeholders in the value-for-money debate (Lomas, 2007; Woodall et al., 2014).

In essence, these developments point to a transparency problem in higher education similar to what economists identify as an "information asymmetry" problem (Van Damme, 2015). The system provides little information to the user (the student), the stakeholders (taxpayers, employers), or the government. Data-driven transparency systems in higher education overly rely on metrics related to the research function of universities. The rankings built on such systems define the power balances in the global higher education arena and drive the reputation race, without addressing the teaching and learning function of universities or of the vast bulk of institutions serving the large majority of students below the absolute global top.

In this context, the interest in direct assessment of learning outcomes is rapidly growing. In recent years, various approaches have been developing, among them the Collegiate Learning Assessment + (CLA+) International, developed by the Council for Aid to Education (CAE). Endorsed by the OECD, the CAE has enrolled a significant number of postsecondary institutions in several countries to participate in the launch of CLA+ International, an assessment of generic skills. In this chapter, we illustrate the relevance of and outline the process for developing and administering a higher education generic skills assessment in an international context.

THE CASE FOR GENERIC SKILLS ASSESSMENT

Institutions of higher education around the world are being challenged to improve instruction so that tomorrow's workforce will have the knowledge and skills necessary to meet the demands of modern careers and contribute to the global economy. Indeed, a higher education degree has never been more necessary for productive participation in society. Employers now seek individuals able to think critically and communicate effectively to meet the requirements of the new knowledge economy (Hart Research Associates, 2006; Levy & Murnane, 2004; Tremblay et al., 2012). Therefore, the skills taught in higher education are changing; more emphasis is being placed on so-called generic skills (Clanchy & Ballard, 1995; Crebert et al., 2004; Hart Research Associates, 2013; Kearns, 2001), such as analytic reasoning and evaluation, problem solving, and written communication.

Because generic skills are so critical to workforce productivity, one of the best alternatives to solve the globally problematic skills mismatch issue (Montt, 2015) is to emphasize the development of generic skills in the education and training of all students. This will equip them to "learn field- or job-specific skills on the job."

This alternative is aligned with and supports the most basic rationale for focusing on generic skills. In the knowledge economy, where the service sector is dominant, definitions of knowledge and learning have shifted from an emphasis on content to the ability to apply what one knows to new situations. Human capital, the most important asset nations have, includes the knowledge, education, experience, and skills a nation's citizens possess. In today's knowledge economy, this privileges the ability to access, structure, and use information not merely recall facts. This places the focus squarely on the importance of generic skills in every occupation.

MEASURING GENERIC SKILLS

Increasing recognition of the essential role of generic skills in the knowledge economy portends significant changes in teaching and learning, as reflected in the educational reform movement now underway and assisted by education technology. Although this reform movement is present in elementary and secondary education, most advances have occurred in higher education in Europe and the United States. The reform movement can be characterized along three dimensions: (a) the shift from the long-standing lecture format to a student-centered approach emphasizing students' active class participation, (b) the change in the balance of curricular and textbook focus from its current emphasis on content to case and problem-based materials requiring students to apply what they know to novel situations, and (c) the innovation in assessment instruments from multiple-choice tests that are best used for measuring the level of content absorbed by students to open-ended assessments that are aligned with several goals of the reform initiative (Hillman et al., 2015; Jacobs & van der Ploeg, 2006; McLendon, 2003).

Although significant advances have been made on the first two dimensions of this educational reform movement (Wright, 2011), assessment has lagged behind (Ku, 2009). As universities focus increasingly on developing generic skills in their students, assessments need to evolve to measure how well students are learning—and institutions are teaching—such skills. The recall, recognition, and regurgitation paradigm is no longer sufficient.

Multiple-choice and short-answer assessments remain the dominant testing regime, not only for facts but also for generic skills (Liu et al., 2014). As a result, in higher education and elsewhere, the testing regime is not assessing the most critical skills required in the workplace and—just as importantly—is not supporting the other two dimensions of reform. We believe the promise of educational reform developing in today's knowledge economy cannot be achieved without employing open-ended, performance-based assessments, not only in higher education, but in primary and secondary education as well as other points along the education-to-work continuum (Lai, 2011; Liu et al., 2014). In the workplace and in contemporary human resources management approaches to recruitment, selective and upskilling performance-based assessments have become standard practice, as in so-called assessment centers.

Another important advantage of performance assessments is that they are seen as tests worth teaching to (Benjamin & Klein, 2006). The practice of "teaching to the test" is generally frowned upon when referring to traditional multiple-choice and short-answer assessments (Lazear, 2006; Moloney, 2006; Popham, 2001; Volante, 2004), but there is ample evidence that this practice occurs, especially when educators are held accountable for their students' test performance. However, "teaching to the test" for performance assessments should be encouraged. That is, class time spent preparing students to apply knowledge and analysis and problem-solving skills to complex, real-world problems is time well spent. If performance assessments are integrated into accountability systems, this has the potential to encourage teachers to foster the development of competencies in generic skills. This effect has yet to be established, so it would be worthwhile to investigate whether the introduction of performance assessment for accountability purposes has the desired effect. One potential barrier to investigate is the perceived level of effort required to use performance assessments regularly.

In addition to negative effects on pedagogy, a critical shortcoming of today's assessment regime is that it pays little attention to how much an institution contributes to developing the competencies students will need after graduation.

For instance, the outcomes that are typically looked at by higher education accreditation teams, such as retention, graduation rates, and percent tenured faculty, say nothing about how the school fosters the development of its students' analytic reasoning, problem-solving, and communication skills. This situation is unfortunate, because the ways in which institutions are evaluated significantly affect institutional priorities. If institutions were held accountable for student learning gains and student achievement, they would likely direct greater institutional resources and effort toward improving teaching and learning. All these conditions point to the need to support advances in performance assessment. If the human capital school demonstrates the importance of education, the implications of the knowledge economy and recent theories of learning place the focus on improving generic skills in the next generation of students. These developments create an urgent need to generate and implement a testing paradigm that measures and simulates these skills. To address this need, there is an excellent opportunity to demonstrate the effective use of performance assessment to measure generic skills through the use of CLA+ International.

CLA+: PERFORMANCE-BASED ASSESSMENTS OF GENERIC SKILLS

The CLA+[1] is a performance-based assessment of critical thinking and written communication. Traditionally, the Collegiate Learning Assessment (CLA) was an institutional-level assessment that measured student learning gains (Klein & Benjamin, 2008; Klein et al., 2007), specifically using a value-added model (Steedle, 2010a, 2012) within a university. The CLA employed a matrix sampling approach, under which students were randomly distributed either a Performance Task (PT) or an Analytic Writing Task, for which students were allotted 90 min and 75 min, respectively. The CLA PTs presented real-world situations in which an issue, problem, or conflict was identified, and students were asked to assume a relevant role to address the issue, suggest a solution, or recommend a course of action based on the information provided in a document library. Analytic Writing Tasks consisted of two components— one in which students were presented with a statement around which they had to construct an argument (Make an Argument), and another in which students were given a logically flawed argument that they then had to critique (Critique an Argument).

In its original form, the utility of the CLA was limited. Because the assessment consisted of just one or two responses from each student, reliable results were only available at the institutional level, and students' results were not directly comparable. Likewise, reporting for the CLA was restricted to the purposes of its value-added measure; institutions were not eligible for

---

[1]https://cae.org/flagship-assessments-cla-cwra/cla/

summary results, unless they had tested specified class levels in the appropriate testing windows.

Thus, the CLA+ was created, which contains a PT similar to the original CLA PT as the anchor of the assessment. There is an additional set of 25 selected-response questions (SRQs) to increase the reliability of the instrument (Zahner, 2013) for reporting individual student results. (The CLA+ does not include the analytic writing tasks of the CLA.) The SRQ section is aligned to the same construct as the PT and is intended to assess higher order cognitive skills rather than the recall of factual knowledge. Similar to the PT, students are presented with a set of questions and one or two documents to refer to when answering. The supporting documents include a range of information sources (e.g., letters, memos, photographs, charts, newspaper articles). Each student receives both components (PT and SRQ) of the assessment.

Subscores

The CLA+ has six separate subscores. The open-ended student responses from the PT are scored on three subscores (ranging from 1 to 6): (a) Analysis and Problem Solving, (b) Writing Effectiveness, and (c) Writing Mechanics.[2] The SRQs also consist of three subsections: (a) Scientific and Quantitative Reasoning, (b) Critical Reading and Evaluation, and (c) Critiquing an Argument. Students have 60 minutes to complete the PT and 30 minutes to complete the SRQs. There is a short demographic survey following the assessment, which should take 15 minutes to complete.

Additionally, CLA+ includes a new metric in the form of mastery levels. The mastery levels are qualitative categorizations of total CLA+ scores, with cut scores that were derived from a standard-setting study (Zahner, 2014). The five mastery level categories are: Below Basic, Basic, Proficient, Accomplished, and Advanced. CLA+ International is the translated and adapted version of the U.S. domestic CLA+.

Distribution of Mastery Levels by Race/Ethnicity

One of the first studies using CLA+ was a 1-year postgraduation longitudinal survey that followed students from U.S. institutions who had taken the CLA+ in the spring of 2014. CAE also surveyed the employers of students who were able to provide their managers' contact information and asked about the importance of the skills measured by CLA+. The first major study of the longitudinal data (Zahner & James, 2016) revealed unsurprising results. In previous research, Arum and Roksa (2014) had found better outcomes for engineering and computer science majors, but only by comparison to the bleak outcomes of their fellow student graduates. In comparison, Zahner and James reported that CLA+ was found to be a positive predictor of postuniversity

[2]https://cae.org/images/uploads/pdf/CLA_Plus_Scoring_Rubric.pdf

outcomes as measured by employment, full-time employment, salary, or enrollment in a graduate school program (Zahner & James, 2016). However, there are racial biases with respect to hiring, salary, and enrollment in continuing education. White, male business majors had the best postuniversity outcomes when compared with other students. These biases, though, may be conflated with whether students from underrepresented or minority groups attend selective or nonselective colleges.

Race/Ethnicity by Generic Skills by Institution Competitiveness

Race/ethnicity was self-reported by students in the demographic survey from the CLA+. Four categories were selected for analysis: Asian; African American/Black, non-Hispanic; Hispanic or Latino; and White, non-Hispanic. Students were also categorized into two groups on the basis of their mastery of the skills measured on CLA+: those proficient in critical thinking and written communication and those with only basic or below basic skills. The final variable was whether the student attended a competitive or noncompetitive institution (Barron's College Division Staff, 2014). Figure 14.1 depicts these results.

Basically, there are large proportions of minority students who have proficient and above mastery of the critical-thinking and written-communication skills attending noncompetitive institutions. Approximately 35% of African American/Black (non-Hispanic) and 25% of Hispanic or Latino students attending these noncompetitive institutions have proficient, accomplished, or advanced skills. Although these proportions may not seem large, the number of minority students in less- or noncompetitive institutions far exceeds the

FIGURE 14.1. Distribution of CLA+ Proficiency and Institution Competitiveness by Race/Ethnicity

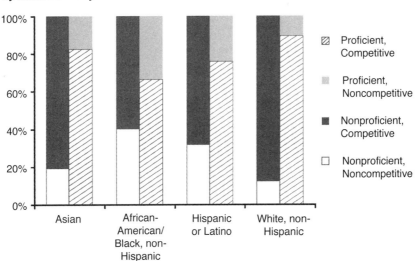

Note. CLA+ = Collegiate Learning Assessment +.

number who attend the competitive institutions. This means that there is a significantly large group of qualified university graduates from under-represented or minority groups who may be overlooked as viable candidates due to the school they attended.

Benchmarking Students From Universities

As an extension of the above analysis on race/ethnicity and university competitiveness, there are approximately 144 competitive higher education institutions in the United States, with 950,000 places for undergraduate students (Barron's College Division Staff, 2014). The remaining 13 million to 14 million 4-year students attend less competitive or noncompetitive institutions that are largely public or not renowned. About 30% of the students in the competitive universities fall into the high-ability category as measured by the CLA+, as compared with 9% of the students in the less competitive colleges (Benjamin, 2015). However, simple arithmetic indicates that there are approximately 1.2 million high-ability students in the less-competitive institutions versus 300,000 in the selective ones (see Figure 14.2). As a point of reference, the average CLA+ score for graduating seniors in the 2017–2018 academic year was $M = 1101$ ($SD = 71$; CAE, 2018). The 1.2 million high-ability students in the less competitive institutions with generic skills similar to their counterparts in the competitive colleges do not get the opportunity to compete for the higher value-added jobs for which their skills qualify them, because the employers do not know how to find them.

Grade inflation has made the undergraduate degree less useful in discriminating students' absolute skills (Rojstaczer & Healy, 2012), so employers settle on students from selective (branded) colleges. The OECD finds similar

FIGURE 14.2. Projected National Student Attendance and CLA+ Total Scores

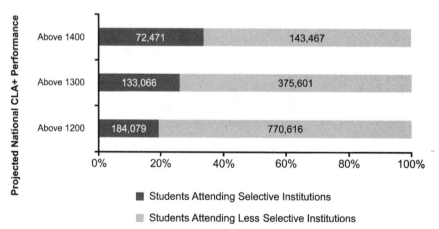

Note. CLA+ = Collegiate Learning Assessment +. Reprinted with permission from the Council for Aid to Education.

problems in their research of grade inflation globally (OECD, 2016). This example illustrates just how many students who are proficient in critical thinking are potentially being overlooked because the playing field for hiring is not level. Many of these students, as shown in Figure 14.1, are from under-represented groups, typically first-generation university students or ethnic minorities. These individuals would be great candidates to employ and also to help organizations fulfill their goal to increase diversity. Oftentimes, organizations are not able to identify these individuals due to their lack of awareness that these talented and able candidates are attending these less selective institutions. Organizations recruit from the same set of institutions from which they have previously recruited, but this doesn't help with the goal of increasing workforce diversity. CLA+ offers an opportunity to close this gap.

There are potentially millions of students graduating from these institutions (Benjamin, 2015) who are proficient in the skills that employers say they desire (Hart Research Associates, 2013, 2015). Given that there is increasing enrollment at these non- and less selective institutions, which have higher proportions of minority students (Benjamin, 2015), employers should expand their recruitment searches beyond the elite colleges and universities in order to have a representative and diverse workforce.

Employers could also consider hiring students from varied fields of study for entry-level positions. It appears that business majors are more likely to obtain full-time positions within 3 months of graduation (Zahner & James, 2016). However, these students have the lowest CLA scores and grade point averages (GPAs; Steedle & Bradley, 2012). If employers want to hire candidates with generic skills (Hart Research Associates, 2013, 2015), they should seek candidates with degrees in the social sciences, humanities and languages, and science and engineering fields of study. This will also increase diversity in the workplace, because students coming from varied fields of study will bring different perspectives to a team, which has been shown to be true when applied to diversifying based on gender (Badal, 2014) and other demographics (Ellemers & Rink, 2016; Herring, 2009; Woolley et al., 2015).

Researchers from this current study offer support for the conclusion that critical-thinking and written-communication skills are important in predicting career placement and workplace success (Arum & Roksa, 2014). Additionally, assessments like the CLA+ serve as effective instruments for identifying high-achieving students from less- and noncompetitive institutions and making their skills more visible to employers. High-performing students who attend non- and less-competitive institutions do, in fact, have the same critical-thinking skills as do their peers at competitive institutions (Hoxby & Avery, 2012). Future studies will include continued longitudinal tracking of this cohort of students, as well as surveys of employers who have hired graduates with verified skills. This will likely corroborate evidence of the findings from this study, furthering the validity of these skills as predictors of postcollege outcomes.

What Do the Employers Think?

In a follow-up study to Zahner and James (2016), CAE asked the 2014 longitudinal survey participants for the contact information of their manager or graduate advisor. The 89 managers/advisors who agreed to participate were asked how important they felt analysis and problem solving, writing effectiveness, and writing mechanics were for their employees. They were also asked to rate the students who were participating in the longitudinal survey on these skills and to rank students' performance compared with other recent college graduates within their organization. Only a small subset of participants' employers provided this information for the students they advised/managed; however, they were demographically relatively similar to the original cohort of students, with the exception of having slightly higher average GPA and SAT scores (Table 14.1). The survey consisted of a series of questions (Table 14.2) regarding the importance of critical thinking and written communication skills to successful performance by the student, the proficiency of the student as measured by these skills, and how the student ranked in comparison with his or her peers in the workplace or graduate program. Results indicated that employers and graduate advisors indeed found critical thinking and written-communication skills to be important, as measured by analysis and problem solving, writing effectiveness, and writing mechanics (see Figure 14.3).

Additionally, Table 14.3 shows the ordinal logistic regression coefficients, their standard errors, the 95% confidence intervals, and the t-statistics ($p > .001$ for all analyses). The regression coefficients can be interpreted as the log-odds of being rated higher given a 1-point increase in CLA+ total score. For instance, in the analysis and problem-solving model, the estimated coefficient is given as .0033. Thus, for a 1-point increase in CLA total score, the log-odds of "jumping" to a higher rating category ("Good" instead of "Satisfactory or worse," or "Outstanding" instead of "Good") increase by .0033. The regression coefficients are small because CLA+ total scores are on a large scale (400–1,600), so one extra point is not expected to make much of a difference. Two factors would increase the interpretability of the results: (a) using a more meaningful score increase (e.g., 50 points), and (b) converting the log-odds to odds by exponentiating the coefficient. Thus, if one student scored 50 points higher than a second student, the log-odds of being rated one category higher than the second student would be 50 * .0033 = .165, and the odds would be

TABLE 14.1. Demographic Descriptive Statistics

Demographics	Employer surveys	All participants
N	89	21,513
% Female	66.3	60.0
% White	66.3	59.2
% English primary language spoken at home	89.5	84.5
% Parent with at least bachelor's degree	66.2	51.9
Mean (*SD*) cumulative GPA (out of 4.0)	3.37 (.45)	3.24 (.48)
Mean (*SD*) SAT (or converted ACT)	1114 (153)	1066 (172)

TABLE 14.2. Employer Survey Questions

How important are the following skills to successful performance in the participant's position:	1 = Unimportant	2 = Of little importance	3 = Moderately important	4 = Important	5 = Very important
Analysis and problem solving					
Writing effectiveness					
Writing mechanics					

How would you rate the participant on the following skills:	1 = Unsatisfactory	2 = Needs improvement	3 = Satisfactory	4 = Good	5 = Outstanding
Analysis and problem solving					
Writing effectiveness					
Writing mechanics					

	1 = Well below other employees	2 = Below other employees	3 = About the same as other employees	4 = Above other employees	5 = Well above other employees
Overall, where does the participant's performance rank compared with other recent college graduates in your workplace?					

FIGURE 14.3. Distribution of Responses to "Importance" Question

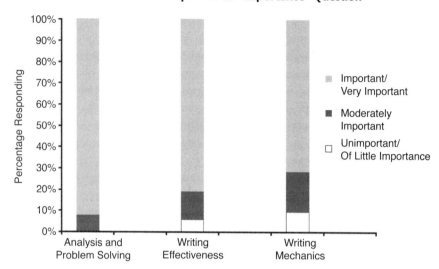

exp(.165) = 1.18. This first student would be 18% more likely than the second student to be rated one category higher ("Good" rather than "Satisfactory or worse," or "Outstanding" rather than "Good") due to the higher CLA+ total score.

The students with higher scores from their managers and advisors tended to have higher CLA+ scores. This is important to note because despite approximately 1.8 million individuals graduating within the United States each year (Hussar & Bailey, 2014), employers are still finding a skills gap (Hart Research Associates, 2015). We offer support for the conclusion that critical-thinking and written-communication skills are seen by hiring managers and employers as important for success in the workplace (Hart Research Associates, 2006, 2013). These findings offer additional evidence that these skills are important

TABLE 14.3. Ordinal Logistic Regression Models for Predicting Participants' Postcollege Performance as Measured by Their Managers or Graduate Advisors

Covariate	Est. coefficient	Std. error	*t*-statistic	95% CI Lower	Upper
		Analysis and problem solving			
CLA+ Score	.0033	.0002	14.33	.0029	.0038
		Writing effectiveness			
CLA+ Score	.0043	.0002	18.36	.0039	.0048
		Writing mechanics			
CLA+ Score	.0046	.0002	19.33	.0041	.0051
		Rank comparison of participant			
CLA+ Score	.0049	.0002	22.18	.0045	.0053

Note. Estimated coefficients are log-odds of being rated one category higher given a 1-point increase in CLA+ total score. CLA+ = Collegiate Learning Assessment +.

in predicting career placement and workplace success (Arum & Roksa, 2014). CLA+ can serve as an effective instrument not only for identifying those high-achieving students but also for making their critical-thinking and written-communication skills more visible to prospective employers, thereby allowing employers to identify skilled individuals who may be overlooked in a talent search based solely on GPA and the brand name of their institution.

IMPLEMENTATION OF CLA+ IN AN INTERNATIONAL CONTEXT

Due to CAE's abundant research and development (Benjamin, 2008, 2014, 2015; Klein & Benjamin, 2008; Klein, Liu, et al., 2009; Klein et al., 2013; Steedle, 2010a, 2010b, 2010c; Steedle et al., 2014; Zahner, 2013, 2014; Zahner & James, 2016; Zahner, Ramsaran, & Steedle, 2012; Zahner & Steedle, 2014, 2015) and the quality of the CLA+ instrument for measuring higher education students' generic skills, in March 2016, the OECD and CAE entered into an agreement to collaborate on CLA+ International. The goal was to attract a sufficient number of international participants for the first administration to support a strong research design, which was intended to address some of the major challenges encountered in OECD's Assessment of Higher Education Learning Outcomes (AHELO) Feasibility Study (OECD, 2013a; Tremblay et al., 2012), such as motivation, sampling, and scoring equivalency (Zahner & Steedle, 2014). The AHELO study attempted to measure teaching quality globally in three different strands and is often described as the higher education equivalent to PISA, discussed earlier. Two of the strands, engineering and economics, were domain specific, but the third was considered to measure "generic skills." The CLA was used to anchor the generic skills strand.

In the international context, institutions are facing the same challenges that their counterparts encounter in the United States. More students are entering university than ever before (OECD, 2013b). Grade inflation has been reported internationally (Bachan, 2017; OECD, 2016; Wissenschaftsrat, 2012), and graduates must find employment. Anecdotally, researchers in these countries report that the graduation rates for students are problematic, because students remain in school to continue to receive support. Students who may be unable to obtain employment postgraduation are not necessarily motivated to graduate. Perhaps employers globally are also finding it difficult to identify qualified students. An assessment like CLA+ International might be able to close the gap between students seeking employment and employers seeking personnel.

CAE and the OECD completed implementation of CLA+ International for the 2017–2018 academic year. The process of implementing CLA+ International was developed following best-practice recommendations (American Educational Research Association, American Psychological Association, & National Council on Measurement in Education, 2014), as well as recommendations about improvements and modifications to address some of the limitations of the AHELO Feasibility Study (OECD, 2012; Tremblay et al., 2012).

Sampling

Because the goal of CLA+ International is not to be a feasibility study, not all participating countries and institutions need to follow the same exact model of assessing their students' generic skills. CLA+ International allows for multiple sampling models to accomplish the specific goals of the institutions and ministries. If participants are interested in using the cross-sectional model, then CAE recommends sampling and testing 200 entering students and 400 exiting students in the same year. This will yield an institutional-level measure of student learning gains within 1 academic year. If participants are interested in using the longitudinal model, then CAE recommends annually sampling and testing 600 entering students tracked longitudinally. This will yield both student and institutional measures of student learning gains. However, this will take up to 3 or 4 academic years to yield results.

A hybrid sampling plan is also recommended, which requires a minimum of 2 years. During the first year, institutions sample 500 incoming (longitudinal cohort) and 100 exiting (cross-sectional cohort) students. The subsequent years require sampling a minimum of 100 entering and 100 exiting students to maintain the cross-sectional cohort, as well as the persisting 500 students from the original longitudinal cohort. This model will yield both student and institutional measures of student learning gains, but institutional measures will be available within 1 academic year.

Translation and Adaptation

Translation and adaptation of a performance assessment is a process that is more complex than a simple word-for-word replacement from one language to another. Translation and adaptation experts must ensure not only that the assessments are consistent with the original version in the source language but also that the tasks will be interpreted by students in their native language as the developers intended. These experts will confirm that the assessment topics maintain their authenticity and meaning for the target student population. CAE uses an internationally accepted five-step translation process that is in compliance with International Translation Committee guidelines (Gregoire, 2018). CAE follows the guidelines used for the localization process of major international studies, such as PISA, Trends in International Mathematics and Science Study, Progress in International Reading Literacy Study, PIAAC, and AHELO. The process includes translatability review, double translation and reconciliation, client review, focused verification, and cognitive labs.

During the translatability review, source material is reviewed to confirm that the text will adapt well to the native language and culture. Particular attention is paid to disambiguation of sources, respecting key correspondences between stimuli and questions, and deciding what should or should not be adapted to local context. Two independent translators then review the text and provide translations, which are reconciled and sent to the lead project manager for review and an opportunity to provide minor suggestions. The translated

CLA+ items are then sent for a focused verification. Cognitive labs are then carried out with the assistance of participating institutions to ensure the translation and adaptation process was effective.

Administration[3]

CLA+ International is administered through an internet-based test platform. Students enter the exam through a secure browser that locks down computer functions and distributes a 60-minute Performance Task and a 30-minute, 25-item Selected-Response Question section to each student. All testing sessions require a proctor to authorize students into the interface and to manage the testing environment. The assessment is designed to be completed in approximately 90 minutes. The assessment includes an optional tutorial that students can scroll through. The assessment must be administered under standardized, controlled testing conditions. CAE provides training materials for institutional administrators and proctors.

Scoring

For CLA+ International, all responses are double-scored by human scorers. CAE staff direct the training for the scoring process. This starts with an in person group training for lead scorers from all participating institutions. This training is conducted in English with exemplary responses from American students. The lead scorer then undergoes rigorous training in order to become a CLA+ International scorer. Training includes an orientation to the prompts and scoring rubrics/guides, repeated practice grading a wide range of student responses, and extensive feedback and discussion after scoring each response. Then CAE serves as a resource for the lead scorer, who is responsible for recruiting and training the in-country team of scorers. This ensures quality and consistency both within and across institutions. The scorers should be recruited from participating institutions and will need to be able to judge university students' generic skills. Institutions will often appoint professors, institutional research fellows, postdoctoral associates, or doctoral students to score the student responses. Once trained, the scorers will receive a randomized selection of anonymized student responses and will enter the score results directly into CAE's internet-based scoring platform. The scorers will not know the institution to which each student belongs. CAE's system automatically monitors human scorer calibration and interrater reliability and notifies the lead scorers of any problems through the E-Verification system.

The E-Verification system was developed to improve and streamline scoring. Calibration of scorers through the E-Verification system requires scorers to score previously scored results, or "verification papers," when they first start scoring, as well as throughout the scoring window. The system periodically

---

[3]This section is adapted with permission from CAE (2020a).

presents verification papers to scorers in lieu of unscored student responses, although they are not flagged to the scorers as such. The system does not indicate when a scorer has successfully scored a verification paper, but if the scorer fails to accurately score a series of verification papers, he or she will be removed from scoring and must participate in a remediation process. At this point, scorers are either further coached or removed from scoring.

Subscores are assigned on a scale of 1 (*lowest*) to 6 (*highest*). Blank responses or responses that are entirely unrelated to the task are flagged for removal from results.

Reporting

Each participating institution receives its own set of reports and data files. If agreed upon by all participating institutions, a collective data file for all students from all participating institutions within the country, along with comparative information of CAE's domestic national data, will be provided. In addition, individual institutional reports and data files for each participating institution, as well as comparative data across all institutions within the country, will be prepared. Finally, there are individual student reports for all participating students.

In addition to these reports, for any new items or forms that are piloted, CAE provides a detailed item analysis of the native language SRQ section. CAE also provides scaling and equating analyses for the PT and SRQ section of the national forms to the English language forms. No data will be shared without the explicit permission of a particular institution.

Standard Setting

CAE will conduct a standard-setting validation study for one form of CLA+ (one PT and 25 SRQs that consist of one Critical Reading and Evaluation set, one Scientific and Quantitative Reasoning set, and one Critique an Argument set) based upon the already established standards for CLA+ (Zahner, 2014). The design and execution of the standard-setting study for CLA+ International will be consistent with procedures adopted in the Standards for Educational and Psychological Testing (American Educational Research Association et al., 2014). This study will require a meeting, facilitated by CAE, with subject matter experts (SMEs) selected collectively by the participating institutions, who will review student responses and determine various cut scores for the tests using the Bookmark standard-setting procedure (Lewis et al., 1999). The SMEs will consist of professionals who have experience working with graduating university students who are entering the workforce or continuing their studies in graduate school. The goal of the standard-setting study is to obtain a consensus on the international standards of mastery of generic skills that students need. CAE recognizes that this may be an extremely challenging task and is, therefore, open to having country-specific standard-setting studies.

However, this approach also has limitations, because it will not be possible to easily compare these results cross-nationally.

International Benchmarking and Cross-Country Comparisons[4]

By participating in CLA+ International, institutions that are taking part have the opportunity to obtain international benchmarking information (for comparisons beyond their native country and the United States). Those in participating countries who are interested in international benchmarking and cross-country comparisons will have the opportunity to share their results and collaborate on research projects. CAE has a rich research history of investigating international comparative studies (Benjamin et al., 2012; Klein et al., 2013; Wolf & Zahner, 2016; Wolf et al., 2014, 2015; Zahner & Kostoris, 2016; Zahner & Steedle, 2014) and hopes to continue this line of research with global partners. No data will be shared without the explicit permission of a particular institution or country.

Certificates and Badging

Using the results from the standard-setting study, students earning Proficient, Accomplished, or Advanced scores will be eligible to receive digital badges (Figure 14.4). These badges will allow students to showcase their generic skills achievement levels to potential employers. The students will also be able to share their CLA+ scores directly on employment boards, through social media, and on their resumes.

Research and Development Efforts

In addition to the administration of CLA+ International, all participating institutions will have the opportunity to contribute to the ongoing research and development initiative at CAE. This will include identifying the topics for future PTs and SRQs and innovating new assessments for additional skills, such as creativity and collaboration. There will also be opportunities for participants to jointly author research articles and chapters (e.g., Zahner & Ciolfi, 2018).

Participation

The CLA+ International initiative functions as a loose network of institutions, systems, and countries, supported jointly by the OECD and CAE. No formal process of registration or accession is in place. By the time of drafting this chapter, the CLA+ International initiative connects the following institutions, systems, and countries. Finland decided to do a system-wide implementation

---

[4]This section is adapted with permission from CAE (2020b).

FIGURE 14.4. CLA+ Mastery Level Badges

Note. CLA+ = Collegiate Learning Assessment +. Reprinted with permission from the Council for Aid to Education.

of the CLA+ in 2019. Two language versions (Finnish and Swedish) were developed and tested in 17 higher education institutions during the 2019–2020 academic year. In Italy, the national quality assurance and accreditation agency Agenzia Nazionale di Valutazione del Sistema Universitario e della Ricerca (ANVUR) has implemented the CLA+ in two rounds of the TEst sulle COmpetenze (TECO) project and is continuing using a modified version of CLA+ in its assessment tools. In Mexico, the University of Guadalajara is testing several cohorts of students with CLA+. A group of universities in Latin America, including Chile, Peru, Paraguay, and Colombia is also starting testing (Chile has begun their testing during the 2019–2020 academic year). In England, a group of post-1992 universities is using the CLA+ within the Teaching Excellence Framework.

SUMMARY AND CONCLUSION

The collaboration between the OECD and CAE in the development and implementation of the CLA+ International certainly is not the only promising initiative in the field of assessing higher education students' and graduates' learning outcomes. At an international level, the situation probably can be best described as one in which institutions, systems, and countries are exploring various conceptual and methodological approaches. It is clear that the interest is growing, most notably among governments and stakeholders in higher education. At the same time, there continues to be resistance and outright opposition among higher education institutions.

Compared with alternative and competing approaches and initiatives, the CLA+ International stands out in several aspects. It is based on a clear argument about generic skills assessment. It focuses on assessing those skills where higher education is supposed to make a real difference, while at the same time being critically important in the context of skills demand in the knowledge economy. The assessment connects very well to core academic values and to what the higher education community itself considers to be its added value. It has a long history of development and fine-tuning, as well as a long and successful history of implementation in the U.S. higher education system. The assessment methodology, as well as the translation, adaptation, implementation, and scoring, is based on state-of-the-art approaches. Participating institutions, systems, and countries can easily benchmark their results against a rich and growing database of assessment data for the United States and other countries.

At the same time, there still are hurdles to overcome. In several countries, motivating students to participate to the best of their abilities can be a challenge, and certificates and badges are not yet familiar enough to students and employers, although they might become so in the future. The support of employers in recognizing the value of the assessment and its outcomes at both the system level and individual level will be critically important.

Still, the benefits for institutions and systems are clear. Assessing students' and graduates' learning outcomes offers an invaluable point of comparison with the internal selection, assessment, examination, and certification processes and can add tremendous value to evaluating the quality and equity of these processes. To institutions, it offers a unique external point of reference for internal quality improvement. To students, it offers an additional attestation of skills that are valued by employers in addition to the certification acquired from university. Finally, to governments and external stakeholders, it offers an exceptionally rich dataset to assess the quality, equity, and value-added of higher education institutions and systems, including to parents and potential applicants to college.

REFERENCES

American Educational Research Association, American Psychological Association, & National Council on Measurement in Education. (2014). *Standards for educational and psychological testing*. American Educational Research Association.

Arum, R., & Roksa, J. (2014). *Aspiring adults adrift*. University of Chicago Press. https://doi.org/10.7208/chicago/9780226197142.001.0001

Bachan, R. (2017). Grade inflation in UK higher education. *Studies in Higher Education, 42*(8), 1580–1600. https://doi.org/10.1080/03075079.2015.1019450

Badal, S. (2014, January 20). The business benefits of gender diversity. *Gallup Workplace*. http://www.gallup.com/businessjournal/166220/business-benefits-gender-diversity.aspx

Barron's College Division Staff. (2014). *Barron's profiles of American colleges* (31st ed.). Barron's Educational Series.

Benjamin, R. (2008). *The contribution of the Collegiate Learning Assessment to teaching and learning*. Council for Aid to Education. https://cae.org/images/uploads/pdf/The_Contribution_of_the__Collegiate_Learning_Assessment_to_Teaching_and_Learning.pdf

Benjamin, R. (2014). Two questions about critical-thinking tests in higher education. *Change: The Magazine of Higher Learning, 46*(2), 24–31. https://doi.org/10.1080/00091383.2014.897179

Benjamin, R. (2015). *Leveling the playing field from college to career.* https://files.eric.ed.gov/fulltext/ED582130.pdf

Benjamin, R., & Klein, S. (2006). *Assessment versus accountability in higher education: Notes for reconciliation* [Draft manuscript]. Council for Aid to Education. https://www.semanticscholar.org/paper/Assessment-Versus-Accountability-in-Higher-%3A-Notes-Benjamin-Klein/6f5115e5bde3ddfe08bc72f79785ce7df4b4bd55

Benjamin, R., Klein, S., Steedle, J. T., Zahner, D., Elliot, S., & Patterson, J. A. (2012). *The case for generic skills and performance assessment in the United States and international settings.* CAE-Occasional Paper. Council for Aid to Education. https://cae.org/images/uploads/pdf/The_Case_for_Generic_Skills_and_Performance_Assessment.pdf

Clanchy, J., & Ballard, B. (1995). Generic skills in the context of higher education. *Higher Education Research & Development, 14*(2), 155–166. https://doi.org/10.1080/0729436950140202

Council for Aid to Education. (2018). *CLA+ national results, 2017–2018.* https://cae.org/images/uploads/pdf/CLA_Summary_Report_2017-18.pdf

Council for Aid to Education. (2020a). *Operational details.* https://cae.org/flagship-assessments-cla-cwra/flagship-assessments-cla-cwra/operational-details/

Council for Aid to Education. (2020b). *Reports & data analytics.* https://cae.org/flagship-assessments-cla-cwra/flagship-assessments-cla-cwra/reports-data-analytics/

Crebert, G., Bates, M., Bell, B., Patrick, C.-J., & Cragnolini, V. (2004). Developing generic skills at university, during work placement and employment: Graduates' perceptions. *Higher Education Research & Development, 23*(2), 147–165. https://doi.org/10.1080/0729436042000206636

Ellemers, N., & Rink, F. (2016). Diversity in work groups. *Current Opinion in Psychology, 11*, 49–53. https://doi.org/10.1016/j.copsyc.2016.06.001

Gregoire, J. (2018). ITC guidelines for translating and adapting tests (2nd ed.). *International Journal of Testing, 18*(2), 101–134. https://doi.org/10.1080/15305058.2017.1398166

Hart Research Associates. (2006). *How should colleges prepare students to succeed in today's global economy? Based on surveys among employers and recent college graduates.* https://www.aacu.org/sites/default/files/files/LEAP/2007_full_report_leap.pdf

Hart Research Associates. (2013). *It takes more than a major: Employer priorities for college learning and student success.* https://www.aacu.org/leap/documents/2013_Employer-Survey.pdf

Hart Research Associates. (2015). *Falling short? College learning and career success.* http://www.aacu.org/sites/default/files/files/LEAP/2015employerstudentsurvey.pdf

Herring, C. (2009). Does diversity pay? Race, gender, and the business case for diversity. *American Sociological Review, 74*(2), 208–224. https://doi.org/10.1177/000312240907400203

Hillman, N. W., Tandberg, D. A., & Fryar, A. H. (2015). Evaluating the impact of "new" performance funding in higher education. *Educational Evaluation and Policy Analysis, 37*(4), 501–519. https://doi.org/10.3102/0162373714560224

Hoxby, C. M., & Avery, C. (2012). *The missing "one-offs": The hidden supply of high-achieving, low-income students.* https://www.brookings.edu/wp-content/uploads/2016/07/2013a_hoxby.pdf

Hussar, W. J., & Bailey, T. M. (2014). *Projections of education statistics to 2022.* https://nces.ed.gov/pubsearch/pubsinfo.asp?pubid=2014051

Jacobs, B., & van der Ploeg, F. (2006). Guide to reform of higher education: A European perspective. *Economic Policy, 21*(47), 536–592. https://doi.org/10.1111/j.1468-0327.2006.00166.x

Kearns, P. (2001). *Generic skills for the new economy. Review of research.* National Centre for Vocational Education Research. https://www.ncver.edu.au/research-and-statistics/publications/all-publications/generic-skills-for-the-new-economy-review-of-research

Klein, S., & Benjamin, R. (2008). *The Collegiate Learning Assessment (CLA)*. Council for Aid to Education.

Klein, S., Benjamin, R., Shavelson, R., & Bolus, R. (2007). The Collegiate Learning Assessment: Facts and fantasies. *Evaluation Review, 31*(5), 415–439. https://doi.org/10.1177/0193841X07303318

Klein, S., Liu, O. L., Sconing, J., Bolus, R., Bridgeman, B., Kugelmass, H., Nemeth, A., Robbins, S., & Steedle, J. T. (2009). *Test validity study (TVS) report.* https://cae.org/images/uploads/pdf/13_Test_Validity_Study_Report.pdf

Klein, S., Zahner, D., Benjamin, R., Bolus, R., & Steedle, J. T. (2013). *Observations on AHELO's generic skills strand methodology and findings.* Council for Aid to Education.

Ku, K. Y. L. (2009). Assessing students' critical thinking performance: Urging for measurements using multiple-response format. *Thinking Skills and Creativity, 4*(1), 70–76.

Lai, E. R. (2011). *Critical thinking: A literature review.* Pearson. https://images.pearsonassessments.com/images/tmrs/CriticalThinkingReviewFINAL.pdf

Lazear, E. P. (2006). Speeding, terrorism, and teaching to the test. *The Quarterly Journal of Economics, 121*(3), 1029–1061. https://doi.org/10.1162/qjec.121.3.1029

Levy, F., & Murnane, R. J. (2004, October). Education and the changing job market: An education centered on complex thinking and communicating is a graduate's passport to prosperity. *Educational Leadership, 62,* 80–83. https://www.humbleisd.net/cms/lib/TX01001414/Centricity/Domain/8712/Changing_Business.pdf

Lewis, D. M., Mitzel, H. C., Green, D. R., & Patz, R. J. (1999). *The bookmark standard setting procedure.* McGraw-Hill.

Liu, O. L., Frankel, L., & Roohr, K. C. (2014). *Assessing critical thinking in higher education: Current state and directions for next-generation assessment* (Research Report ETS RR-14-10). Educational Testing Service. https://doi.org/10.1002/ets2.12009

Lomas, L. (2007). Are students customers? Perceptions of academic staff. *Quality in Higher Education, 13*(1), 31–44. https://doi.org/10.1080/13538320701272714

McGowan, M. A., & Andrews, D. (2015). *Skill mismatch and public policy in OECD countries* (OECD Economics Department Working Paper No. 1210). https://www.oecd-ilibrary.org/economics/skill-mismatch-and-public-policy-in-oecd-countries_5js1pzw9lnwk-en

McLendon, M. K. (2003). State governance reform of higher education: Patterns, trends, and theories of the public policy process. In J. C. Smart (Ed.), *Higher education: Handbook of theory and research* (Vol. 18, pp. 57–143). Springer. https://link.springer.com/chapter/10.1007/978-94-010-0137-3_2

Moloney, K. (2006). Teaching to the test. *International Journal of Learning, 13*(6), 19–25.

Montt, G. (2015). The causes and consequences of field-of-study mismatch: An analysis using PIAAC (OECD Social, Employment and Migration Working Papers, No. 167). Organisation for Economic Cooperation and Development. https://doi.org/10.1787/5jrxm4dhv9r2-en

Organisation for Economic Cooperation and Development. (2012). *Testing students and university performance globally: OECD's AHELO.* http://www.oecd.org/edu/skills-beyond-school/testingstudentanduniversityperformancegloballyoecdsahelo.htm

Organisation for Economic Cooperation and Development. (2013a). *AHELO Feasibility Study Report: Volume 2–Data analysis and national experiences.* https://www.oecd.org/education/skills-beyond-school/AHELOFSReportVolume2.pdf

Organisation for Economic Cooperation and Development. (2013b). *How are university students changing?* OECD Education Indicators in Focus 2013/06. https://www.oecd.org/education/skills-beyond-school/EDIF%202013—N%C2%B015.pdf

Organisation for Economic Cooperation and Development. (2016). *Skills matter: Further results from the Survey of Adult Skills.* http://www.oecd.org/skills/piaac/skills-matter-9789264258051-en.htm

Popham, W. J. (2001). Teaching to the test? *Educational Leadership, 58*(6), 16–21.

Rojstaczer, S., & Healy, C. (2012). Where A is ordinary: The evolution of American college and university grading, 1940–2009. *Teachers College Record, 114*, 1–23.

Steedle, J. T. (2010a, April 30–May 4). *Advancing institutional value-added score estimation* [Paper presentation]. American Educational Research Association 2010 Annual Meeting, Denver, CO, United States.

Steedle, J. T. (2010b, April 30–May 4). *Improving the reliability and interpretability of value-added scores for post-secondary institutional assessment programs* [Paper presentation]. American Educational Research Association 2010 Annual Meeting, Denver, CO, United States.

Steedle, J. T. (2010c, April 30–May 4). *Incentives, motivation, and performance on a low-stakes test of college learning* [Paper presentation]. American Educational Research Association 2010 Annual Meeting, Denver, CO, United States.

Steedle, J. T. (2012). Selecting value-added models for postsecondary institutional assessment. *Assessment & Evaluation in Higher Education, 37*(6), 637–652. https://doi.org/10.1080/02602938.2011.560720

Steedle, J. T., & Bradley, M. (2012, April 13–17). *Majors matter: Differential performance on a test of general college outcomes* [Paper presentation]. American Educational Research Association 2012 Annual Meeting, Vancouver, British Columbia, Canada.

Steedle, J. T., Zahner, D., & Kuglemass, H. (2014, April 3–7). *Test administration procedures and their relationship with effort and performance on a college outcome test* [Paper presentation]. American Educational Research Association 2014 Annual Meeting, Philadelphia, PA, United States.

Tremblay, K., Lalancette, D., & Roseveare, D. (2012). *AHELO feasibility study report: Volume 1—Design and implementation*. http://www.oecd.org/education/skills-beyond-school/AHELOFSReportVolume1.pdf

Van Damme, D. (2015). Global higher education in need of more and better learning metrics. Why OECD's AHELO project might help to fill the gap. *European Journal of Higher Education, 5*(4), 425–436. https://doi.org/10.1080/21568235.2015.1087870

Volante, L. (2004). Teaching to the test: What every educator and policy-maker should know. *Canadian Journal of Educational Administration and Policy, 35*.

Wissenschaftsrat. (2012). *Prüfungsnoten an Hochschulen im Prüfungsjahr 2010*. [Examination marks at universities in the examination year 2010] (Work report Drs. 2627-12). Science Council. https://www.wissenschaftsrat.de/download/archiv/2627-12.pdf

Wolf, R., & Zahner, D. (2016). Mitigation of test bias in international, cross-cultural assessments of higher-order thinking skills. In Y. Rosen, S. Ferrara, & M. Mosharraf (Eds.), *Handbook of research on technology tools for real-world skill development* (pp. 472–501). IGI Global. https://doi.org/10.4018/978-1-4666-9441-5.ch018

Wolf, R., Zahner, D., & Benjamin, R. (2015). Methodological challenges in international comparative post-secondary assessment programs: Lessons learned and the road ahead. *Studies in Higher Education, 40*(3), 471–481. https://doi.org/10.1080/03075079.2015.1004239

Wolf, R., Zahner, D., Kostoris, F., & Benjamin, R. (2014, April 3–7). *A case study of an international performance-based assessment of critical thinking skills* [Paper presentation]. American Educational Research Association 2014 Annual Meeting, Philadelphia, PA, United States.

Woodall, T., Hiller, A., & Resnick, S. (2014). Making sense of higher education: Students as consumers and the value of the university experience. *Studies in Higher Education, 39*(1), 48–67. https://doi.org/10.1080/03075079.2011.648373

Woolley, A. W., Aggarwal, I., & Malone, T. W. (2015). College intelligence and group performance. *Current Directions in Psychological Science, 24*(6), 420–424. https://doi.org/10.1177/0963721415599543

Wright, G. B. (2011). Student-centered learning in higher education. *International Journal on Teaching and Learning in Higher Education, 23*(3), 92–97.

Zahner, D. (2013). *Reliability and validity of the CLA+*. Council for Aid to Education. http://cae.org/images/uploads/pdf/Reliability_and_Validity_of_CLA_Plus.pdf

Zahner, D. (2014). *CLA+ standard setting study final report*. Council for Aid to Education. http://cae.org/images/uploads/pdf/cla_ss.pdf

Zahner, D., & Ciolfi, A. (2018). International comparison of a performance-based assessment in higher education. In O. Zlatkin-Troitschanskaia, M. Toepper, H. A. Pant, C. Lautenbach, & C. Kuhn (Eds.), *Assessment of learning outcomes in higher education* (pp. 215–244). Springer International. https://doi.org/10.1007/978-3-319-74338-7_11

Zahner, D., & James, J. K. (2016, April 8–12). *Predictive validity of a critical thinking assessment of post-college outcomes* [Paper presentation]. American Educational Research Association 2016 Annual Meeting, Washington, DC, United States.

Zahner, D., & Kostoris, F. (2016, April 8–12). *International testing of a performance-based assessment of higher education* [Paper presentation]. American Educational Research Association 2016 Annual Conference, Washington, DC, United States.

Zahner, D., Ramsaran, L. M., & Steedle, J. T. (2012, April 13-17). *Comparing alternatives in the prediction of college success* [Paper presentation]. American Educational Research Association 2012 Annual Meeting, Vancouver, British Columbia, Canada.

Zahner, D., & Steedle, J. T. (2014, April 3–7). *Evaluating performance task scoring comparability in an international testing program* [Paper presentation]. American Educational Research Association 2014 Annual Meeting, Philadelphia, PA, United States.

Zahner, D., & Steedle, J. T. (2015, Aptil 15–19). *Comparing longitudinal and cross-sectional school effect estimates in postsecondary education* [Paper presentation]. National Council on Measurement in Education 2015 Annual Meeting, Chicago, IL, United States.

15

Interdisciplinary Innovations in Formative and Summative Assessment

The Beliefs, Events, and Values Inventory; VALUE Rubrics; and the Cultural Controllability Scale

Kris Acheson, Ashley Finley, Louis Hickman, Lee Sternberger, and Craig Shealy

Assessment has long been integral to psychological research and practice. Even lay audiences are familiar with some of the famous psychological assessments (e.g., personality and psychopathology tests, measures of IQ). However, assessment has expanded far beyond these traditional approaches to include novel usage across a wide range of domains and contexts. Here we explore three examples of such innovations used for both formative and summative assessment. The Beliefs, Events, and Values Inventory (BEVI) is a grounded theory-driven, mixed-methods, whole-person psychometric instrument with a rich, complex set of scales; the Association of American Colleges & Universities' (AAC&U) Valid Assessment of Learning in Undergraduate Education (VALUE) rubrics are used for comprehensive and qualitative analyses; and the Cultural Controllability Scale (CCS) is a short, "stackable," Likert-type survey that focuses on a single construct.

Although these instruments represent dramatically different processes of development and application, they share a focus on the global, both in terms of constructs and implementation—they open new avenues in international assessment to evaluate and facilitate human learning, development, and transformation. The BEVI, for instance, was distilled from a richly diverse

https://doi.org/10.1037/0000183-016
Assessing Undergraduate Learning in Psychology: Strategies for Measuring and Improving Student Performance, S. A. Nolan, C. M. Hakala, and R. E. Landrum (Editors)

cross-cultural data set of authentic statements about beliefs; its Full Scale Score has been utilized as a proxy for globalized identity, and it is employed comparatively in a number of countries at individual and institutional levels as well as in international contexts such as globally connected classrooms. The VALUE rubrics were developed iteratively by a diverse team of scholars with a focus on globally contextualized knowledge and social responsibility beyond national borders, and they have been implemented internationally in higher education. The CCS is in the infancy of its development and to this point only in use internationally via administration at a U.S. university with a very high international student population. Nonetheless, it serves goals of internationalized curricula, specifically learning outcomes of greater acceptance and respect across cultural differences. We present each instrument in further detail below as international exemplars of assessment innovations.

THE BELIEFS, EVENTS, AND VALUES INVENTORY

How do we humans become who we are? Where do our beliefs and values come from, and how do they influence actions, policies, and practices around the world? Can we measure these processes in a way that captures our complexity as human beings while cultivating globally sustainable selves and the capacity to care? These are among the questions that the BEVI seeks to explore (e.g., Acheson et al., in press; Cozen et al., 2016; Dyjak-LeBlanc et al., 2016; Shealy, 2016, in press; Shealy et al., 2012; Wandschneider et al., 2015). Based on over 2 decades of research and application in the United States and internationally, and with excellent psychometric and test development properties, the BEVI consists of a series of statements about beliefs, values, and life events—often with global implications. Through a wide range of statistical procedures, it has been found repeatedly that BEVI questions cluster or group into specific factors or scales, which make up the larger BEVI.

What Does the BEVI Measure, and How Is It Used?

The BEVI assesses a number of relevant processes and constructs including (but not limited to)

> basic openness; receptivity to different cultures, religions, and social practices; the tendency (or not) to stereotype in particular ways; self and emotional awareness; and preferred but implicit strategies for making sense of why "other" people and cultures "do what they do." (Shealy, 2005, p. 99)

In research and practice, the BEVI is used nationally and internationally in a wide range of settings, populations, and purposes, from therapeutic assessment in the realms of mental health and well-being, to leadership, organizational, and program development to the evaluation of international, multicultural, and transformative learning (see http://thebevi.com). More specifically, the BEVI is used to

- evaluate learning (e.g., study abroad, multicultural courses, general education, training programs, mental health/well-being interventions, service learning),

- understand change (e.g., who learns what and why and under what circumstances),

- pursue goals (e.g., increased awareness of self, others, and the larger world),

- enhance quality (e.g., which experiences, courses, programs, interventions, etc., have what impact, and why, and how they may be improved),

- conduct research (e.g., how, why, and under what circumstances people become more "open" to different cultures),

- demonstrate compliance (e.g., for accreditation, link objectives to outcomes),

- address needs (e.g., assess and resolve conflict, staff/leadership development), and

- facilitate growth (e.g., of individuals, couples, groups, and organizations).

BEVI Theory, Structure, and Scales

The model underlying the BEVI is called equilintegration (EI) theory, a needs-based framework that

> draws upon a wide range of theoretical, empirical, and applied perspectives to account for the dialectic process between the "transmission" and "internalization" of beliefs and values, and constituent aspects of self-regulation, content, structure, affect, attribution, and development. . . . EI theory "explain[s] the processes by which beliefs, values, and worldviews are acquired and maintained, why their alteration is typically resisted, and how and under what circumstances their modification occurs" . . . the BEVI is "designed to identify and predict a variety of developmental, affective, and attributional processes and outcomes that are integral to EI Theory." (Shealy, 2004, p. 1075)

From a structural standpoint, the BEVI consists of four interrelated components: (a) a comprehensive set of demographic/background items that may be modified for particular projects; (b) a life history questionnaire, built into the measure; (c) two validity and 17 "process" scales; and (d) three qualitative "experiential reflection" items. Specific scales are clustered, for theoretical and empirical reasons, underneath nine separate domains that are described in Table 15.1.

BEVI Psychometrics

In development for over 25 years, the BEVI has been evaluated, revised, and refined through a wide array of analyses and procedures, including multiple factor analyses and item review by international subject matter experts. As it has been published and presented in multiple forums in the United States and internationally, there is strong evidence for the BEVI's stability, reliability, and

TABLE 15.1. BEVI Structure, Scales, and Sample Items

Domain	Scale	Description	Sample items
Validity scales	Consistency	Responses consistent for items assessing similar content	"People change all the time." "People don't really change."
	Congruency	Response patterns correspond to that which would be predicted statistically	"I have real needs for warmth and affection." "I take my own feelings very seriously."
Formative variables	Background Information	Demographic and experience items	"What is your gender?" "What is your ethnicity?"
	Negative Life Events	Difficult childhood; parents were troubled; life conflict/struggles; many regrets	"I have had a lot of conflict with one or more members of my family." "My family had a lot of problems with money."
Fulfillment of core needs	Needs Closure	Conflictual/disturbed family dynamics; stereotypical thinking/odd causal explanations	"I had a wonderful childhood." "Some numbers are luckier than others."
	Needs Fulfillment	Open to experiences, needs, and feelings; deep care/sensitivity for self, others, and the larger world	"We should spend more money on early education programs for children." "I like to think about who I am."
Tolerance of disequilibrium	Basic Openness	Open and honest about the experience of basic thoughts, feelings, and needs	"I don't always feel good about who I am." "I have felt lonely in my life."
	Self-Certitude	Strong sense of will; impatient with excuses for difficulties; emphasizes positive thinking; disinclined toward deep analysis	"You can overcome almost any problem if you just try harder." "If you play by the rules, you get along fine."
Critical thinking	Basic Determinism	Prefers simple explanations for differences/behavior; believes people don't change	"AIDS may well be a sign of God's anger." "It's only natural that the strong will survive."
	Socioemotional Convergence	Open, thoughtful, pragmatic, determined; sees world in shades of gray	"We should do more to help those who are less fortunate." "Too many people don't meet their responsibilities."

Self-access	Physical Resonance	Receptive to corporeal needs/feelings; experientially inclined	"I am a free spirit." "My body is very sensitive to what I feel."
	Emotional Attunement	Emotional, sensitive, social, affiliative; values the expression of affect	"I don't mind displays of emotion." "Weakness can be a virtue."
	Meaning Quest	Searching for meaning; seeks balance; resilient/persistent; concerned for less fortunate	"I think a lot about the meaning of life." "I want to find a better sense of balance in my life."
Other access	Religious Traditionalism	Highly religious; sees self/behavior/events as mediated by God/spiritual forces	"Without religion there can be no peace." "There is one way to heaven."
	Gender Traditionalism	Men and women built to be a certain way; prefers traditional/simple views of gender/gender roles	"Women are more emotional than men." "A man's role is to be strong."
	Sociocultural Openness	Progressive/open regarding a wide range of actions, policies, and practices in the areas of culture, economics, education, environment, gender/global relations	"We should try to understand cultures that are different from our own." "There is too big a gap between the rich and poor in our country."
Global access	Ecological Resonance	Deeply invested in environmental/sustainability issues; concerned about the earth/natural world	"I worry about our environment." "We should protect the land no matter who owns it."
	Global Resonance	Invested in learning about/encountering different individuals, groups, languages, cultures; seeks global engagement	"It is important to be well informed about world events." "I am comfortable around groups of people who are very different from me."
Experiential reflection items		Three qualitative/free responses questions	"Please describe which aspect of this experience has had the greatest impact upon you and why?" "Is there some aspect of your own 'self' or 'identity' that has become especially clear or relevant to you or others as a result of this experience?" "What have you learned and how are you different now?"

validity (e.g., content, predictive, construct; Acheson et al., in press; Shealy, 2016; Wandschneider et al., 2015).

Most recently, a shortened, 185-item version of the BEVI was created, which takes about 30 minutes to complete online. A standardized measure, the BEVI was renormed in 2019 with a sample of over 20,000 respondents from around the world. Table 15.2 summarizes model fit information, including calculations for chi-square, degrees of freedom, statistical significance, and two fit measures (i.e., comparative fit index and root mean square error of approximation).

BEVI Projects

Over the years, the BEVI has been used in a range of contexts and settings in the United States and around the world, to illuminate the possibilities of depth-based, psychometrically rigorous, and ecologically valid assessment. For instance, the Forum BEVI Project is a 6-year collaboration between two nonprofit organizations: the Forum on Education Abroad (an association of over 800 institutional members representing higher education institutions, consortia, and organizations; https://forumea.org) and the International Beliefs and Values Institute (a "non-partisan organization that addresses real-world issues of conflict resolution, human rights, sustainability, global education, and religious and cultural understanding"; http://ibavi.org). The Forum BEVI Project is a prime example of how the BEVI helps us understand how and why human learning, growth, and development do, and do not, occur. The implications and applications of the Forum BEVI Project resulted in

TABLE 15.2. Model Fit Information for BEVI Scales

Scale	Chi-square	df	p value	CFI	RMSEA
Negative Life Events	428.612	27	0.000	.977	.080
Needs Closure	2993.316	225	0.000	.911	.073
Needs Fulfillment	2855.248	248	0.000	.912	.067
Identity Diffusion	28.973	2	0.000	.983	.076
Basic Openness	619.225	54	0.000	.956	.067
Basic Determinism	536.465	41	0.000	.927	.072
Ecological Resonance	456.526	9	0.000	.967	.147
Self-Certitude	634.634	62	0.000	.937	.064
Religious Traditionalism	166.821	9	0.000	.995	.087
Emotional Attunement	654.891	62	0.000	.960	.064
Physical Resonance	40.557	2	0.000	.984	.091
Self-Awareness	598.360	54	0.000	.948	.066
Socioemotional Convergence	3523.339	369	0.000	.901	.061
Sociocultural Openness	2596.628	225	0.000	.935	.067
Global Resonance	93.898	14	0.000	.994	.050
Gender Traditionalism	765.686	44	0.000	.948	.084
Meaning Quest	836.661	61	0.000	.925	.074

Note. df = degrees of freedom; CFI = comparative fit index; RMSEA = root mean square error of approximation. From http://thebevi.com. Copyright 2016 by C. N. Shealy. Adapted with permission.

"over 20 publications (e.g., articles, chapters, dissertations), 50 presentations (e.g., symposia, papers, posters), and hundreds of separate analyses" (Wandschneider et al., 2015, p. 160).

Additional collaborations have occurred with nonprofit, community-based, and organizational leaders, entities, and individuals across a range of areas (e.g., board of directors of a women's organization, inmates in a department of corrections, community mental health and private-practice clients). Recently, the BEVI was tapped for the Collaborative Online International Learning (COIL) BEVI Project, a grant-based initiative between the Japanese and U.S. governments. The BEVI was selected because it (a) is used widely, not only in the United States but also in other countries and regions of the world (as of this writing, the BEVI has been administered over 50,000 times on five continents); (b) is comprehensive, measuring multiple aspects of learning, growth, and development including, but not limited to, sociocultural and global openness and engagement; (c) is well validated, with a demonstrable track record over the past 25 years of international development and usage with excellent psychometric properties; (d) is highly accessible and cost-effective, with a secure and online system of administration, and individual, group, institutional, and cross-institutional report and analysis options; and (e) includes both evaluative and practical applications, which can examine processes of change within and between institutions, while also facilitating student learning, growth, and development. The COIL BEVI Project seeks to evaluate whether and to what degree COIL helps students who may otherwise not be able to afford or manage study abroad, but who can still benefit from engaging with peers and faculty in other countries through low-cost, accessible, and web-based technologies.

Through projects such as these (see http://thebevi.com), the BEVI is used to research and facilitate engaged, high impact, and transformative learning, though scholarly discourse, real world application, and big picture initiatives, such as the *Cultivating the Globally Sustainable Self Summit Series* (a multiyear, multi-institution, multicountry endeavor including over 20 separate research-to-practice projects; see http://ibavi.org). The BEVI is a proprietary instrument that does require training (for individual administrators) and licensing (for the institution). Current information about training and licensing processes and fees can be found at http://thebevi.com.

BEVI Innovations

The BEVI is innovative at a number of levels. For example, as a grounded theory measure (i.e., its EI theoretical framework emerged from empirical observations and was informed by subsequent statistical analyses), the BEVI is able to illuminate not only what human beings believe and value, but why. Moreover, the diverse origins of its formulation means it lends itself well to multiple applications (e.g., items were derived from actual statements by a highly diverse group of human beings uttered over many years across a wide range of settings and contexts in the United States and internationally). Likewise, the underlying EI theoretical framework is deeply informed by literatures within and beyond psychology (e.g., from abnormal, clinical, cognitive, cultural, developmental, and social psychology to interdisciplinary scholarship on the etiology and nature of beliefs and values). More specifically, EI theory seeks to

> account for the dialectic process between the "transmission" and "internalization" of beliefs and values, and constituent aspects of self-regulation, content, structure, affect, attribution, and development [to] explain the processes by which beliefs, values, and "worldviews" are acquired and maintained, why their alteration is typically resisted, and how and under what circumstances their modification occurs. (Shealy, 2005, p. 98)

At a complementary level, the BEVI is "designed to identify and predict a variety of developmental, affective, and attributional processes and outcomes that are integral to EI Theory" (Shealy, 2004, p. 1075). Finally, the report system for the BEVI is sophisticated and adaptable to a wide array of populations, settings, and needs and may be used for both research and assessment purposes (e.g., to determine what sorts of interventions or programs are having what sort of impact for whom), as well as for real world application to facilitate learning, growth, and development (e.g., Acheson et al., in press; Shealy, 2016, in press; Wandschneider et al., 2015).

These aspects of the BEVI may be illustrated through a fairly typical example of a Time 1/Time 2 (T1/T2) analysis of change over a 3- to 4-month study abroad (a standardized measure, BEVI scores are converted to percentages ranging from 1 to 100). Specifically, Figure 15.1 shows the T1/T2 results from "Aggregate Profile," one of approximately 20 different indices generated by the BEVI's report system. From an interpretive perspective, it appears that by the conclusion of the study abroad experience, students are: (a) more open to their own experiences, needs, and feelings (Needs Fulfillment increases from 65 to 74); (b) less likely to be experiencing difficulties regarding who they are and where they are going in life (Identity Diffusion decreases from 40 to 30); (c) more open to their own emotions and those of others (Emotional Attunement increases from 62 to 73); (d) more likely to actively searching for a sense of meaning and purpose (Meaning Quest increases from 47 to 65); and (e) more invested in learning about and engaging cultures or groups different from their own (Global Resonance increases from 69 to 78). Space limitations do not permit a full explication of BEVI indices, including a focus on examining within- and between-group differences, but additional information is available at http://thebevi.com.

In terms of limitations, the richness of the data generated by the BEVI is a double-edged sword that appeals to some while overwhelming others. The BEVI and its report systems are complex, requiring training in its theoretical foundations and practical applications for successful implementation as

FIGURE 15.1. Example of a Time 1/Time 2 BEVI Aggregate Profile

	Low	High
Congruency Score T1	83	
Congruency Score T2	83	
1. Negative Life Events (T1)	50	
1. Negative Life Events (T2)	52	
2. Needs Closure (T1)	20	
2. Needs Closure (T2)	17	
3. Needs Fulfillment (T1)	65	
3. Needs Fulfillment (T2)	74	
4. Identity Diffusion (T1)	40	
4. Identity Diffusion (T2)	30	
5. Basic Openness (T1)	45	
5. Basic Openness (T2)	51	
6. Self Certitude (T1)	41	
6. Self Certitude (T2)	43	
7. Basic Determinism (T1)	40	
7. Basic Determinism (T2)	34	
8. Socioemotional Convergence (T1)	67	
8. Socioemotional Convergence (T2)	72	
9. Physical Resonance (T1)	80	
9. Physical Resonance (T2)	80	
10. Emotional Attunement (T1)	62	
10. Emotional Attunement (T2)	73	
11. Self Awareness (T1)	81	
11. Self Awareness (T2)	86	
12. Meaning Quest (T1)	47	
12. Meaning Quest (T2)	65	
13. Religious Traditionalism (T1)	33	
13. Religious Traditionalism (T2)	32	
14. Gender Traditionalism (T1)	24	
14. Gender Traditionalism (T2)	14	
15. Sociocultural Openness (T1)	89	
15. Sociocultural Openness (T2)	91	
16. Ecological Resonance (T1)	78	
16. Ecological Resonance (T2)	74	
17. Global Resonance (T1)	69	
17. Global Resonance (T2)	78	

a formative and/or summative assessment at individual and group levels. As Roy et al. (2014) observed, it may be

> difficult to interpret some its scales [but] it also has many customizations that can be useful for a university or other organizations to more specifically target certain areas or to add questions that will be useful to the goals of the organization. (p. 2)

Overall, the psychometric, formulation, and applied innovations of the BEVI method and EI model may be summarized as follows:

- theoretically and practically grounded in more than 2 decades of research and assessment,
- normed upon an international sample ($N = 20,000+$), and
- adherent to psychometric best practices.

AUTHENTIC, DIRECT ASSESSMENT OF STUDENT LEARNING USING THE AAC&U VALUE RUBRICS

In 2005, the AAC&U released its Liberal Education and America's Promise (LEAP) essential learning outcomes framework. The LEAP learning outcomes were culled from the AAC&U's 1300 member institutions, employer data, and other sources. The outcomes identified within the LEAP framework are those most frequently identified for student learning and success across all sectors of higher education and by employers (Hart Research Associates, 2018). The LEAP framework is organized into four broad "Goal Areas" with specific suggested outcomes: (a) Knowledge of Human Cultures and Physical and Practical Worlds (e.g., general knowledge, in addition to disciplinary ways of knowing); (b) Intellectual and Practical Skills (e.g., critical thinking, quantitative reasoning, information literacy); (c) Personal and Social Responsibility (e.g., intercultural knowledge and competence, global learning, ethical reasoning, civic engagement); and (d) Integrative and Applied Learning (e.g., integration and application of knowledge across contexts). Each of these Goal Areas connects the individual with the international: knowledge and literacies are contextualized within cultural contexts and compared/contrasted across cultures, social responsibility is conceived of as transcending national borders, and integration and application of knowledge emphasize the global as well as the local. With the wide adoption of the LEAP outcomes framework, attention rightly turned to how the learning outcomes should be effectively assessed. The LEAP outcomes framework resonated with campuses because the goal categories and outcomes could be authentically linked with institutional missions across a diverse range of universities (i.e., public or private, 2 year or 4 year). Assessment of these outcomes, therefore, needed to be equally adaptable, authentic, and institutionally driven. Thus was born a new AAC&U project—the development of a comprehensive set of rubrics for the VALUE.

Development of the VALUE Rubrics

With the wide adoption of the LEAP outcomes framework, the AAC&U VALUE rubrics were developed to assist campuses in meeting emerging needs for assessment. On the one hand, campuses need authentic, direct assessment of student learning across a diverse set of outcomes, as represented by the LEAP outcomes and institutional mission statements. Campuses also increasingly need a way to respond to mounting pressures for accountability. The course-embedded nature of the VALUE rubrics and adaptability to faculty designed assignments provide a means to achieve both of these needs with learner-centered tools rooted in faculty practice. With funding from the Fund for Improvement of Secondary Education (i.e., within the U.S. Department of Education) and State Farm, the AAC&U VALUE rubrics were released in 2009 following an 18-month development period. To date, 16 VALUE rubrics have been developed. Notably, no rubrics exist for the first Goal Area of the LEAP framework (i.e., Knowledge of Human Cultures and the Physical and Practical Worlds). Because this category primarily addresses students' acquisition and retention of knowledge, particularly within specific disciplines, it was assumed that faculty largely have the tools to evaluate learning in this domain. Thus, the VALUE initiative focused on the broad skills and capacities that transcend disciplines, connect general education and the majors, and are widely endorsed by employers, but for which faculty often lack tools for direct assessment. Each of the 16 rubrics was developed by an interdisciplinary team composed primarily of faculty and other educational professionals from a diverse range of colleges and universities (see AAC&U; https://aacu.org/value). Each rubric underwent multiple rounds of revision, including campus-based testing. Feedback from a total of nearly 100 campuses was provided directly to the development teams to inform each stage of revisions (see Rhodes, 2010).

Structurally, the VALUE rubrics enable complex outcomes, such as critical thinking and lifelong learning, to be articulated and assessed in two fundamental ways. First, the rows of each rubric delineate the dimensions that comprise a particular learning outcome. It is expected that students will demonstrate ability on up to five or six dimensions of a learning outcome, not just one. For example, effective written communication requires demonstrated not only competency with syntax and mechanics but also the ability to develop content, communicate purpose, display adeptness with different disciplinary conventions, and appropriate deployment of sources and evidence (e.g., the Written Communication VALUE rubric in Table 15.3). The rubric underwent multiple rounds of revision, and feedback from nearly 100 campuses was provided directly to the development teams to inform each stage of revisions.

The rubrics' columns explicate the developmental trajectory of students' competency across dimensions *over time*. Reading from left to right, columns begin at Level 4, the expected performance when students graduate with a 4-year degree. "Milestone" markers (i.e., Columns 2 and 3) signify benchmarks for gauging students' progress throughout their baccalaureate path or for those transitioning from 2- to 4-year institutions. Finally, Level 1 represents expected performance at the beginning of a baccalaureate or associate's degree. The rubrics were intended to be read from *high* (4) to *low* (1), so that scorers (including students) would start with the highest level of cognitive complexity in mind as they reviewed student work. The underlying philosophy is to forefront high expectations for learning over time, rather than starting with the scorer's (or the student's) expectations for where they *think* they are.

The VALUE rubrics are widely accessible via free download from AAC&U's website (see https://aacu.org/value). Since 2009, the VALUE rubrics have been downloaded by more than 70,000 individuals, representing nearly 6,000 organizations (over 2,000 of which are colleges and universities; McConnell & Rhodes, 2017). The rubrics have also been used internationally in countries such as Australia and China in addition to being translated into Japanese (see https://tinyurl.com/vmy4785). Additionally, there are examples of U.S. colleges and universities that have used the VALUE rubrics to assess learning in global partnerships. St. Edwards University, for example, has used the global

TABLE 15.3. Excerpt From the Written Communication VALUE Rubric

	Capstone	Milestones		Benchmark
	4	3	2	1
Dimension				
Context of and purpose for writing	Demonstrates a thorough understanding of context, audience, and purpose that is responsive to the assigned task(s) and focuses all elements of the work.	Demonstrates adequate consideration of context, audience, and purpose and a clear focus on the assigned task(s) (e.g., the task aligns with audience, purpose, and context).	Demonstrates awareness of context, audience, purpose, and to the assigned tasks(s) (e.g., begins to show awareness of audience's perceptions and assumptions).	Demonstrates minimal attention to context, audience, purpose, and to the assigned tasks(s) (e.g., expectation of instructor or self as audience).
Content development	Uses appropriate, relevant, and compelling content to illustrate mastery of the subject, conveying the writer's understanding, and shaping the whole work.	Uses appropriate, relevant, and compelling content to explore ideas within the context of the discipline and shape the whole work.	Uses appropriate and relevant content to develop and explore ideas through most of the work.	Uses appropriate and relevant content to develop simple ideas in some parts of the work.

Note. From VALUE: *Valid Assessment of Learning in Undergraduate Education,* by the Association of American Colleges and Universities, 2020 (https://www.aacu.org/value/).
Copyright 2020 by the Association of American Colleges and Universities. Reprinted with permission.

learning VALUE rubric to assess such a partnership in Japan (see NAFSA: International Association of Educators, 2020).

The rubrics have been endorsed by all of the major regional accrediting associations in the United States, as well as the Voluntary System of Accountability, a nonprofit organization that provides transparency in educational outcomes across public institutions, as viable tools for evaluating student learning and success. Although dense, the VALUE rubrics are broadly seen as useful by an array of campus stakeholders, most specifically faculty and administrators who are most often tasked with assessing student learning. Beginning in 2021, the VALUE rubrics will undergo a feedback and revision process to update and clarify language and improve upon common areas of concern.

The next phase of implementation for the VALUE rubrics will focus on scale of adoption and aggregation of data, particularly at state and national levels. In 2014, a pilot project, called the Multi-State Collaborative, was launched to understand the feasibility of state-level adoption of the VALUE rubrics. Working with state systems of higher education and the State Higher Education Executives Organization, this project gathered insights on state level adoption processes across 13 states and 100 2- and 4-year institutions (McConnell & Rhodes, 2017). The success of this state-level initiative led to the 2017 launch of the VALUE Institute and the development of national benchmarks on broad learning outcomes using the VALUE rubrics and student work samples. Campuses identify outcomes for assessment and follow defined protocols for developing a sampling plan and organizing student data. Samples of student work are scored by nationally trained, campus-based scorers (i.e., faculty, staff, administrators). Results are provided back to campuses and aggregate data are used to create multicampus reports on student achievement, including disaggregated results to expose equity gaps across populations.

Strengths of the VALUE Rubrics Approach

The wide adoption of the VALUE rubrics across higher education is due in many ways to the rubrics' multiple utilities. Though not perfect, the VALUE rubrics have provided campus stakeholders significant benefits at multiple levels. At the student level, rubrics provide essential measurement of students' demonstrated learning. Much assessment of learning is indirect, reflecting students' perceived learning, either through surveys, course evaluations, or the occasional focus group. It is critical to couple indirect data on campuses with students' directly demonstrated ability to execute learning outcomes over time. Because the rubrics were developed with the intent that students would see them, they also provide a means through which students can reflect on their own learning. All students benefit from self-reflection, but this may be particularly powerful for students from traditionally underserved populations who benefit from added layers of transparency in the classroom and awareness of their strengths. In addition to providing helpful transparency for performance expectations between students and faculty, the rubrics also offer the opportunity for students from all backgrounds to recognize relative areas of strength and highlight demonstrated growth.

At the faculty level, the interdisciplinary orientation of the rubrics offers faculty much needed opportunities to discuss student learning with colleagues from different disciplines. These conversations can be especially helpful in the development and assessment of general education curricula and at the program level. Finally, because effective use of the VALUE rubrics hinges on well-constructed assignments, faculty professional development includes discussions of effective assignment design. The combination of the student-centered structure of the rubrics with effective assignments underscores the authentic approach of the VALUE rubrics to the assessment of student learning by locating assessment at the core of faculty creativity.

At the institutional level, all stakeholders (i.e., administrators, faculty, and student affairs professionals) benefit from the ability to modify the rubrics to fit an institution's culture and mission. Such modification may involve developing new rubrics that replicate the structure of the 16 nationally created rubrics. For example, campus-developed versions of the VALUE rubrics for outcomes such as "work ethic," "personal and social development," and "pluralism" demonstrate how campuses can use authentic, direct assessment to target their own institutional priorities. For campuses that have adopted nationally developed VALUE rubrics, there is promise of comparability of assessment across campuses. Findings from the MSC project and the VALUE Institute showcase the potential in using the VALUE rubrics as tools for national and state-level benchmarking of student learning and equity across a spectrum of learning outcomes.

Ultimately, the best measure of any assessment of student learning is the degree to which findings are used for institutional and programmatic improvement. Evidence not used is nearly the same as evidence not collected, except that the former actually requires resources. Perhaps the greatest measure of the VALUE rubrics will be the degree to which these data will function as catalysts for change. After a decade of national use, the utility of VALUE rubric data only continues to grow at individual (course) and institutional (program) levels. This is because the VALUE approach to assessment invites stakeholder engagement, particularly faculty, at every step—from the selection of outcomes, to evaluating the proper rubric, to assignment design, and discussion of results. All of this ought to result in the ultimate promise of authentic assessment of student learning; the engagement of campus leaders and educators from wanting to see *whether* learning is happening, to conversations about how to *improve* learning and for *whom*.

THE CULTURAL CONTROLLABILITY SCALE

Implicit theories, or "naive assumptions about the self and social reality" (Dweck et al., 1995, p. 267), determine how individuals respond to stimuli. Beliefs regarding fixedness (*entity* theories) and malleability (*incremental* theories) regarding certain attributes may affect intercultural competence development. Malleable beliefs increase motivation to interact with outgroups (Williams & Eberhardt, 2008), improve response to ambiguous cross-cultural situations (Chao et al., 2017), and improve intergroup attitudes among members of conflicting ethnic groups (Halperin et al., 2011). To date, such implicit theories focused exclusively on whether attributes, such as intelligence and personality, are fixed or malleable. However, Dweck and Leggett (1988) defined them as beliefs about whether a given attribute is "malleable, increasable, controllable" or "fixed [and] uncontrollable" (p. 262); yet, beliefs about attribute malleability are independent from beliefs about attribute controllability. Recently, we developed the CCS, a publicly available scale focused on cultural *controllability* rather than *malleability*, that contributes to our understanding of when and why individuals are tolerant of diversity, including at an international level. This tolerance has become a key learning outcome on increasingly internationalized campuses that are preparing students for careers in a globalized workforce and life in diverse and mobile communities.

Scale Development

Attribution theory (Weiner, 1986) posits three primary dimensions of causal ascription: locus (internal vs. external), stability (fixed vs. malleable), and controllability (controllable vs. uncontrollable). Among these, controllability is the most critical dimension for interpersonal interactions (Smith et al., 1993; Weiner, 2000). For example, if we perceive poverty to be controllable, we tend to blame and feel anger toward the lower class, whereas, if we perceive it to be uncontrollable, we tend not to blame them and are more likely to support social policies that help them (Zucker & Weiner, 1993).

Malleable beliefs tend to relate to positive intergroup attitudes, and uncontrollable beliefs should as well. Implicit controllability beliefs can help explain why the outcomes of entity/incremental beliefs reverse over time. Specifically, although malleable beliefs decrease blame following failure, when failure repeats over time, attitudes reverse: Incremental theorists blame individuals for repeated failure, whereas entity theorists are accepting of repeated failure because they believe fixed traits are responsible for behavior (Ryazanov & Christenfeld, 2018). Similarly, beliefs that culture is uncontrollable should lead to greater acceptance of failure to adapt culturally, but incremental beliefs will increase initial acceptance of diverse others.

Culture, including habitual responses to external stimuli (Geertz, 1973), has several dimensions. Culture influences ascription, behavior, beliefs, communication, goals, perspective, and values (Hofstede, 2001; Smith & Bond, 1998). Two of this chapter's authors (Hickman and Acheson) iteratively drafted scale items to tap into each of these dimensions. We then presented the items at a conference of intercultural experts and incorporated their suggestions for revision.

Item Reduction and Convergent/Discriminant Validity

We piloted the initial set of items with two samples: undergraduate students as part of a larger study and Amazon Mechanical Turks (MTurks) to obtain a large, diverse sample for initial evidence of construct validity. Students were paid $20 and MTurks were paid $2. We describe the pilot item dimensions above but do not present the entire pilot scale here. Both samples were administered the 32-item pilot scale, and the MTurks were administered several other scales, namely, cultural intelligence (CQ; Ang et al., 2007), ethnocultural empathy (Wang et al., 2003), and intercultural sensitivity (IS; Chen & Starosta, 2000). Although the original implicit theories (e.g., intelligence, person, morality) show a one-factor structure, several newer implicit theories of change have best fit a two-factor structure due to low subscale correlations (e.g., Burnette & Pollack, 2013). Following recent findings in implicit theory research, we tested ($N = 560$) both a one- and two-factor version of the shortened eight-item scale. The data fit a one-factor solution poorly (root mean square area of approximation [RMSEA] = .22; standardized root mean residual [SRMR] = .16; comparative fit index [CFI] = .52; Tucker-Lewis Index [TLI] = .33). The data fit a two-factor solution specifying the controllability and uncontrollability subscales as separate factors well (RMSEA = .06, SRMR = .05, CFI = .96, TLI = .94). Treating the subscales as distinct but related factors enables each to have independent relationships with theoretically connected constructs. The two subscales, along with scale dimensions and the items retained in the final short scale, are presented in Table 15.4.

The scale expands implicit theory measurement by assessing beliefs about the controllability of cultural influences, which is associated with intercultural attitudes (see Table 15.5) and, theoretically, the development of intercultural competence. Understanding beliefs that foster positive expectations toward the behavior of others is vital for adapting to cross-cultural

TABLE 15.4. The Final Eight Scale Items

Scale	Dimension	Item
Uncontrollability	Ascription	When people act differently than I expect, I generally assume their culture is driving their behavior.
	General	Culture has a stronger impact on the average person than their choices do.
	Behavior	Cultural influences, not intentional decisions, largely determine people's daily behavior.
	Goals	A person's goals are mostly shaped by cultural influences.
Controllability	Behavior	Cultural upbringing doesn't strongly influence people's behaviors.
	Beliefs	The attitudes and beliefs of most people are not influenced by their home culture.
	Values	Cultural values are fairly easy for people to change.
	Perspective	Cultural background does not construct a person's perspective.

TABLE 15.5. Means, Standard Deviations, and Correlations

Dimension	M	SD	1	2	3	4	5	6	7	8	9	10	11
1. CU	3.64	.89	.77										
2. CC	2.63	.89	-.15	.77									
3. EFE	4.34	.95	.09	-.21	.92								
4. EPT	4.01	.86	.08	.02	.53	.74							
5. ACD	4.79	1.00	-.09	-.29	.59	.48	.83						
6. EA	4.60	1.09	.08	-.24	.71	.41	.49	.86					
7. IS	4.37	.57	-.01	-.18	.67	.55	.63	.50	.91				
8. MCCQ	4.93	1.18	.18	-.02	.46	.43	.29	.43	.59	.84			
9. CCQ	3.89	1.29	.25	.24	.23	.41	.08	.20	.36	.64	.89		
10. MotCQ	5.09	1.17	.05	.06	.51	.49	.42	.38	.73	.68	.55	.88	
11. BehCQ	4.61	1.25	.14	.06	.35	.25	.17	.33	.45	.70	.49	.54	.88

Note. CU = Cultural Uncontrollability; CC = Cultural Controllability; EFE = Empathic Feeling & Expression; EPT = Empathic Perspective Taking; ACD = Acceptance of Cultural Differences; EA = Empathic Awareness; IS = intercultural sensitivity; MCCQ = Metacognitive Cultural Intelligence; CCQ = Cognitive Cultural Intelligence; MotCQ = Motivational Cultural Intelligence; BehCQ = Behavioral Cultural Intelligence. MTurk Data, N = 321. Cronbach's alpha reliabilities in diagonal. $r \geq .11$ significant at $p < .05$.

260 Acheson et al.

situations (Chao et al., 2017). Cross-cultural attitudes and the ability to adapt are increasingly important due to the connectedness of our world. At the individual level, the scale can be used for formative assessment in learning interventions designed to increase learners' self-awareness of beliefs important in their development of intercultural competence, as well as in summary to measure the effectiveness of such learning interventions. Likewise, the scale is useful both formatively and in summary at the institutional level, especially in higher education institutions increasingly concerned with documenting intercultural learning outcomes (Deardorff, 2011).

The scale's interdisciplinarity of theoretical foundations provides a wide range of other applications, including corporate, governmental, nonprofit organizations, military, and other institutions committed to the development of intercultural competence or diversity and inclusion. The applicability of the CCS for diversity/inclusion work is a particular advantage because professionals in this realm have fewer options of measures for formative and/or summative assessment than can be brought to bear. Finally, the CCS also may flexibly be used in combination with other short, open-source Likert-type instruments. From a design perspective, such an approach allows for measurement configurations that are responsive to different theoretical foundations of a research project.

CONCLUSION

Assessment often gets a bad rap for lamentably legitimate reasons. Among other critiques, measures may be conceptualized, developed, and implemented in a manner that is dehumanizing, reductionist, and unresponsive to the diversity and depth of the human condition. On the other hand, when done right and well, assessment can be powerfully illuminating and transformative, revealing complexities and facilitating processes that simply would not otherwise be accessible (Deardorff, 2011). Without such an ecologically valid assessment, which accurately captures and communicates the nature of reality in the real world, we have no reliable way of illustrating or demonstrating where we are and where we may go (Shealy, 2016). Such concerns are magnified in international contexts and projects because of the subjective and culture-dependent nature both of the experience of assessment and of the interpretations of assessment results.

Although no test can be perfect, the three innovative and interdisciplinary measures described here—the BEVI, VALUE Rubrics, and the CCS—strive to be ecologically valid. From the user standpoint, these measures seek to be responsive to human complexity and genuinely useful in the real world, across a range of local and global populations and contexts (Hanson et al., in press; Wandschneider et al., 2015). That said, no measure, including these three, is ever "done," as test development is an ongoing process of assessing the assessment to ensure that our instruments are what we say they are and do what we say they do. It is our hope that the models and methods described here are helpful for those who wish to keep learning with us how we may best demonstrate the power and potential of ecologically valid assessment both at home and abroad.

REFERENCES

Acheson, K., Dirkx, J., & Shealy, C. (in press). High impact learning in higher education: Operationalizing the self-constructive outcomes of transformative learning theory. In E. Kostara, A. Gavrielatos, & D. Loads (Eds.), *Transformative learning theory and praxis: New perspectives and possibilities.* Taylor & Francis.

Ang, S., Van Dyne, L., Koh, C., Ng, K. Y., Templer, K. J., Tay, C., & Chandrasekar, N. A. (2007). Cultural intelligence: Its measurement and effects on cultural judgment and decision making, cultural adaptation and task performance. *Management and Organization Review, 3*(3), 335–371. https://doi.org/10.1111/j.1740-8784.2007.00082.x

Association of American Colleges and Universities. (2020). *Valid Assessment of Learning in Undergraduate Education (VALUE).* https://aacu.org/value

Burnette, J. L., & Pollack, J. M. (2013). Implicit theories of work and job fit: Implications for job and life satisfaction. *Basic and Applied Social Psychology, 35*(4), 360–372. https://doi.org/10.1080/01973533.2013.803964

Chao, M. M., Takeuchi, R., & Farh, J.-L. (2017). Enhancing cultural intelligence: The roles of implicit culture beliefs and adjustment. *Personnel Psychology, 70*(1), 257–292. https://doi.org/10.1111/peps.12142

Chen, G.-M., & Starosta, W. J. (2000). The development and validation of the Intercultural Sensitivity Scale. *Human Communication, 3,* 1–15. https://digitalcommons.uri.edu/com_facpubs/36/

Cozen, J., Hanson, W., Poston, J., Jones, S., & Tabit, M. (2016). The Beliefs, Events, and Values Inventory (BEVI): Implications and applications for therapeutic assessment and intervention. In C. N. Shealy (Ed.), *Making sense of beliefs and values: Theory, research, and practice* (pp. 575–621). Springer.

Deardorff, D. K. (2011). Assessing intercultural competence. *New Directions for Institutional Research, 2011*(149), 65–79. https://doi.org/10.1002/ir.381

Dweck, C. S., Chiu, C.-Y., & Hong, Y.-Y. (1995). Implicit theories and their role in judgments and reactions: A world from two perspectives. *Psychological Inquiry, 6*(4), 267–285. https://doi.org/10.1207/s15327965pli0604_1

Dweck, C. S., & Leggett, E. L. (1988). A social-cognitive approach to motivation and personality. *Psychological Review, 95*(2), 256–273. https://doi.org/10.1037/0033-295X.95.2.256

Dyjak-LeBlanc, K., Brewster, L., Grande, S., White, R. P., & Shullman, S. L. (2016). The EI Leadership Model: From theory and research to real world application. In C. N. Shealy (Ed.), *Making sense of beliefs and values: Theory, research, and practice* (pp. 531–574). Springer.

Geertz, C. (1973). *The interpretation of cultures.* Basic Books.

Halperin, E., Russell, A. G., Trzesniewski, K. H., Gross, J. J., & Dweck, C. S. (2011). Promoting the Middle East peace process by changing beliefs about group malleability. *Science, 333*(6050), 1767–1769. https://doi.org/10.1126/science.1202925

Hanson, W. E., Leighton, J. P., Donaldson, S. I., Oakland, T., Terjesen, M. D., & Shealy, C. N. (in press). Assessment: The power and potential of psychological testing, educational measurement, and program evaluation around the world. In C. Shealy, M. Bullock, & S. Kapadia (Eds.), *Going global: How psychology and psychologists can meet a world of need.* American Psychological Association.

Hart Research Associates. (2018). *Fulfilling the American dream: Liberal education and the future of work.* Association of American Colleges and Universities. https://www.aacu.org/sites/default/files/files/LEAP/2018EmployerResearchReport.pdf

Hofstede, G. (2001). *Culture's consequences: Comparing values, behaviors, institutions and organizations across nations* (2nd ed.). Sage.

McConnell, K. D., & Rhodes, T. (2017). *On solid ground.* Association of American Colleges and Universities. https://www.aacu.org/OnSolidGroundVALUE

NAFSA: Association of International Educators. (2020). https://www.nafsa.org/professional-resources/learning-and-training/assessing-global-learning-measurement-implications-and-applications

Rhodes, T. L. (Ed.). (2010). *Assessing outcomes and improving achievement: Tips and tools for using rubrics.* Association of American Colleges and Universities.

Roy, P., Wandschneider, E., & Steglitz, I. (2014). *Assessing education abroad outcomes: A review of the BEVI, IDI, and GPI. White paper.* Michigan State University Office of Study Abroad. https://educationabroad.isp.msu.edu/files/2914/9486/1612/Assessing_EA_Outcomes_WhitePaper.pdf

Ryazanov, A. A., & Christenfeld, N. J. S. (2018). Incremental mindsets and the reduced forgiveness of chronic failures. *Journal of Experimental Social Psychology, 76,* 33–41. https://doi.org/10.1016/j.jesp.2017.12.003

Shealy, C. N. (2004). A model and method for "making" a Combined-Integrated psychologist: Equilintegration (EI) Theory and the Beliefs, Events, and Values Inventory (BEVI). *Journal of Clinical Psychology, 60*(10), 1065–1090. https://doi.org/10.1002/jclp.20035

Shealy, C. N. (2005). Justifying the justification hypothesis: Scientific-humanism, Equilintegration (EI) Theory, and the Beliefs, Events, and Values Inventory (BEVI). *Journal of Clinical Psychology, 61*(1), 81–106. https://doi.org/10.1002/jclp.20092

Shealy, C. N. (Ed.). (2016). *Making sense of beliefs and values: Theory, research, and practice.* Springer.

Shealy, C. N. (Ed.). (in press). *Cultivating the globally sustainable self: How the human species might fulfill its potential.* Oxford University Press.

Shealy, C. N., Bhuyan, D., & Sternberger, L. G. (2012). Cultivating the capacity to care in children and youth: Implications from EI theory, EI self, and BEVI. In U. S. Nayar (Ed.), *Child and adolescent mental health* (pp. 240–255). Sage.

Smith, C. A., Haynes, K. N., Lazarus, R. S., & Pope, L. K. (1993). In search of the "hot" cognitions: Attributions, appraisals, and their relation to emotion. *Journal of Personality and Social Psychology, 65*(5), 916–929. https://doi.org/10.1037/0022-3514.65.5.916

Smith, P. B., & Bond, M. H. (1998). *Social psychology across cultures* (2nd ed.). Pearson/Prentice Hall Europe.

Wandschneider, E., Pysarchik, D. T., Sternberger, L. G., Ma, W., Acheson, K., Baltensperger, B., Good, R. T., Brubaker, B., Baldwin, T., Nishitani, H., Wang, F., Reisweber, J., & Hart, V. (2015). The Forum BEVI Project: Applications and implications for international, multicultural, and transformative learning. *Frontiers: The Interdisciplinary Journal of Study Abroad, 25,* 150–228.

Wang, Y.-W., Davidson, M. M., Yakushko, O. F., Savoy, H. B., Tan, J. A., & Bleier, J. K. (2003). The scale of ethnocultural empathy: Development, validation, and reliability. *Journal of Counseling Psychology, 50*(2), 221–234. https://doi.org/10.1037/0022-0167.50.2.221

Weiner, B. (1986). *An attributional theory of motivation and emotion.* Springer-Verlag. https://doi.org/10.1007/978-1-4612-4948-1

Weiner, B. (2000). Intrapersonal and interpersonal theories of motivation from an attributional perspective. *Educational Psychology Review, 12,* 1–14. https://doi.org/10.1023/A:1009017532121

Williams, M. J., & Eberhardt, J. L. (2008). Biological conceptions of race and the motivation to cross racial boundaries. *Journal of Personality and Social Psychology, 94*(6), 1033–1047. https://doi.org/10.1037/0022-3514.94.6.1033

Zucker, G. S., & Weiner, B. (1993). Conservatism and perceptions of poverty: An attributional analysis. *Journal of Applied Social Psychology, 23*(12), 925–943. https://doi.org/10.1111/j.1559-1816.1993.tb01014.x

Afterword

What's Next?

Susan A. Nolan, Christopher M. Hakala, and R. Eric Landrum

The imperative to assess is here to stay. We can approach assessment in a lackluster way, or we can do it in a way that informs our teaching and our students' learning. Assessment *can* be exciting and incredibly useful. Here are some ways that these chapters make us, as coeditors, think about the future of assessment.

RECRUITMENT TO THE CAUSE

Through their writing, the chapter authors convey their enthusiasm for assessment, particularly when it is done creatively and effectively. Their valuable, empirically-informed advice acts as recruitment material, proselytizing that assessment is valuable not just for external validation from governing and accrediting bodies, but for teaching, learning, and for student success. Unfortunately, such proselytizing is sorely needed in most institutions throughout most parts of the world. In their chapter, for example, Jane S. Halonen and Dana S. Dunn talk about the "assessment hero," the professor or administrator who takes on the task of overseeing assessment for a department or other unit. Although they note the merits of the often selfless hero, they also outline the sometimes detrimental effects on colleagues who may slack off on assessment when they realize someone else is doing the heavy lifting. All of the chapter authors in this volume are convincing in their encouragement of active, thoughtful engagement in assessment activities that are beneficial for our

https://doi.org/10.1037/0000183-017
Assessing Undergraduate Learning in Psychology: Strategies for Measuring and Improving Student Performance, S. A. Nolan, C. M. Hakala, and R. E. Landrum (Editors)

students, pedagogy, courses, and curricula. Those of us who already "believe" must take on the sometimes difficult, often thankless work of recruiting colleagues to join us as assessment advocates.

INTRA-INSTITUTIONAL CONNECTIONS

Faculty members and unit administrators are often at loggerheads when it comes to assessment. Administrators might demand assessment without always appearing to care in what form it occurs. Faculty members feel like they must deliver "or else," which can have the side effect of encouraging less-than-thoughtful assessment efforts. These standoffs need not occur if professionals at both levels embrace organically created, albeit evidence-based, assessments that simultaneously assist the professor in helping students to attain the learning goals of the course or program and allow unit administrators to provide richly detailed reports to relevant stakeholders. As an analogy, international development projects (e.g., women's rights projects in Uganda) have long emphasized the importance of locally driven solutions that can be bolstered, but should not be dictated, by international sources. Replace "local" with "faculty," and, as Claudia Stanny observes in Chapter 6, "when faculty reflect on evidence about student learning and use evidence to inform decisions about curriculum and teaching strategies, they can craft programs that facilitate student learning" (p. 77). The bottom-up nature of faculty efforts—the local impetus behind assessment—informs programmatic assessment structures and reports—the "international" angle in this analogy. We can all benefit from working together.

INTERNATIONAL CONNECTIONS

In our opinion as coeditors, one of the most important takeaways from this volume is the need for U.S. faculty to look beyond U.S. borders. We have much to learn from studying assessment models, research, and outcomes outside of the United States, especially with respect to the Bologna Process and related initiatives previously described. In our experience, broader conversations about assessment within the United States, whether at conferences or in other venues, so often fail to consider viewpoints from other countries. This is unfortunate both because we have so much to learn from how others approach assessment and because international connections and collaborations can lead to the kinds of infrastructure that facilitate the mobility that is increasingly important—nay, essential—in higher education.

WHAT WE MISSED

A single volume cannot possibly capture the full range of viewpoints on assessment, particularly because of the broad, international scope of this particular book. We'd like to leave you with a short list of what we'd like to learn more about and what we'd like to see in terms of assessment in higher education. (Volume 2, maybe?) Here's our list:

1. We need to talk more about ways to give students the evidence they need to communicate their skills to employers—as certificates, badges, or powerful rings that unleash speaking holograms attesting to students' proficiencies (that hologram thingie would be cool).

2. Speaking of badges, what if we developed rubrics and credentials to identify faculty members who have developed excellent assessments of the learning outcomes in their courses and programs? And what if they factored into tenure and promotion decisions?

3. We need a better understanding of differences in how assessment is carried out across countries and across regions within a country. We could encourage someone to take on the task of creating a website that compiles this information for faculty and administrator use. Let's make sure this person or organization has the continuous resources to maintain and update the website over time.

4. We have the World Bank, the World Health Organization, and so on. What organization can bring us all together with respect to assessment? The Organisation for Economic Co-operation and Development (OECD) is currently our best hope, and you can read more about their impressive efforts in Chapter 14. But what if we had an international entity focused solely on assessment of higher education around the world?

5. In the United States, a higher education institution might have a Center for Teaching and Learning or a Center for Teaching Excellence. Why not a Center for Assessment? There are some institutions that have this type of institutional support, and sometimes this support is required for a college or school within an institution (e.g., School of Business). Training faculty members and providing support for assessment should become more mainstream, just as training faculty members and providing support for becoming better teachers is mainstream.

CONCLUSION

We believe that the authors of the chapters in this book have succeeded in conveying the richness and complexity of assessment. I hope that you understand why we did, after all, need yet another book on assessment! Whether you are conducting an assessment of your own students' learning, developing an institutional assessment plan, or building bridges across institutions or national borders, these chapters hold lessons for best practices in developing assessments, ways to overcome challenges, and pitfalls to avoid.

Throughout the book, the authors outline the many limitations of assessment, while they encourage flexibility in our thinking about what to assess, how to assess it, how to act on assessment data, and how to communicate it to others. More specifically, the authors offer ideas on how to communicate about assessment in ways that allow for comparisons and, ultimately, mobility. Perhaps most importantly, they promote an idealism in which we can imagine a world in which students obtain the knowledge and skills that they need to be successful global citizens, and in which they can easily communicate what they have learned to employers, other educational institutions, and their communities. After all, we're in this profession because we want this kind of success for our students; assessment is central to this goal. Who would have guessed that assessment could be so exciting?

INDEX

ABOUT THE EDITORS

Susan A. Nolan, PhD, earned her doctorate in psychology from Northwestern University in Evanston, Illinois, and completed her clinical psychology internship through the Vanderbilt University Internship Consortium. She is currently a professor of psychology at Seton Hall University in South Orange, New Jersey. Dr. Nolan studies the stigma associated with psychological disorders and the role of gender in science, technology, engineering, and mathematics (STEM) education and careers, the latter of which has been funded in part by the National Science Foundation. She has long been interested in assessment; she chaired her university's reaccreditation steering committee (for the Middle States Commission on Higher Education) and was a working group chair at the American Psychological Association's (APA's) 2016 Summit on National Assessment of Psychology. Her interest in assessment internationally was furthered when she studied the Bologna Process and EuroPsy at the University of Banja Luka in Bosnia and Herzegovina as a U.S. Fulbright Scholar.

Dr. Nolan's work has resulted in numerous journal articles, chapters, and conference presentations. She is a coauthor of introductory psychology and behavioral statistics textbooks, as well as a book on critical thinking. She coedited a book on women in STEM. Dr. Nolan is a past president of the Eastern Psychological Association (EPA) and the 2021 president of the Society for the Teaching of Psychology. Dr. Nolan is a Fellow of EPA, APA (through Divisions 1, 2, 5, and 52), and the Association for Psychological Science.

Christopher M. Hakala, PhD, earned his doctorate in psychology from the University of New Hampshire. He is currently the director of the Center for Excellence in Teaching, Learning, and Scholarship and a professor of psychology at Springfield College in Springfield, Massachusetts. Dr. Hakala studies teaching and learning in higher education, as well as strategies for effective assessment. His interest in assessment has been long-standing as well; he has worked on several reaccreditation steering committees, including chairing a standard of Springfield College's most recent visit. In addition, he has served as an outside accreditor (for the New England Commission on Higher Education) and has been awarded a grant from The Davis Educational Foundation for work on real-time assessment.

Dr. Hakala's work has resulted in numerous journal articles, chapters, and conference presentations. He has coauthored books on statistics, learning and thinking, and applying psychological theory to education. He is past president of the New England Psychological Association and is a Fellow of the Eastern Psychological Association.

R. Eric Landrum, PhD, is a professor of psychology and department chair at Boise State University in Idaho. He received his doctorate in cognitive psychology from Southern Illinois University-Carbondale. He is a research generalist, broadly addressing the improvement of teaching and learning, including the long-term retention of introductory psychology content, skills assessment, improving help-seeking behavior, advising innovations, understanding student career paths, the psychology workforce, successful graduate school applications, and more. During summer 2008, Dr. Landrum led an APA working group at the National Conference for Undergraduate Education in Psychology studying the desired results of an undergraduate psychology education. With the launch of a new APA journal in 2015—*Scholarship of Teaching and Learning in Psychology*—he served as one of its inaugural coeditors.

Dr. Landrum is a member of the American Psychological Association, a fellow in APA's Division 2 (Society for the Teaching of Psychology; STP), served as STP Secretary (2009–2011) and STP president (2014); he is also a Fellow of Division 1 (General Psychology). He was a charter member of the Association for Psychological Science and was named a Fellow in 2018. During 2016–2017, Dr. Landrum served as president of the Rocky Mountain Psychological Association and he served as president of Psi Chi, the International Honor Society in Psychology in 2017–2018. In August 2019, he received the American Psychological Foundation's Charles L. Brewer Distinguished Teaching of Psychology Award, the highest award given to teachers of psychology in America.